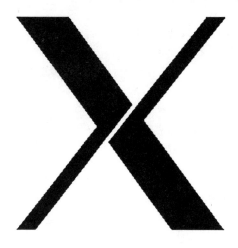

A Guide for Users

Jerry D. Smith

Iris Computing Laboratories
The Spectro Group, Inc.
Albuquerque/Santa Fe, New Mexico

PTR PRENTICE HALL
Englewood Cliffs, New Jersey 07632

Editorial/production supervision: bookworks
Cover design: Karen Marsilio
Manufacturing manager: Alexis R. Heydt
Acquisitions editor: Gregory G. Doench

© 1994 by PTR Prentice Hall
Prentice-Hall, Inc.
A Paramount Communications Company
Englewood Cliffs, New Jersey 07632

The publisher offers discounts on this book when ordered
in bulk quantities. For more information, contact:

Corporate Sales Department
PTR Prentice Hall
113 Sylvan Avenue
Englewood Cliffs, NJ 07632
Phone: 201-592-2863
Fax: 201-592-2249

Printed in the United States of America

10 9 8 7 6 5 4 3 2 1

ISBN 0-13-123795-0

Prentice-Hall International (UK) Limited, *London*
Prentice-Hall of Australia Pty. Limited, *Sydney*
Prentice-Hall Canada Inc., *Toronto*
Prentice-Hall Hispanoamericana, S.A., *Mexico*
Prentice-Hall of India Private Limited, *New Delhi*
Prentice-Hall of Japan, Inc., *Tokyo*
Simon & Schuster Asia Pte. Ltd., *Singapore*
Editora Prentice-Hall do Brasil, Ltda., *Rio de Janeiro*

To my mother

Contents

Preface

The X Window System™ is an incredibly powerful environment. Because X is operating system and hardware independent, it has the potential, at least technically, for delivery to a broad range of computing environments. For a variety of nontechnical reasons, however, it remains unclear whether or not X can achieve widespread penetration into PC environments. There is no question that X's technical potential is vastly superior to that of window systems available with current PCs.

For the time being, X shines on UNIX® platforms. Although there is no particular relationship between X and UNIX, both have been designed and implemented by and for individuals who require the utmost sophistication in their computing environments. Most of us who have worked in both PC and UNIX workstation environments find it difficult to live in a PC environment, even for a day or so, primarily because of the limited support for multiple, concurrently executing applications and the lack of sophisticated networking.

It is quite difficult to remember, or imagine returning to, the world of powerful, client-server computing without X. Although X environments are still maturing in terms of the refinement of their user interfaces, the fundamentals are there. In the client-server computing world, one of the most important fundamentals is network transparency; in this arena, X is the champion. With X, running applications on one machine and displaying them on another is so seamless that the entire client-server process seems trivial—there's nothing to it. In any computing endeavor, this type of simplicity is the by-product of design sophistication. X is a sophisticated, networked window system.

Because X delivers so much, it is easy to become impatient, expecting even more. In this book, we are somewhat susceptible to this affliction. In particular, for the user we think that it is important to point out those aspects of X that are potential trouble spots. This tendency, on occasion, to highlight aspects of X that can be troublesome is warranted because this book is an X user's guide, not a treastise on the technical accomplishments of X. As X matures these trouble spots, all of which are pale in comparison with X's many great features, will largely disappear.

With these issues in mind, we hope you enjoy using X.

Acknowledgments

A number of individuals have contributed to the development of this book including many individuals at Prentice Hall. I would like to thank the entire staff at Prentice Hall for their efforts toward the overall process. In particular, I would like to thank my editor Gregory Doench for his many efforts on behalf of this book.

I would like to thank the X users and programmers (many of whom are our customers) who have regularly called with questions and comments on X. In writing an X user's guide, there is no substitute for daily encounters with a broad range of X users. Your comments and assistance are very much appreciated.

Several readers of early drafts of specific chapters as well as formal reviewers provided comments that were invaluable in determining the final content of this user's guide. To these individuals I would like to express a very large thank you.

On several occasions during the development of this book, software and workstation vendors made their current and upcoming X environments available on a variety of workstations. In particular, I would like to thank the following individuals and groups for their assistance: John Cahill at Quarterdeck; Michael Kantrowitz and Dave Tolman at Human Designed Systems; Karl Kortkamp, John LaBry, Steve Simonds, and the entire staff at Silicon Graphics in Albuquerque; and Gary Van Vranken at Hewlett-Packard.

Next, I would like to thank the staff at UUNET Technologies for their ongoing efforts to distribute noncommercial software including the source code for our previous books and many of the freeware applications mentioned in this book. In particular, I would like to thank James Revell at UUNET for his ongoing assistance. UUNET provides a valuable service for the X user and programming community.

It is important to acknowledge the efforts of the staff at the former MIT X Consortium, now X Consortium. This group of individuals develops the core X software, serves as a clearinghouse for X software contributed by X programmers from around the world, distributes X software ready for installation on a variety of hardware platforms, frequently answers X-related questions for the *comp.windows.x* newsgroup, and many other tasks.

Jerry D. Smith
jsmith@spectro.com
Santa Fe, New Mexico

1

Introduction

In this book we address the X Window System from the user's viewpoint. This chapter provides an overview of X as well as a foundation for subsequent chapters.

1.1 Operating Systems and Windowing Systems

Traditionally, operating systems (OSs) and windowing systems have been distinct software entities. An operating system, as the control program for the computer, provides a series of commands for users at all levels. System administrators issue directives for system maintenance, set up accounts for new users, and so on; end-users, on the other hand, perform more basic tasks such as requesting a listing of files, starting a word processor session, sending files to the printer, and others.

A character-oriented computer terminal might serve as a vehicle for entering commands and receiving feedback from the computer, with both input and output being word oriented. For example, a UNIX® user can request a listing of all files with statistics regarding file ownership, creation date, size, and so on with the command "ls -l"; the output is displayed in table format—as "words" (see Figure 1.1).

A windowing system, on the other hand, provides a mechanism for managing multiple input and output areas within a physical display space, such as that provided by a display screen, keyboard, and pointing device. Thus, if a window system were available, and if that window system allowed/supported windows that emulate traditional command windows, a user could request a listing of files using the previous command. In this sense, a window system can support traditional ASCII- (character-)oriented computing. Figure 1.2 shows an X-based command window provided by the X application *xterm*. In this case, *xterm*'s dimensions are configured to match a traditional terminal window with 24 rows and 80 columns. Also, we are using a traditional character application, the text editor *vi(1)*.

1

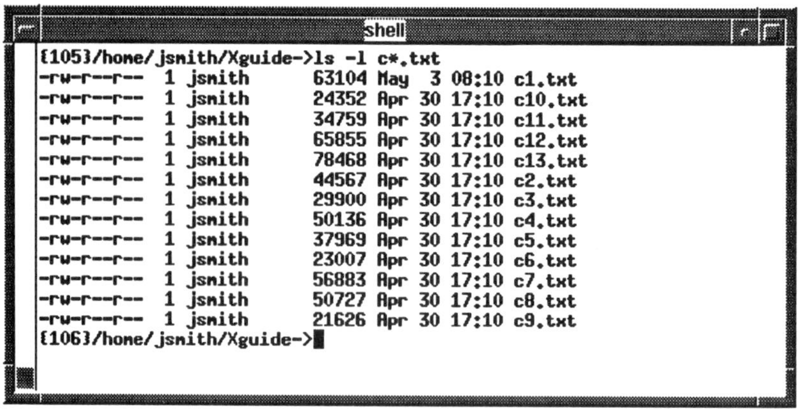

```
┌─────────────────────────── shell ───────────────────────────┐
│ [105]/home/jsmith/Xguide->ls -l c*.txt                       │
│ -rw-r--r--  1 jsmith      63104 May  3 08:10 c1.txt          │
│ -rw-r--r--  1 jsmith      24352 Apr 30 17:10 c10.txt         │
│ -rw-r--r--  1 jsmith      34759 Apr 30 17:10 c11.txt         │
│ -rw-r--r--  1 jsmith      65855 Apr 30 17:10 c12.txt         │
│ -rw-r--r--  1 jsmith      78468 Apr 30 17:10 c13.txt         │
│ -rw-r--r--  1 jsmith      44567 Apr 30 17:10 c2.txt          │
│ -rw-r--r--  1 jsmith      29900 Apr 30 17:10 c3.txt          │
│ -rw-r--r--  1 jsmith      50136 Apr 30 17:10 c4.txt          │
│ -rw-r--r--  1 jsmith      37969 Apr 30 17:10 c5.txt          │
│ -rw-r--r--  1 jsmith      23007 Apr 30 17:10 c6.txt          │
│ -rw-r--r--  1 jsmith      56883 Apr 30 17:10 c7.txt          │
│ -rw-r--r--  1 jsmith      50727 Apr 30 17:10 c8.txt          │
│ -rw-r--r--  1 jsmith      21626 Apr 30 17:10 c9.txt          │
│ [106]/home/jsmith/Xguide->                                   │
└──────────────────────────────────────────────────────────────┘
```

Figure 1.1 Character-oriented Operations Within an *xterm* Command Window

Beyond this basic capability, however, most window systems are designed to support (1) multiple (concurrent) user-computer interactions and (2) something more sophisticated than word-oriented, user-computer interaction. Typically, for example, a window system can start multiple applications, say, a word processor and a calculator, in separate windows such that the user is free to switch between them in an intuitive manner, with both applications remaining on-screen concurrently (see Figure 1.3). Moreover, modern window-based

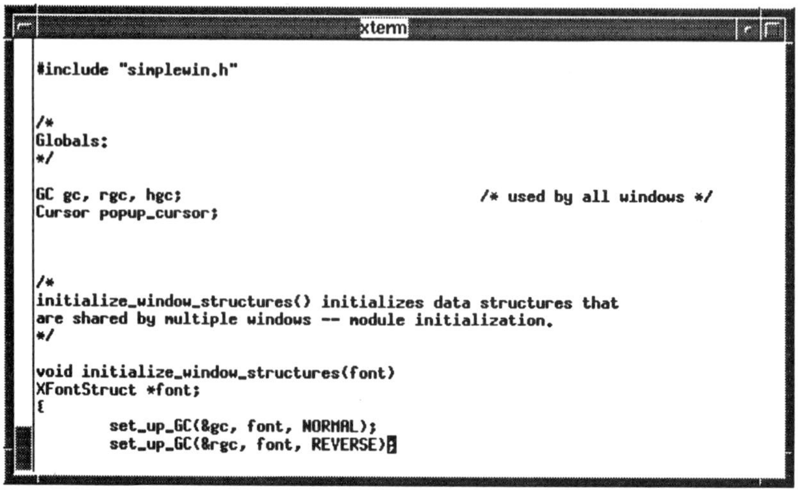

```
┌─────────────────────────── xterm ───────────────────────────┐
│ #include "simplewin.h"                                       │
│                                                              │
│ /*                                                           │
│ Globals:                                                     │
│ */                                                           │
│                                                              │
│ GC gc, rgc, hgc;                    /* used by all windows */│
│ Cursor popup_cursor;                                         │
│                                                              │
│ /*                                                           │
│ initialize_window_structures() initializes data structures that│
│ are shared by multiple windows -- module initialization.     │
│ */                                                           │
│                                                              │
│ void initialize_window_structures(font)                      │
│ XFontStruct *font;                                           │
│ {                                                            │
│         set_up_GC(&gc, font, NORMAL);                        │
│         set_up_GC(&rgc, font, REVERSE)                       │
└──────────────────────────────────────────────────────────────┘
```

Figure 1.2 *vi* from an *xterm* Command Window

applications provide user controls such as pull-down menus and scrollbars that minimize, or in some cases eliminate, the need for word-oriented commands.

In essence, a window system provides multiple views, or points of access, to the computer system. Yet, each window system differs with respect to its philosophy behind and the design of this user-computer interaction, which is often called the *user interface* (UI). In some cases, the user interface is rigid, having a strictly enforced user-computer interaction; with other designs, the user interface may support a very flexible, open-ended style of interaction between the user and the computer, as represented by the computer's operating system.

Modern window systems are either character- or graphics-oriented, the latter being more favored today because of their support for graphical images such as gauges, icons, and slider-type control devices. Some graphical window systems such as the X Window System [Scheifler and Gettys, 1992] allow applications to create windows that fully exploit the

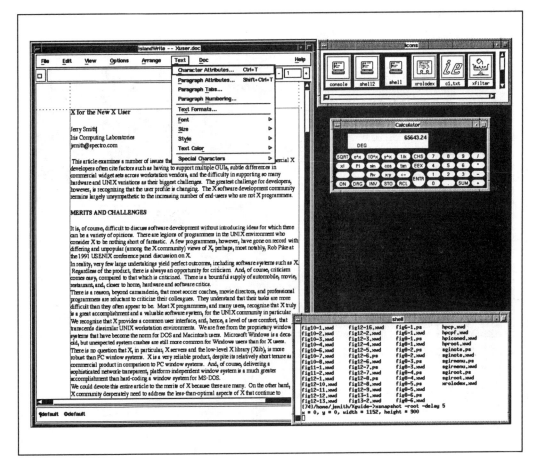

Figure 1.3 Multiple, Concurrent X Applications

graphics capabilities of the hardware yet also support applications that use the computer's graphics capabilities in a very basic way, such as when emulating traditional character-oriented computing within a (command) window. X goes further than many window systems in its application-level flexibility by leaving it up to applications to determine the user-interface policy and design; X is said to provide mechanism, not policy. This design decision has made X somewhat controversial; some critics argue that X should have *forced* a particular high-level user-interface style on its users.

1.2 Division of Labor

With X, the graphical user interface (GUI) that accompanies an application is a function of the window manager (the program that allows you to rearrange applications on the desktop), the GUI objects (components) and the programming toolkit used to develop the application, and other aspects of the application itself—X imposes no window system look-and-feel policies. X per se is best described as a low-level windowing system from which higher

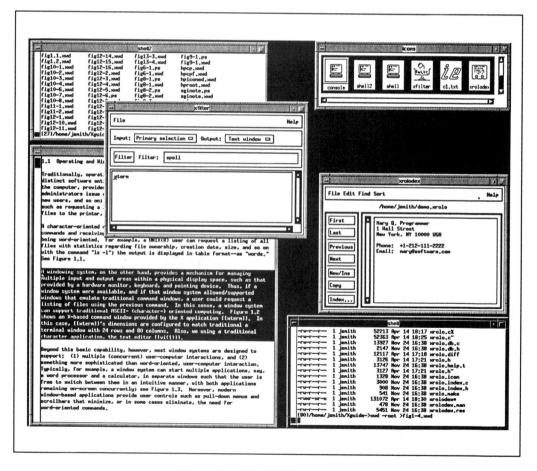

Figure 1.4 A Motif X Environment

level graphical environments can be designed. At present, there are two widely supported commercial user-interface style specifications for X: Motif™ [OSF, 1992b] and OPEN LOOK® [UNIX® System Laboratories, 1992]. Figures 1.4 and 1.5 illustrate X environments based on the Motif and OPEN LOOK style specifications, respectively. In contrast, for the Apple® Macintosh® environment there is only one user-interface style, or look-and-feel, specification. Note that a user-interface style specification proposes the (ideal) look and feel for an application's user interface, as documented in an official style guide. X application developers *independently* provide window managers, widget sets, programming toolkits, and so on that implement the look and feel specified by a style guide. (Widget sets are discussed in Section 1.4.)

Although conventional wisdom suggests that it is desirable to have a consistent user interface across applications, it is, in many cases, unreasonable to apply a generic user interface to an application for which a customized user interface would be more intuitive or user efficient. It is well known, for example, that the stringent user-interface guidelines

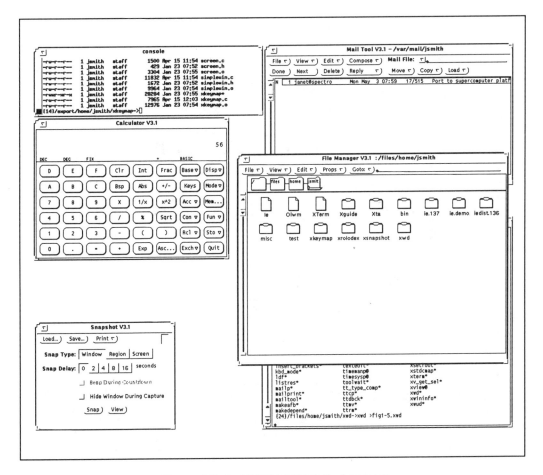

Figure 1.5 An OPEN LOOK X Environment

suggested for Macintosh applications have proved, in some cases, to be too restrictive for application developers as well as users [Dvorak, 1992].

1.3 The Window Manager

Unlike in the Macintosh environment, with X, *generic* window management is handled by a separate application called the window manager. Popular window managers include *mwm*, the Motif™ window manager [OSF, 1992a]; *olwm*, the OPEN LOOK® window manager [UNIX® System Laboratories, 1992]; and *twm*, the tab window manager, which is shipped with the standard X distribution from the X Consortium. Hereafter, we refer to this X distribution as "Consortium X," or the "Consortium X distribution." Figures 1.6 through 1.8 illustrate these window managers. Although most users operate with a window manager, because of X's flexibility, well-behaved X applications do not require a window manager.

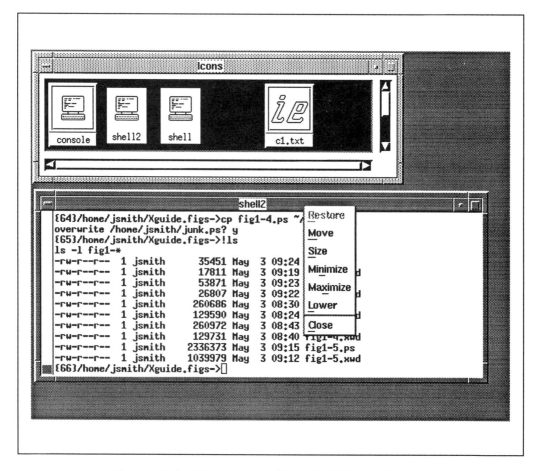

Figure 1.6 An X Environment with the Motif Window Manager

That is, you could design your X environment to start up with, say, one *xterm* command window. From this command window you could start other X applications by typing the appropriate command, as with nonwindow system applications. With this design, each application would pop up in an arbitrary location on the display screen, depending on default configuration settings for your X environment and your X applications (or command-line options). Without the window manager, the look and feel of the X environment would be provided by the application alone. (And, in many cases, the application's look and feel is indirectly provided by a programming toolkit from which many applications are built).

For Macintosh and PC users, it may seem strange to have a window manager that is distinct from the window system itself. The distinction is this. With X, the window system is the software that's responsible for all low-level window management operations such as

- physically creating and destroying windows
- serving as a window system resource manager for the X applications

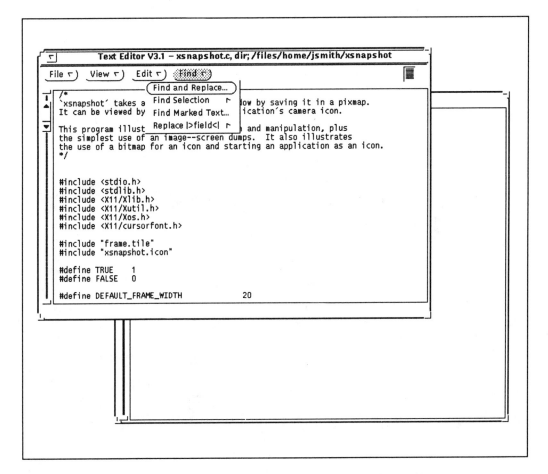

Figure 1.7 An X Environment with the OPEN LOOK Window Manager

□   processing requests to draw a line in a window
□   notifying applications when events occur, such as pressing a key
□   monitoring and reporting window system errors to X applications
□   controlling the display

The window manager, on the other hand, is a separate X application that handles high-level operations that are common to all applications such as

□   resizing a window
□   dragging/moving a window to a new location on the screen
□   converting a window to an icon and vice versa
□   decorating windows with title bars, borders, resize corners, and so on
□   supporting the stack-like manipulation of windows
□   launching (other) X applications

Being able to *iconify* a window is one of the most important facilities provided by a window manager. To iconify an application window is to replace it with a small window (icon) that represents the larger application. Without this capability, most users' desktops would be hopelessly cluttered.

Without a window manager, there would be no convenient way to resize or move your application's window(s), unless this functionality were provided by the application. Figure 1.9 shows the display screen of a UNIX workstation running X without a window manager. Compare the windows in Figures 1.6 and 1.9. The title bars, resize handles on the corners of the windows, and other window manager decoration in Figure 1.6 is absent in Figure 1.9.

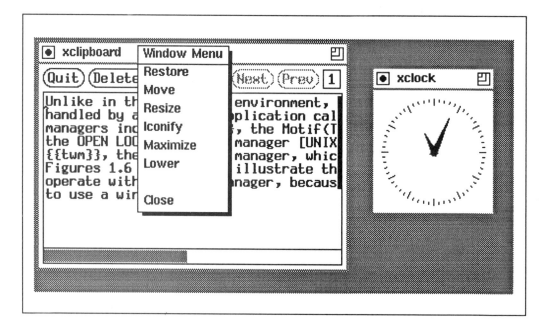

Figure 1.8 An X Environment with the Tab Window Manager

Technically, an X application should not depend on the presence of any window manager. Applications that will not operate *minimally* without a window manager, or that depend on the presence of a specific window manager, are sometimes called ill-behaved applications. It is not necessary for an application to supply its own window manager-like operations because a window manager is normally present; otherwise, however, it should still function without a window manager.

In a sense, a window manager serves as an intermediary between the X server (the X program that manages the computer display) and each application; it functions as a *super-application* issuing X server requests that decorate and manipulate *other* applications' windows. As mentioned, most window managers decorate each X application's windows with title bars, plus window borders that have areas designated as graphical handles for moving or resizing windows. Some window managers also provide a background menu that can be used to start and terminate applications plus a menu attached to the title bar and/or symbols in the title bar that provide shortcuts for operations such as expanding the window to cover the entire screen (a maximize operation).

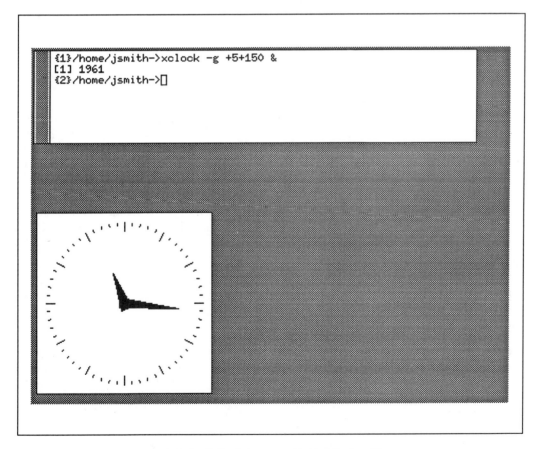

Figure 1.9 An X Environment with No Window Manager

You might ask: How can a window manager, which is just an X application, exert this level of control over other X applications? With X, window system resources (such as windows) can be shared (accessed) cooperatively by all X applications. That is, there is no mechanism in place to prohibit application A from manipulating a window belonging to application B. Thus, the window manager simply "watches" with help from the X server as applications are launched and terminated, adding its own little windows (for example, the title bar across the top of each window) to each application window. Like other X applications, it creates windows by requesting this service from the window system. An application can request a type of "lightweight" window by registering a request that the window manager not decorate a particular window.

1.4 X Toolkits and Widget Sets

It is important to recognize that although the window manager provides the resizing *controls*, the application is responsible for acting on all resize operations in an application-specific manner. For example, consider a Rolodex® (card-file) application. The application must request that the X server provide it with resizing information. When the user resizes a rolodex viewport by, say, dragging the corner of the window with the mouse, the application must redraw itself within the new window size, as requested by the user via interactions with the window manager.

If a rolodex application were developed using a programming toolkit such as the X toolkit (Xt) [Asente and Swick, 1990], the toolkit would support GUI components/objects—called *widgets* with X—that automatically respond to resize requests. There are a variety of widgets (widget sets/libraries) for implementing text-entry fields, scrollbars, dials, and so on. Of course, libraries of UI components have been available for years in character-based environments, originating perhaps with forms packages. The point here is that the use of common, prebuilt widgets for the GUI portion of a program by many application developers provides a degree of uniformity or consistency in the X environment beyond that provided by window managers. For example, scrollbar behavior will be (virtually) identical across all applications built from the same scrollbar widget. Figure 1.10 illustrates button, menu bar, scrollbar, and text-entry widgets that provide the user interface for the freeware X application *xrolodex* [Smith, 1992].

With X, the GUI objects are distinct from the programming toolkit. A widget set provides the data structures and subprograms necessary to display each GUI object and maintain its current state. A toolkit such as Xt is, essentially, a library of subprograms that provide the underlying operations necessary to implement *all* of the user-interface side of an application, beyond that provided by the GUI objects.

For example, X supports several forms of interclient communication, such as copy and paste operations between two independent X applications. In theory, the tasks involved in carrying out a paste operation should be provided by an X toolkit, because they are common to all X applications, regardless of the widget set used to implement the buttons and menus. Thus, suppose an application provides a menu entry for pasting text from the X clipboard. The menu (or menu entry) could be implemented from a widget, but the paste operation typically would be provided by a toolkit routine—the association between the GUI component and the operation is application defined. Unfortunately, in some cases, widget sets that have been developed independent of toolkits provide duplicate functionality, for example, their own copy and paste routines.

In any case, even though much of the look and feel of an application's user interface is provided by the visible components of the user interface, the toolkit is responsible for a significant portion of the application's "feel." For example, the differences between applications developed with the Motif widget set versus OPEN LOOK-based widget sets/toolkits goes beyond differences in the appearance of widgets per se. More specifically, the copy-cut-and-paste philosophy of applications developed with the XView toolkit [Heller, 1991b] is often different from that of Motif-based applications.

It is clear that the separation, or independence, that exists among the operating system, the window system, the window manager, and the application programming toolkits for the X Window System does not exist in all modern computer environments. For example, Microsoft Windows® for IBM-compatible PCs is dependent on MS-DOS® as the computer's

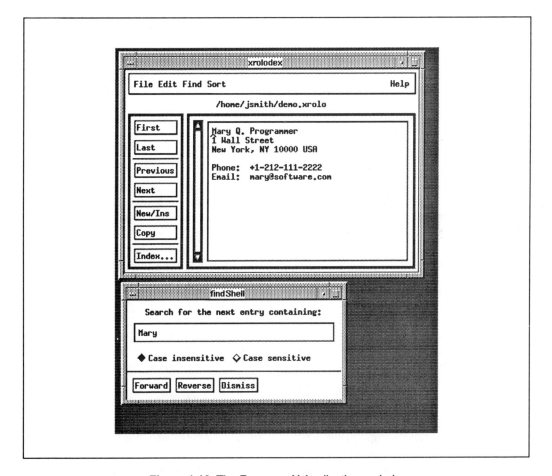

Figure 1.10 The Freeware X Application *xrolodex*

low-level control program; also, it provides a "built-in," proprietary window manager plus toolkit components that dictate the user interface's look and feel of the entire user environment. The Apple Macintosh goes a step further essentially combining the operating system, the window system, and the window manager into one giant monolith. The modular and the monolithic approaches both have advantages and disadvantages.

1.5 The X Window System

From a user's perspective, X is a collection of computer applications, libraries, and resources that provide, or implement, a graphical user environment on top of an existing operating system. X is the enabling technology that has made a common, modern, graphical, window-based user and programming environment possible with UNIX-based computing systems. Recently, however, X has been implemented for MS-DOS environments; one example is DESQ®view/X [Quarterdeck, 1992]. In addition, products such as PC-Xview® [Network Computing Devices, 1992] allow PCs to emulate X terminals (see Section 1.12) when connected to a UNIX workstation network.

Cross-platform implementations are possible because, in addition to being operating system independent, X is hardware neutral. X is also network transparent. X simply requires a reliable network transport service (such as Transmission Control Protocol [TCP] or DECnet [Kochan and Wood, 1989]) over which an X application and an X server can communicate. These issues are described further in the following sections and in Chapter 13.

Technically, X is defined by the X protocol. That is, X is a specification that states exactly how to design a system of software in which one or more programs provide display services and other programs communicate with them following a well-defined messaging system—the X protocol.

An X implementation is not a single program; it is a collection of software from at least three categories (depending on various criteria): (1) the X server, (2) common X applications, and (3) X-related data files (see Figure 1.11). The X server is *the* program that manages the computer display. X applications include utilities installed in most X environments for basic tasks such as capturing screen/window images, viewing available colors, and so on, plus freeware and commercial applications such as electronic mail programs, text editors, and spreadsheets. There are, however, many X-related files that are necessary in any X environment to support basic operations. These files include configuration files, font files, files describing colors, and so on.

We almost always speak of X as a window system, but it is also a graphics system in the sense that it supports a fairly complete library of graphics operations, such as point, line, arc, rectangle, and text drawing, plus related operations such as filling a rectangle, and many others.

1.6 The X Server and X Clients

An X server is typically implemented as software, a program that is loaded into memory each time it is used. It would, however, be possible to implement an X server on a circuit board. In some environments (for example, when a user logs in using an X terminal) the X server is started automatically; that is, the user operates within an X environment all the

time. Although it is becoming increasingly less common, in some workstation environments a user logs in to a traditional command-line prompt and then issues a command that
starts X (the X server). Typically, this command is a script that starts several common
applications in addition to the X server, such as a window manager, a miniconsole window,
a mail tool, and possibly other X applications.

In essence, the X server is a control program that manages a computer display, typically, a
monitor, keyboard, and mouse. As mentioned, the X server is an application; it is not part
of the operating system. If your environment includes a (local area) network of computers,
note that each computer display must run its own X server for users to use X from that node.
It is possible, of course, for some workstations to run X while others run a different window
system. X workstations/terminals and X servers go hand in hand because, by definition, an
X server is *the* program that provides X display services.

An X application is a *client* of the X server in the sense that it requests display services and
the X server then carries out these services on behalf of its client (typically, by sending
requests to lower level software routines that control the hardware). For this reason, X
applications such as *xterm* are often called *X clients*. X is said to follow a client-server
model. Figure 1.12 diagrams these relationships.

Sometimes, users who are new to X are confused by the "X server" terminology because
they make an improper analogy to the more familiar term "file server." Actually, the
comparison can be useful. A server is any device or program that provides services. A file
server is a computer system (typically, hardware and software) that provides large-scale data
storage services for other computers on a network, some of which may have very minimal

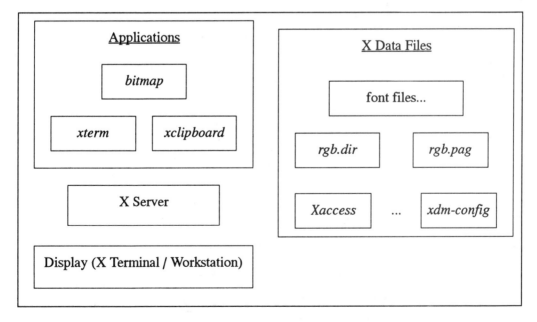

Figure 1.11 Components of an X Environment

data storage capabilities. In other words, a file server *serves* other computers on the network with respect to file management and data storage. Likewise, an X server is a component of a software system (X) that provides display services for X applications; the applications are its clients, hence, "X clients."

For example, an X application/client might issue a request such as "draw a line from coordinate (1,3) to coordinate (45,23)," and then the X server instructs the hardware to perform this task. As part of its normal operations, an X server also issues notifications of (hardware) events, for example, "the user pressed mouse button 1." During start-up operations, each X application informs the X server—on a window-by-window basis—as to which events are relevant to the application. For example, if an application has two windows, but processes keystrokes in only one window, it (typically) notifies the X server to send keystroke event notifications (over the network) for the relevant window only. The X client then performs an application-specific operation in response to each keystroke that "arrives."

1.7 X's Network Transparency

X is network transparent in the sense that X client-server communication is conducted over a network, without any special requirements from the user, via a byte-oriented communication protocol (the X protocol [Scheifler and Gettys, 1992]). It doesn't matter whether messages conforming to this protocol are communicated over a physical network between two computers or via a fixed memory area shared by the X server and client on a single

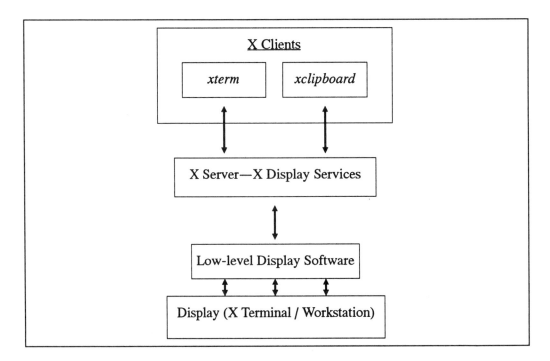

Figure 1.12 The X Server Model

computer. It is commonplace for both the X server and client to reside on the same workstation or on different workstations.

If, for example, a user has access privileges for each workstation on a network, that user can selectively start X applications on his or her workstation that use the display of any of the other workstations, simply by specifying the proper value for the display parameter. It is more common, however, for a user to perform a remote log-in to another workstation on the network and execute an X application on the remote machine, directing the application to "display itself" on the local workstation so that the user can interact with the remote X application using the local screen, mouse, and keyboard. X automatically takes care of the network-oriented details; you simply have to designate where an application should display its output. It is important to point out that X works fine on a stand-alone (non-networked) workstation as well, because with modern UNIX workstations a stand-alone workstation is, essentially, a one-workstation network (see Figure 1.13).

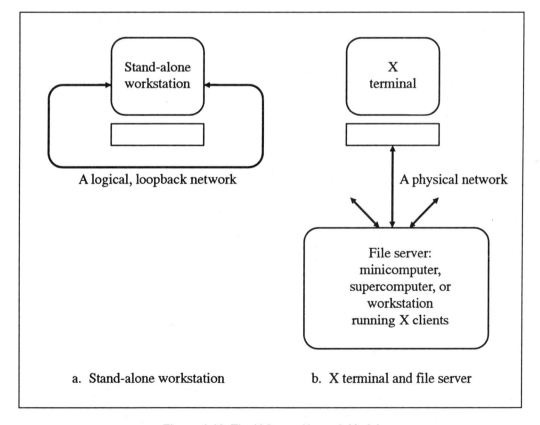

Figure 1.13 The X Server Network Model

1.8 X's Operating System Independence

X is operating system independent in the sense that the X protocol (the messaging system allowing X applications to communicate with an X server) is not designed around any particular operating system. It is true, of course, that an X server, as well as some X applications, may use certain features of the host operating system for their *implementation*. But, once they are developed/implemented as executable programs, they communicate via an operating system-independent messaging system (technically, communication protocol). This independence enables an X server executing under one operating system, say, a PC X server in a MS-DOS environment, to communicate with (provide services for) X applications executing under a different operating system, say, a Silicon Graphics® (SGI) UNIX workstation [Silicon Graphics, 1992].

1.9 X's Hardware/Platform Independence

X is hardware independent in the sense that (1) the message format for the X communication protocol uses standard data types that can be implemented for (virtually) any computer system and (2) the X server acts as an intermediary agent between an X application and the display hardware. In terms of its implementation, an X server must issue control directives for the hardware that differ from one type of hardware to the next, but in terms of communication with its clients (X applications), the X server speaks one language—the X protocol—which is understood by all X clients regardless of the type of hardware they are executing on. Thus, to modify an X server that's been designed for, say, a Sun workstation, so that it will provide the same services for, say, a PC, a programmer would rewrite hardware-dependent sections of the X server program that handle tasks such as building X protocol messages and interacting with the physical display components of the host hardware.

1.10 Look and Feel versus Interoperability

It is quite common in the popular press to advance the idea that the workstation industry should strive for one common look and feel in its software. Moreover, magazine editorials and articles sometimes suggest that there is a direct relationship between software interoperability and user-interface style. Note, however, that the concept of sharing, or transferring, information across database, spreadsheet, electronic mail, or word-processing software is largely *independent* of user-interface style.

From another viewpoint, the computing industry is a long way from the ultimate human-computer interface. In this sense it is ludicrous to suggest that, at this point in time, we should blindly follow one user-interface style. We need competing technologies because they are necessary to produce *real* advancements in user-interface design, as well as their acceptance. Otherwise, we would be stuck forever with the user-interface design offered by one hardware or software manufacturer.

A related argument is that all applications should have (essentially) the same user interface. Following this model, all applications would locate the "Save" option/command within the "File" menu, which would be the left-most menu in a mandatory menu bar. Although there are advantages to having familiar command syntax and/or menus across many applications, it is going too far to suggest that a particular application is poorly designed if it does not prescribe to this design. There are plenty of situations where a customized user-interface design may be more appropriate than one that forces the application to follow a generic user-interface layout.

With respect to interoperability, there is no reason that an X application that provides an OPEN LOOK-compliant GUI could not interoperate with an application having a Motif-compliant GUI. The issue of interoperability is largely an issue of developing standards for interclient communication. At present, X provides basic, low-level interclient communication facilities, for example, copy and paste, but these facilities are not sufficient to provide, or even encourage industry-wide movement toward, interoperability among all X clients. X's interclient communication is based on a primitive data-sharing mechanism whereby X clients can request and deliver data in a finite number of formats by attaching data as properties to the applications' windows. Ultimately, true interoperability among X clients will require considerably more cooperation and standardization than simply sharing public data via windows. (Appendix B discusses the X property concept.) The upcoming CDE initiative may rekindle an interest in interoperability (see Chapter 4).

1.11 X and the Desktop Metaphor

The X Window System, in conjunction with typical window managers, supports the so-called desktop metaphor for user-computer interaction. That is, in the typical X environment you can rearrange your applications' windows much as you would rearrange papers on your desk. A window system could be designed to support *tiled windows*, that is, windows that do not overlap each other, much like bathroom or floor tiles. This design introduces severe limitations for the user, however, because (unlike floor tiles) applications' windows typically vary in size. Thus, a tiled window design would lead to unused areas on the screen (desktop). Moreover, it is extremely convenient to have overlapping windows, just as with overlapping papers on your desk. Figure 1.14 illustrates an "out-of-control" X desktop with many overlapping windows, not unlike the desk of someone that each of us knows.

X per se supports the desktop metaphor because it supports: (1) the management of windows that are partially obscured by other windows and (2) window-move and window-resize operations. As mentioned, however, X leaves it up to the window manager to implement specific policies regarding: (1) how to request that one window be moved to a new position on the screen, for example, dragging a window by its title bar; (2) how to bring a partially hidden window forward, for example, clicking the mouse on the window's title bar or border area; (3) how to throw away a window, for example, choosing the "Close" or "Quit" entry in a menu attached to the title bar; and so on.

In terms of implementation, X is designed such that the X server honors a variety of requests by the window manager, such as a request to move application A's window. For example, the window manager might issue a request to "move window `1123497` (which the X server identifies as the main window for application A) to a position such that the top-left corner of the window is at position (45,97) on the screen." The X server carries out this request, and then generates several events that the application is responsible for monitoring. For example, a word processor should be designed to operate properly from any location on the screen; thus, an event notifying it that its window has been moved is typically of little consequence.

On the other hand, if the left half of the word processor's main window were previously obscured by a spreadsheet application's window, this portion of the word processor's window must be redisplayed. (Typically, when you move a window to a new location, a window manager will place it on top of other windows—the entire window will be viewable.) With X (and an efficient application or a powerful workstation), the user has the illusion that the window's text persists across periods of movement in front of and behind other windows. Actually, however, X provides no guarantee that it can maintain the contents of any application's window(s); this task is the responsibility of the application.

That is, each time a portion of a window is *exposed*, the X server sends the application an *exposure* event—more precisely, a notification that an exposure has occurred. The message carrying the event notification includes information that identifies the window and describes

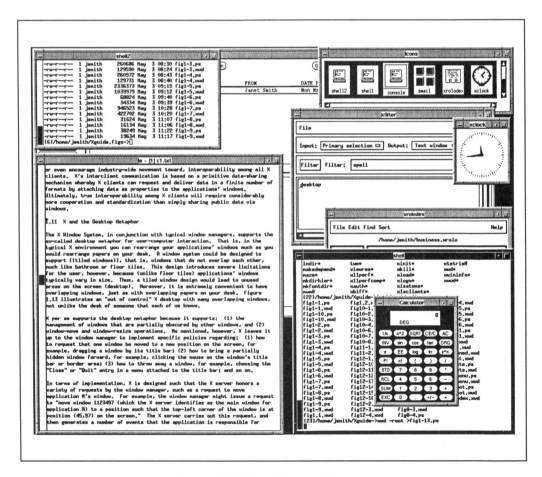

Figure 1.14 The X Desktop Metaphor

the portion of the window that has been exposed. The application can decide whether to redisplay the entire window or to rebuild/redisplay the image for the exposed window area only. A well-designed application includes rules (heuristics) that make these display-all-or-part-of-the-window determinations, based on a variety of efficiency-related issues.

If you use an inefficient application on a heavily loaded workstation, you can see an application's exposure-handling strategy in operation. Simply cover one corner of a window with some other window, and then click on the title bar to expose the entire window. The application should then either (1) generate the window image for the exposed area or (2) redisplay the entire window. The exposure handling strategy is particularly noticeable with text editors and word processors that support automatic/continuous scrolling when the text is partially hidden by a small window from another application.

During normal interaction with an X application, you generate many events indirectly, via the window manager, as well as directly (typing text in an application window generates keystroke events). For the most part, you can think of the window manager as the principal application that exploits the desktop metaphor in your X environment, because it manages the common desktop-like operations/events. On the other hand, X applications should be designed to take advantage of the desktop metaphor as well. For example, X applications that make use of multiple top-level windows, so that seldom-used functionality is hidden away except when needed, are demonstrating good use of the desktop metaphor but in an application-specific fashion. In both cases, the X server, the window manager, and applications work together to provide the illusion that tasks such as moving or resizing a window are effortless and spontaneous operations.

1.12 X Terminals versus Workstations

An X terminal is a graphics display station, typically, including a monitor, keyboard, and mouse, for user-computer interaction. Computationally, an X terminal includes one or more microprocessors that provide the computing power for graphics display operations, as well as high-speed memory for storing information. X terminals execute a customized X server; during start-up operations the X server is either downloaded from a file server somewhere on the network, or stored locally (in the X terminal), possibly in read-only memory. Regardless of where the X server is physically stored between user sessions, the X server (an executable program—software) is designed for and executes on the X terminal's microprocessor(s).

A workstation can execute any program designed for its hardware: operating systems, window systems, word processors, and so on. X terminals, on the other hand, primarily accommodate X-related programs. Minimally, an X terminal executes an X server, which manages its monitor, keyboard, and mouse. We've mentioned that because of X's network transparency X applications can execute on one workstation and "display themselves" on another workstation. Actually, X applications can "display themselves" on any (known) display station on the network that has an X server managing the display. For example, with the proper hardware and software support, a PC can serve as an X display station. An X terminal is simply a display station with hardware and software that is designed for X.

In addition to executing an X server, X terminals often provide other X and non-X services. In particular, most X terminals also support traditional, character-oriented terminal services, which may be useful during system installation, or later as a tool for communicating with computers on the network that are not X-aware. Other X-related services include providing a local window manager and X-oriented system diagnostics and statistics for X resource usage.

Local window managers are now quite common. A local window manager is an X application that executes on the X terminal, much like the X server. The X server manages the display and the window manager manages the windows of X applications (which run on the workstation), as described earlier in Section 1.3. During most X sessions you use a varied and unpredictable array of X applications, so it makes sense that they are designed to execute from a workstation. The window manager, on the other hand, typically runs continuously, and many users use the same window manager day after day.

For these reasons, in many X environments it makes sense for the X terminal to provide its own window manager, custom designed for efficient co-operation with its X server. With this set-up, communication between the X server and the window manager is local to the X terminal, as opposed to occurring over the network. Thus, X applications may perform more efficiently because of reduced network overhead. If a user prefers a window manager residing on the workstation, the X terminal can be configured easily to use the alternate window manager at the expense of additional network overhead.

1.13 X Terminals versus PC Display Stations

PC X-server software provides another type of X display station. X-server software for PCs provides an X server customized for PC hardware, for example, VGA monitors, as well as for the PC environment, for example, hotkeys for breaking out to a DOS shell and so on. As in an X terminal environment, X applications execute on the workstation and use the PC for display services. In some cases, this type of hardware/software solution is appropriate because it allows an organization to make use of an existing base of PCs. On the other hand, the performance of first-generation PC X servers has been inferior to that of the average X terminal. It would be unfortunate if a PC user's impression of X were based solely on using X via these early X display stations. We should point out, however, that as faster PCs and second-generation PC X servers become available, PC-based X display stations provide a viable alternative to X terminals in some environments.

Lastly, PC X-server software should not be confused with software that provides a complete X implementation for PCs, for example, DESQview/X. The former primarily provides display services for an X client running on a remote machine, whereas the latter provides an X server, a window manager, X libraries, and a suite of X applications (utilities). With the former, it may be possible to interrupt the X server program to execute DOS commands, and so on, but X applications must be executed on a remote machine. In contrast, with a complete X implementation for PCs such as DESQview/X, all of the X-related software can execute locally on the PC, independent of any other computer system. Moreover, if the proper physical network is in place linking DESQview/X PCs with other X environments, such as UNIX workstations running X, users in both environments can execute local X clients, as well as remote X clients.

See Chapter 13 for more information on X terminals. Also, Appendix A includes additional, somewhat in-depth, information on various aspects of X.

2

***

Getting Started with X

This chapter focuses on start-up and initialization-related issues, as well as setting up and customizing your X environment. Each computer system provides its own slight variation(s) on the X initialization process. In this chapter, to add a degree of concreteness, we describe the X start-up process for two operating system environments, but the emphasis is on the generic aspects of X Window System initialization.

2.1 Two Approaches to the X Initialization Process

Even though X is independent of the host operating system, it is fairly straightforward to set up an X user environment in which X is well integrated with and complements the non-X computing facilities. For example, with PCs, DESQview/X provides a single command, *dvx*, that starts up the X environment. If you want X to be started automatically when you turn on your PC, you can include this command in your *autoexec.bat* file (actually, the installation process will do this for you). When your PC executes *dvx*, it automatically starts the X server and a window manager, providing a menu from which you can start other X clients such as an application manager, a DOS command window, or even Microsoft Windows.

The start-up process is slightly more involved with UNIX workstations because UNIX provides user-accounting services, requiring you to log in via a log-in name and password. That is, a user must first qualify for access to the computer by way of the operating system before X can be started. Most X implementations for UNIX provide at least two ways to start X: (1) *xdm* (X display manager) and (2) *xinit* (X initialization). These programs are *not* traditional X clients; they work with the operating system to start the X server and perform other tasks. (You cannot run traditional X clients until the X server is running.)

xdm manages the complete session-oriented process of logging in to a computer, using X as your user interface to the computer, and then terminating the user session. *xinit*, in contrast, is a more simplistic program that starts X for a user who is already logged in (conducting a user session), and, typically, works from the bare console. In terms of common functionality, both utilities start the X server (thus preparing an X environment that is initialized for communication with X clients), plus X clients as specified in their respective start-up (configuration) files.

2.2 xdm

xdm is a complete display and, marginally, a session manager. A system administrator can include the appropriate commands in an operating system start-up file so that *xdm* is automatically started each time the computer is restarted. *xdm* works with the operating system to present a log-in screen that prompts for the log-in name and password; this log-in screen can be customized by the system administrator. *xdm* uses this information to (1) coordinate password verification with the operating system including reprompting the user if the log-in information is incorrect, (2) starting a user session after the log-in is verified, (3) setting up the X environment, and (4) terminating the user session and re-presenting the log-in screen for the next user. Figure 2.1 shows a UNIX workstation's screen immediately after the completion of system start-up.

xdm provides default operations for setting up the X environment, but, typically, system administrators install a start-up script (a file containing a series of operating system commands) in either a system-wide directory or in each user's home directory. Users can substitute their own customized initialization scripts in the control file *.xsession* (in their home directories). If no *.xsession* file is found, and if the system administrator has not modified the default system-wide script file (typically, */usr/lib/X11/xdm/Xsession*), the default X environment will include the *twm* window manager, plus one *xterm* command window. You could, for example, provide a script that starts a miniconsole window, a larger command window for entering UNIX commands, a mail tool, an analog clock, and other X applications. Some workstation vendors customize the log-in screen extensively.

xdm is ideal for workstation environments in which users want to run X all the time. When a workstation is configured to run *xdm* automatically, it is impractical to alternate among window systems during the course of daily operations. An obvious occasion to use *xdm* is when you're computing from an X terminal. Virtually all X terminals are designed to communicate with *xdm*, which runs on a remote computer. *xdm* manages a user session (on the remote computer) in which X clients (also running on the remote computer) are displayed at the X terminal. See Chapter 13 for more information on X terminals and *xdm*.

2.3 xinit

xinit differs from *xdm* primarily in that (1) it does not manage a user session (logging in and out), and (2) it kills the X server (and all other X processes) and terminates when the operations specified in its control file, *.xinitrc*, have completed, whereas *xdm*, in effect, manages the X server from one user session to the next. Hence, *xinit* is used chiefly by traditional UNIX users (UNIX old-timers) who want to start and stop X manually from a command-line environment. In particular, it's important to point out that *xinit* is not intended to be used directly by end-users. Rather, it is provided as part of the X distribution because it gives system administrators tremendous flexibility in setting up an X environment for their users, assuming they don't want to use *xdm*—system administrators should build a high-level user interface to X hiding the lower level *xinit*.

xinit, like *xdm*, processes an optional start-up script in the user's home directory; for *xinit*, it is named *.xinitrc*. If no *.xinitrc* file is found, the default X environment will include one *xterm* window—that's all, no window manager is started. Figure 2.2 shows an *xinit*-based X initialization with the default *xterm* window, which originates at screen coordinate (0,0). When you terminate the *xterm* window (actually, the command shell running in the *xterm* window using the command "exit"), *xinit* terminates the X session, returning you to the command shell from which you started X. [A command shell is simply a program that provides a system prompt and processes commands; common UNIX shell programs include *csh(1)*, *ksh(1)*, and *sh(1)*.]

Despite the greater sophistication of *xdm* over *xinit*, we should point out that Sun workstations as recently as OpenWindows™ 3.x were still using an *xinit*-based process to start the X environment (see Section 2.5).

Figure 2.1 The *xdm* Log-in Screen

2.4 X Initialization and Termination

Both *xdm* and *xinit* first start the X server. The X server in turn creates a large background window, the *root window*, that covers the entire screen. After the X server is running, both programs process the commands in their respective start-up scripts. When the last command in the start-up script completes (typically because of termination by the user), *xinit* simply kills the X server process (terminating any X clients running in the background) and then terminates. *xdm*, on the other hand, logs the user out and manages the next log-in prompt via the X-based log-in window, still under the control of the X server.

Consider the following hypothetical start-up script for either *xdm* or *xinit*:

```
<command to start a window manager>  &
<command to start an on-screen clock>  &
<command to start a command window>  &
<command to start a command window>
```

Figure 2.2 An *xinit*-based X Session

Here, the first three commands are started as background, or asynchronous, processes (by appending a "&" to the tail of the command). That is, as soon as each X client starts, the next command is started without waiting for the previous one to complete, providing multiple concurrent X applications. Note that the fourth command is started as a foreground, or synchronous, process; hence, *xdm/xinit* will not proceed with the next operation until this command window completes (that is, until it is terminated by the user). When the user exits this particular command window, the script is completed and the X session is finished.

Although many system administrators follow this command window-oriented convention for user termination of an X session, you can use an *.xsession/.xinitrc* script to tailor your X session to match your particular preferences. For example, suppose you'd like to end your X session by choosing the "Quit" option from your window manager's background menu, as with Sun's OpenWindows X environment. For this type of exit, simply place the command to start the window manager as the final entry in your script and run it as a foreground process:

```
<command to start an on-screen clock>  &
<command to start a command window>  &
<command to start a command window>  &
<command to start a window manager>
```

Here's an *.xsession* (or *.xinitrc*) file that provides a concrete example for a window manager-oriented termination of an X session:

```
xclock -geometry 120x120+500+2  &
sleep 2
xsetroot -solid "dark slate gray"
sleep 2
xterm -sb -geometry 70x30-1-1 -fn 7x13bold -n shell -iconic  &
sleep 2
xterm -sb -geometry 66x8+2+2 -fn 6x10 -C -n console -iconic  &
sleep 2
exec mwm
```

Note that *xsetroot*, which sets the root window to your preferred background color, terminates as soon at it performs its task, so there is no need to start it as a background process. Also, for some X environments, the *sleep(1)* commands may speed up the X start-up process because they provide "breathing room" between the invocation of each X client, reducing the number of simultaneous requests for many system resources and the contention among X clients for the X server's attention. Lastly, the use of *exec* to execute a command (in this case, the window manager) allows the operating system to start the requested command and terminate the shell process that's associated with this script, in effect, replacing the shell process with that for the program given as the final command in the script. See Appendix G for a list of X toolkit command-line options.

In conjunction with an X initialization script that is terminated via the window manager, the customization script for *mwm*, *.mwmrc*, contains (among other things) a menu specification for the root window:

```
...
Menu RootMenu
{
    "Root Menu"         f.title
    no-label            f.separator
    "Shuffle Up"        f.circle_up
    "Shuffle Down"      f.circle_down
    "Refresh"           f.refresh
    no-label            f.separator
    "xterm"             f.exec "/usr/bin/X11/xterm &"
    "xman"              f.exec "/usr/bin/X11/xman &"
    no-label            f.separator
    "Restart..."        f.restart
    "Quit X / mwm"      f.quit_mwm
}
...
```

(We've modified our root menu; the root menu defined in the default *.mwmrc* has fewer entries.) The "Quit X / mwm" menu option asks *mwm* to perform the *f.quit_mwm* operation, directly terminating the window manager and indirectly terminating X via either *xdm* or *xinit* (because "exec mwm" was the last operation in the script).

In this case, we're using the Motif window manager, *mwm*, but the same concept applies with other window managers such as *twm*, the default window manager for the X Consortium distribution of X11. For example, here is the menu definition for our root menu from a *.twmrc* customization file for *twm*:

```
...
menu "RootMenu"
{
    "Root Menu"         f.title
    "Raise"             f.raise
    "Lower"             f.lower
    "Refresh"           f.refresh
    "Applications"      f.menu "ApplicationMenu"
    "Root Background"   f.menu "BackgroundMenu"
    ""                  f.nop
    "Restart twm"       f.restart
    "Quit X / twm"      f.quit
}
...
```

2.5 Vendor-related Issues

We're taking our X examples primarily from UNIX environments, mostly because the X Window System was originally developed and first achieved widespread acceptance among UNIX workstation users. To qualify as an X implementation, a window system must honor the X protocol, the communication protocol used by the X server and X clients. Beyond this minimal requirement, however, there are many informal conventions relating to system configuration and usage that constitute an informal, standard X environment for users. In the UNIX arena, many vendors provide an X environment in which initialization and customization are similar to what we're describing here, in large part, because many vendors' X implementations are derived from the X implementations for popular workstation platforms that are distributed by the X Consortium.

A few UNIX vendors seem compelled to introduce unnecessary variations in their X implementations, and hence in the X configuration and initialization process. Some vendors "flavor" their X implementations to some degree with bits and pieces of older, sometimes proprietary, window systems, partly because they want to maintain conventions established with earlier window systems and partly because they are reluctant to provide an X environment that's almost identical to that offered by the X Consortium.

There have been several superficial modifications to the standard X environment. Examples of superficial modifications include modifying the directory structure (file organization) for X, eliminating standard X clients such as *xev*, replacing standard X clients such as *xterm* with vendor-specific command-window applications.

We should also point out, however, that several X implementations from workstation vendors provide *very significant* enhancements without introducing incompatibilities with X software from the Consortium distribution. Two examples are the control panel and associated applications that accompany the VUE™ X environment [Hewlett-Packard, 1992] and the Toolchest™ facilities provided with Silicon Graphics workstations [Silicon Graphics, 1992].

The OpenWindows X environment (Version 3.1) combines an X11 server with a NeWS® server forming one giant program, *xnews*, that honors both the X and NeWS protocols. (NeWS is a Sun Microsystems-promoted alternative to X that failed to attract a significant following.) X users who don't use NeWS clients incur a significant performance penalty (unless they have a large amount of memory in their workstations) because the X11/NeWS server is necessarily much larger than an X-only server. Many Sun users cannot elect to replace the X11/NeWS server with the Consortium X server because (at this time) Sun's online help and documentation system requires the NeWS-half of the server. Sun will soon provide a Consortium X-based desktop and has announced its participation in the CDE initiative [X/Open, 1993].

As an aside, nonstandard X implementations often have more errors than the "sample" implementations distributed by the X Consortium, introducing significant porting problems for software developers, which leads to delays in software delivery for certain hardware platforms. It is possible to enhance a product with unique features without introducing incompatible features; the HP VUE X environment is an example of a robust X-based desktop (see Section 4.12.1).

In contrast, X implementations for non-UNIX computer systems should not be expected to mirror those on UNIX platforms. That is, the X implementation should reflect conventions that already exist for that computer/operating system. For example, consider DESQview/X, an X implementation for MS-DOS-based PCs. After installing DESQview/X, a user starts the DESQview/X server simply by entering "dvx" at the DOS command prompt. If you want DESQview/X to be your default user environment, you simply add this command to your *autoexec.bat* file. In particular, DESQview/X does not make use of an *.xinitrc* file. In the PC tradition, you customize the DESQview/X environment via a set-up program and a menu-customization facility.

2.6 Starting X and X Clients

The steps you must take to configure your computer system so that X and the various X clients are available differs from one system to the next. To start DESQview/X on a PC, assuming you have installed it, you must ensure that the top-most directory in which you installed DESQview/X, typically, *c:\dvx*, is a component of your search path, which is set in your *autoexec.bat* file. The directories in which you install DESQview/X clients must be added to your search path as well, as with other DOS applications. DESQview/X suggests and provides one directory, typically, *c:\dvx\bin*, to which you can add DESQview/X clients. Hereafter, we refer to the top-most DESQview/X directory as ...*dvx*, where "..." represents the location in your directory hierarchy where you've installed DESQview/X. Once DESQview/X has been installed, you simply type "dvx" to start X and then follow the DESQview/X user's guide for information on how to start X clients from a menu or from a DOS command window.

Most UNIX systems now come with X installed, and each user environment is preconfigured with a satisfactory default X environment. If your system is not configured for X, before you can start X using either *xdm* or *xinit* you should make sure that the X11 *bin* directory is part of your search path. (A "bin" directory is a directory that has been designated for binary, or executable, files.) Typically, the *bin* directory has the path specification */usr/bin/X11*, although the location varies with certain UNIX systems. For example, with OpenWindows, the *bin* directory has the path specification *$OPENWINHOME/bin*, where $OPENWINHOME is the value of the OPENWINHOME environment variable, typically, "/usr/openwin". Search paths should be set in log-in and start-up scripts such as *.cshrc*, *.login*, and *.profile*; see your system's documentation or your system administrator for details.

With DESQview/X, X server-related files are stored in the ...*dvx\server* directory. With UNIX X implementations, the X server is typically in the file */usr/bin/X11/X*, or this filename may simply point to another executable file. For example, with Consortium X11R5 for Sun workstations the *bin* directory contains two X servers: *Xsun* and *XsunMono*. With the default installation, *X* is a symbolic pointer to *Xsun*. If you use a monochrome workstation (screen), you should probably repoint *X* at *XsunMono* because the monochrome-only X server is considerably smaller:

```
lrwxrwxrwx   1 root          8 Oct 26 10:15 X -> XsunMono*
-rwxr-xr-x   1 root    1671168 Oct 21 08:13 Xsun*
```

```
-rwxr-xr-x  1 root        827392 Oct 21 08:13 XsunMono*
```

Note that this has no bearing on whether or not you can access the workstation from color X terminals, because X terminals provide their own X servers.

If you're not already running X, you should seek help from your system administrator, if necessary, to make sure that X is properly installed. Also, if you're not running X, *xdm* is probably not active on your system. In this case you can start X with *xinit*. You can do so simply by typing "xinit" from the console:

```
{your system prompt} xinit
```

In this case, *xinit* is running as a foreground process, overtaking the entire workstation screen. When you terminate X, based on the design of your start-up script as described in Section 2.4, you should get the system prompt again. With some systems, you may have to press **<Enter>** one or two times to get the prompt.

With Sun workstations and Consortium X, you should use a text editor to create a script with the following two commands:

```
xinit
kbd_mode -a
```

kbd_mode with the -a option resets the state of the keyboard after X terminates. You should *not* execute *xinit* as a background process because you want *kbd_mode* to execute *after xinit* finishes. In some cases, without this command, your system may hang. After creating this file (suppose you've named it *start_x*), you should inform your system that it is to be used as a script/executable file:

```
{your system prompt} chmod 755 start_x
```

If you use the C shell, you should rebuild the list of executables:

```
{your system prompt} rehash
```

Then, each time you want to start X simply enter:

```
{your system prompt} start_x
```

With OpenWindows/*xnews*, you have to set the proper environment variables, as described in the OpenWindows documentation, and then type "openwin" at the console:

```
{your system prompt} openwin
```

If you decide you want to run X all the time, you can put these commands in your log-in script.

Be careful *not* to create a dependency in which your script terminates when the window manager terminates, but the window manager is configured without a "Quit" menu option. In this situation, the only way to terminate X is to list the currently running processes, find the process number for the window manager, and then kill that process.

Initially, you may want to use a script in which you terminate X via an *xterm* miniconsole window. When you're comfortable with X and you're *sure* that your window manager has a "Quit" entry in its menu system, you can modify your script. The following *.xinitrc* is quite simple and should work for just about any UNIX/X environment:

```
<window manager>  &
xclock -geometry 120x120+500+2  &
xterm -sb -geometry 70x30-1-1 -fn 7x13bold -n shell -iconic  &
exec xterm -sb -geometry 66x8+2+2 -fn 6x10 -C -n console -iconic
```

where *<window manager>* is your window manager, for example, *mwm*, *swm*, or *twm*. In this case, you terminate X by typing "exit" in the small command window (named "console" here).

Note for X terminal users: It is important to point out that if you're working from an X terminal environment, your X terminal may automatically start a local window manager, as discussed in Section 1.12. Hence, you would start a window manager from your *.xsession* script only if you prefer the window manager residing on the file server over the X terminal's default window manager. In this case, you should use your X terminal's set-up window to disable activation of the local window manager.

2.7 Customizing Your X Environment

Throughout the remainder of this book we'll address issues that have a bearing on X customization. For now, we'll mention several configuration-related details that are useful during preliminary customization of your X environment.

2.7.1 Geometry Specifications

In our sample start-up scripts we've used the `-geometry` command-line option to control where the X client first appears on the screen. If you omit the geometry specification, an X client may pop up in the top-left (0,0) position of the screen, or in a completely arbitrary location. Some window managers have configuration options (X resources) that control where the X client's window is placed in the absence of a geometry specification. Also, for some X clients, their placement may be specified in one or more resource files, as addressed in subsequent chapters. The command *appres* (application resources) will list X's current assessment of resource settings for a particular X client:

```
{your system prompt} appres XTerm
*vtMenu*altscreen*Label:    Show Alternate Screen
*vtMenu*appcursor*Label:    Enable Application Cursor Keys
*vtMenu*softreset*Label:    Do Soft Reset
*vtMenu*appkeypad*Label:    Enable Application Keypad
*vtMenu*hardreset*Label:    Do Full Reset
```

```
*vtMenu*scrollbar*Label:        Enable Scrollbar
. . .
*fontMenu*font6*Label:          Huge
*fontMenu*font2*Label:          Tiny
*fontMenu.Label:                VT Fonts
*borderContext:                 off
*resizeBorderWidth:             8
```

Here, we've requested the current X resource database settings for any X client belonging to the class *XTerm*, which includes *xterm*. In Chapter 5 we investigate X resources in detail; for now, we simply note that resource specifications often have multiple components, separated by "*" or ".". Another point is that when there are multiple components in the resource setting, a right-hand component provides specificity that can override a more general specification that includes only those components that occur to the left in the hierarchy of UI components. For example, consider a hypothetical X word processor with multiple menu systems. The following X resource would set the background color to blue for each of the application's UI components:

```
xwp*background:  blue
```

To configure the background color for specific UI components, you must name them:

```
xwp*mainWindow*popupMenu*background:    blue
xwp*spellWindow*popupMenu*menuTitle*background:   green
```

In any case, command-line options take precedence over all X resource specifications. Some command-line options such as -iconic require no trailing value; that is, the mere presence of "-iconic" on the command line signals that the application should start up as an icon.

For other command-line options such as -geometry, the X client expects the geometry specification immediately after the -geometry keyword (with at least one space in between), for example,

```
xclock -geometry 120x700+500+2   &
```

The format of the geometry specification is

```
<width>x<height>{+,-}<horizontal-offset>{+,-}<vertical-offset>]
```

The horizontal and vertical offsets may be omitted, but are important when you want an application to be placed automatically on the screen in a prescribed location.

In the previous example using *xclock*, the clock's window is 120 pixels wide and 700 pixels high. The clock's window is offset from the left edge of the screen with a displacement of 500 pixels and offset from the top edge of the screen with a displacement of 2 pixels. That is, it originates near the top-center of the screen. Here we've used different width and height values for the sake of illustration; typically, square analog clocks are more common.

A positive horizontal displacement signifies that the displacement is measured from the left side of the screen; a negative value indicates that the offset should be taken from the right edge of the screen. Similarly, a positive vertical displacement is relative to the top of the screen, and a negative offset is relative to the bottom of the screen. Figure 2.3 illustrates how X clients interpret geometry specifications. Figure 2.4 shows a workstation screen with several *xclock* clients running at various screen locations.

Most X applications use pixel metrics in interpreting geometry specifications, for example, *xclock*. For character-oriented applications, however, it is often more appropriate to use row-column metrics for the width and height specifications; command windows and text editors are examples of X clients that often use row-column metrics. For example, consider the geometry specification for one of the *xterm* command windows specified in our sample start-up script:

```
xterm -sb -geometry 70x30-1-1 -fn 7x13bold -n shell -iconic  &
```

With this specification, the command window will be 70 columns wide and 30 columns high. If you're using an X application for the first time, you may want to consult the documentation to determine how it will interpret your geometry specification.

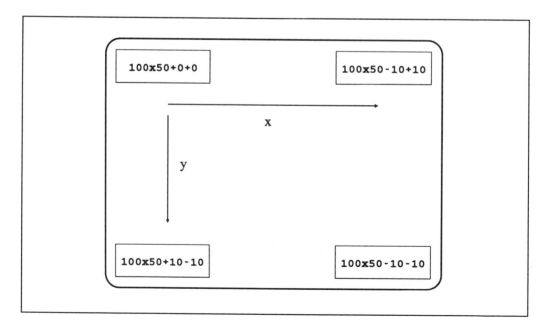

Figure 2.3 X Client Geometry Specification

2.7.2 Scrollbars

Some X clients automatically add and remove scrollbars depending on the width or height of the text. Figure 2.5.a shows *xclipboard*, the X clipboard application, displaying the first three words of this paragraph. (The text was copied to the X clipboard using a text editor.) Figure 2.5.b shows *xclipboard* displaying a longer text segment; this segment is too long for the text window (viewport), so *xclipboard* adds a horizontal scrollbar automatically.

Other X clients such as *xterm* do not provide a scrollbar in their default configuration and do not automatically add a scrollbar. For these clients, you must request a scrollbar, as we did in our sample start-up scripts, for example,

```
xterm -sb -geometry 70x30-1-1 -fn 7x13bold -n shell -iconic  &
```

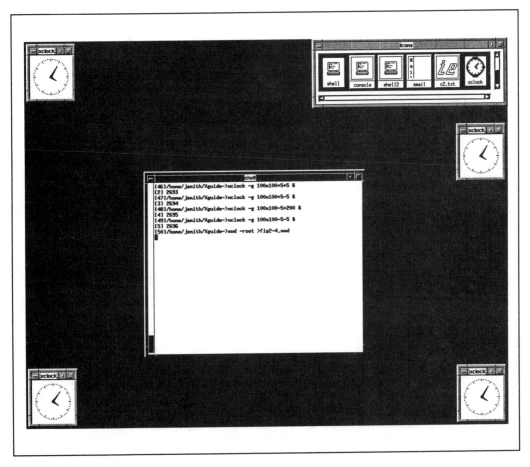

Figure 2.4 *xclock*s with Various Geometry Specifications

With *xterm*, you enable the scrollbar with the `-sb` option; as with `-iconic`, you do *not* provide a trailing on/off value. Most users prefer scrollbars for their command windows, so if you aren't using them, you may want to give them a try.

2.7.3 Fonts

Most X clients allow you to specify your preferred font, which may differ from time to time depending on how much screen area you'd like to use. If, for example, you'd like to have your X session include *xclipboard*, you simply include a line similar to the following in your start-up script:

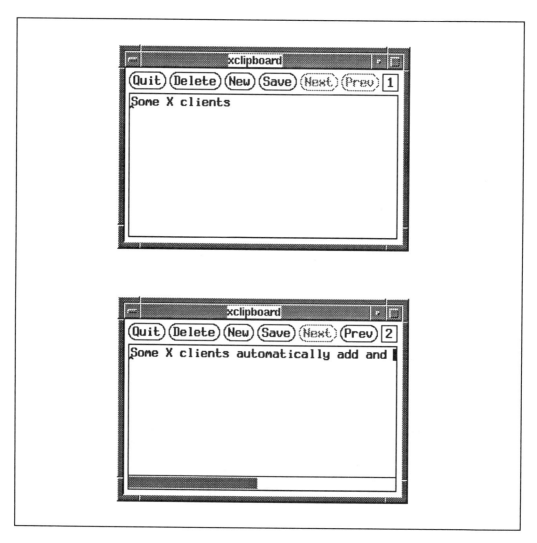

Figure 2.5 *xclipboard* with and without Scrollbars

```
xclipboard -fn 8x13bold &
```

Many X clients (but not Motif applications) accept either the `-fn` or `-font` command-line option followed by a legitimate fontname. Fontnames are quite long; therefore, X provides a mechanism for establishing short aliases for fontnames and most X implementations should be supplied from the vendor with a reasonable set of fontname aliases, for example, "fixed", "7x13bold", "9x15", and so on. X also supports incomplete, or partial, specification of fontnames using wildcard characters. For example, in the command

```
xclipboard -fn '*courier*' &
```

X will choose the first fontname that matches the font specification. In this case, we've asked for "any Courier font." The single quotes are necessary to prevent the command processor from interpreting wildcard characters as file specifications. Your system probably has several simple fontname aliases such as "7x13bold", "9x15bold", and others that don't require you to specify long fontnames or use wildcard specifications. Of the X clients we've mentioned so far, *xterm* "prefers" a monospaced font, as opposed to a proportional font. You can tell whether a font is monospaced or proportional by examining its complete fontname, which includes an "m" for monospaced fonts and a "p" for proportional fonts. For example, for the two fontnames that follow, the first font is proportional and the second font is monospaced:

```
. . .
-bitstream-charter-bold-r-normal--33-240-100-100-p-206-iso8859-1
. . .
-b&h-lucidatypewriter-bold-r-normal-sans-24-240-75-75-m-140-iso8859-1
. . .
```

We address various font issues in subsequent chapters; for now, you can use *xlsfonts* from a command window to get a listing of the available fonts. *xfd* will display the "attributes" for a specific font, as well as each character in the font; *xfd* is sometimes useful for previewing a particular font, although its primary purpose is to provide point-and-click feedback for font-level and character-level attributes of a specific font.

2.7.4 Application and Icon Names

When we address X resources in depth, we will provide a complete discussion of application names. In terms of configuring your start-up scripts, however, it is often convenient to have multiple sessions of an application, each with a different icon name. Distinct icon names are important, of course, so that you can distinguish among them at times when multiple sessions of an application are reduced to icons.

For this reason, many X applications provide an X resource, typically called *iconName*, as well as a command-line option for setting the icon name. With *xterm*, for example, the default icon name is "xterm"; you can override the title bar and icon names with the command-line option `-n`. In our sample start-up script we use the `-n` option to start one *xterm* named "shell" and another named "console":

```
...
xterm -sb -geometry 70x30-1-1 -fn 7x13bold -n shell -iconic  &
exec xterm -sb -geometry 66x8+2+2 -fn 6x10 -C -n console -iconic
```

Our primary objective at this point is to distinguish `-n` from `-name`. The latter option sets the application name for an X client, which affects the manner in which X searches for an application's configuration values. Thus, if you inadvertently use `-name` instead of `-n`, it's likely that the *xterm* client's configuration will differ in some way from your other *xterm* clients, so be aware of this distinction. There is another option, `-title`, that can be used to set the title of an *xterm* window, provided that the window manager honors the request, but it does *not* affect the icon name. Typically, however, if you want to modify the name displayed in the title area, you also want the icon name to match it. The command-line option `-name` is discussed further in Section 5.7.

2.7.5 Border Width

Each user has his or her personal preferences with respect to "cosmetic" issues, such as the border width for an application's window(s). Keep in mind that the border width of top-level windows is controlled, essentially, by the window manager. For example, if you're using *mwm* as your window manager and you set the border width for *xterm* with the `-bw` command-line option, for example,

```
xterm -bw 5 &
```

(or with the X resource *borderWidth*), it will probably have no effect on your top-level windows, because it will be masked by *mwm*'s *resizeBorderWidth* resource. In other words, window manager configuration parameters affect many top-level application windows, so the effect of setting things like border width may be limited to an application's subordinate (interior or nested) windows. Thus, if it appears that a command-line option is being ignored, especially for anything that seems somewhat related to the window manager, make a mental note that you may need to check for a related X resource supplied by your window manager.

2.8 Remote Display Operations

In most X environments, particularly with UNIX workstations, you don't have to specify the display explicitly. That is, the hardware device from which you interact with the X application is determined automatically; common displays include workstations, X terminals, and PC-based X display stations.

2.8.1 The DISPLAY Environment Variable

Both *xdm* and *xinit* set the DISPLAY environment variable to "unix:0.0", ":0.0", or something similar to this, which is understood by X to represent your local host (the machine you're working from). Subsequently, each X client will use the value of the DISPLAY environment variable, unless otherwise specified, in choosing the appropriate X server (display).

Parenthetically, if you're a UNIX/X user with *csh(1)* as your command shell, you can use the *setenv* command with no arguments, that is,

```
{your system prompt} setenv
```

for a listing of all environment variables and their current values. (With the Bourne shell [*sh(1)*], use *set* to examine environment variables.) Or, you can simply test the value of this one environment variable:

```
{your system prompt} echo $DISPLAY
```

The format of the display value is `host:x-server.screen-number`, for example, `pluto:0.0`. *host* refers to the workstation's hostname as returned by the command *hostname(1)* for Berkeley UNIX derivatives, or by *uname(1)* with the `-n` command-line option for UNIX System V derivatives. *x-server* is the number of the X server to which the application should connect. Because an X server serves a particular display, you can think of this field as representing the display. *screen-number* is the screen number on the specified display.

2.8.2 Real and Artificial Hostnames

We should emphasize that the default value used by *xdm/xinit* is not the actual hostname; as mentioned, it is an artificial value, possibly null, that *represents* the local workstation. If, however, you want to work with an X client on your local display that is running on a remote computer, you must identify your local display station by its official network name. If your display is a workstation, use its official hostname; if your display is an X terminal, use its network node name (not the hostname of the remote computer that is hosting the X terminal).

The display value includes a component for the X server number because it is theoretically possible to have multiple displays (screen, keyboard, and mouse combinations) attached to one CPU; in this case, each display would be under the control of a distinct X server. This type of configuration is very uncommon in practice, but it is nevertheless reassuring that X supports multiple displays. On the other hand, it is not uncommon to connect multiple screens to a workstation, for example, one color screen and one monochrome screen. Note that a single X server can manage multiple screens; some X servers can manage one physical screen as two virtual screens (for example, color and monochrome screens).

X is designed so that over-the-network execution and/or display of X clients is almost effortless. Note that determining/specifying the machine on which an X client will *execute* is not really an X-related issue. That is, arranging access to the *bin* directories where X applications are located is the same for both X and traditional applications. Executables could reside in one or more directories local to your workstation, or they could be accessed (mounted) over the network from a file server.

Assuming that you have the proper file access so that you can execute X clients, let's consider the possibilities for interacting with an X application from a computer other than the one where it's executing.

2.8.3 Executing/Displaying X Clients from an X Terminal

The first situation that we should mention is an X terminal environment. That is, you're sitting at an X terminal, but the X client is running on a file server. Most X terminals are configured such that when you log in to the file server (via *xdm*) the `DISPLAY` environment variable will be set to the X terminal's network name. Moreover, `DISPLAY`'s value will be set properly for the command shell associated with each *xterm* command window, as well as for X clients launched from your start-up script. Here's the value of `DISPLAY` taken from an *xterm* window for one of our X terminals:

```
{your system prompt} echo $DISPLAY
hds1:0.0
```

With this X terminal, configured as node "hds1" on our network, there is one display and one screen (display number 0 and screen number 0).

2.8.4 Displaying X Clients on a Remote Workstation

Next, suppose you're sitting at a workstation named "saturn" and would like start an X client on saturn and display it on a workstation named "jupiter" in the next room. For example, suppose both workstations are on the same local area network, it's late in the day, you're tired of sitting down, and the chair at jupiter is much more comfortable than the one at saturn. First, you (or someone else with an account on jupiter) must activate/authorize remote access to jupiter from saturn:

```
{the system prompt on jupiter} xhost +saturn
saturn being added to access control list
```

This command adds saturn to the list of network nodes that is authorized to connect to (display on) jupiter. *xhost* is a component of X's host-based access control facilities; see Section 13.15 for more information.

Typically, jupiter will have one hardware display system and one screen. So, to start an *xterm* on saturn that you can interact with from jupiter, and its comfortable chair, you would enter the following in a command window on saturn:

```
{your system prompt on saturn} xterm -display jupiter:0.0 &
```

At this point, you could walk to the next room and work comfortably.

Another example of this particular configuration of over-the-network display of X clients is the devious situation in which you would like to activate the freeware X client *xroach* on the display of pluto, a workstation used by one of your colleagues. (*xroach* displays bugs on the root window that hide behind application windows. When the user iconifies a window, the bugs are suddenly exposed and they scurry for cover behind another window.) First, you should authorize a connection from your machine, saturn, while your colleague was gone to lunch (pluto was left unattended and unprotected):

```
{the system prompt on pluto} xhost +saturn
saturn being added to access control list
```

You can now surprise your unsuspecting colleague:

```
{your system prompt on saturn} xroach -display pluto:0.0 &
```

Of course, before your colleague can retaliate, you should disable access to your workstation from pluto (if it exists):

```
{the system prompt on saturn} xhost -pluto
pluto being removed from access control list
```

2.8.5 Running X Clients on a Remote Workstation

A common remote-display situation is when you need to run an X application on a remote workstation, but you want to interact with it from your workstation. There are many situations that give rise to this type of remote-on-local display operation: (1) your chair is better than the one at the remote workstation; (2) you don't have the required application on your workstation, but you prefer to work from your office; or (3) the application is a gigantic number cruncher that requires the fastest possible CPU, but your machine is a midrange workstation.

For this type of situation, you have essentially two ways to get the X client going: (1) walk/drive/fly to the location of the faster workstation and start the X application in the manner we described in Section 2.8.4 or (2) start the application on the faster workstation (jupiter) remotely from your workstation (saturn), directing it to saturn for display services. The first step is to authorize jupiter to use your display, if you haven't already done so:

```
{your system prompt on saturn} xhost +jupiter
jupiter being added to access control list
```

The next step is to log in to the remote workstation:

```
{your system prompt on saturn} rlogin -l <your-user-id> jupiter

<jupiter responds with a message of the day, and so on>

{your system prompt on jupiter}
```

The last step is to start the X application on jupiter, directing it to saturn:

```
{your system prompt on jupiter} <xapplication> <other-args> -display
saturn:0.0 &
```

2.8.6 Running X Clients on an Alternate Workstation

There is another potentially confusing situation. Suppose that you normally work from an X terminal named "ncd1" configured for host (log-in) services on saturn. On occasion, however, you need to log in to your account on jupiter from ncd1, to make use of jupiter's faster CPU. In this case, you want to direct the X application to display on ncd1.

With this type of configuration your X terminal is already associated with saturn. So, should you direct the application on jupiter to saturn? No. With X, it immaterial that there is an existing "log-in relationship" between saturn and ncd1. From ncd1, you can do a remote log-in to jupiter, analogous to that demonstrated in Section 2.8.5. When you start the application on jupiter, you should direct it to ncd1:

```
{your system prompt on saturn via ncd1} xhost +jupiter
jupiter being added to access control list
{your system prompt on saturn via ncd1} rlogin -l jsmith jupiter

<jupiter responds with a message of the day, and so on>
. . .
{your system prompt on jupiter via ncd1} <xapp> <other-args> -display
ncd1:0.0 &
```

Depending on your environment, there may be other opportunities for remote-display operations, but the previous situations are the most common ones. With these examples as guidelines, you should be able to handle any over-the-network X environment.

2.9 Access to X Applications

We mentioned *bin* directories in Section 2.6. A final note is that if you have a problem executing common X clients such as *xev*, *xdpyinfo*, *xedit*, and others, there are several considerations:

1. Do they exist in an unreferenced *bin* directory; see Section 2.6?
2. Do they require access to certain shared operating system and X libraries?
3. Have they been relocated to, say, a demonstration directory?
4. Are they missing from your X software distribution?
5. Have configuration files been placed in nonstandard locations?

As mentioned earlier, with OpenWindows, the *bin* directory has the path specification "$OPENWINHOME/bin", where $OPENWINHOME is the value of the OPENWINHOME environment variable, typically "/usr/openwin". In particular, there is no *usr/bin/X11* directory.

In a UNIX environment, X applications are often designed to access common subprograms from a library that's shared by all X applications. If these libraries are unavailable, an X application will not start, even if the *bin* directory and executable file are in well-known locations. X client failure resulting from missing libraries is common when applications are started from window manager menus, because these libraries may not be known in the command environment in which the window manager was launched—even though the same X clients start properly from a command window after X is up and running.

In certain vendor-specific X environments, numerous X clients are often relocated to a demonstration directory, or omitted from the X distribution altogether because the vendor made the decision for you that you wouldn't need that client, or because there is a vendor-specific alternative to a standard X client such as *xterm*. If they exist in out-of-the-way locations, you can have your system administrator make them available. If they are nonexistent, he or she will have to obtain the original X program(s) and build them locally.

The last scenario that we mention is the one in which an X client fails to start properly because it depends on various configuration parameters that it reads from configuration (X resource) files. If these files are missing, or located in nonstandard directories, the application could fail.

For each of these situations there are numerous site- and vendor-specific issues that could have a bearing on getting your system fully operational. The best plan of action is to consult with your system administrator. X is a large and sophisticated software system. If your X environment has been configured properly, it is a joy to use; if not, it is simply too complex for trial-and-error configuration.

3

Window Manager Fundamentals

In this chapter we focus on basic window manager operations and issues. In subsequent chapters we address the many ways of customizing the X environment, which include various window manager issues. In particular, a discussion of window manager customization must await our coverage of X's resource database facility.

3.1 The Window Manager as a Look-and-feel Contributor

In Chapter 1 we mentioned that the look and feel of the X environment is provided by (1) the window manager and (2) the application(s). And, the look and feel of an application is typically a function of (1) the toolkit and (2) the widget set from which it is built. Not all applications, however, are built from the X toolkit and the Athena [MIT X Consortium, 1992] or the Motif widget set. There are other popular toolkits and widget set (object library) combinations including InterViews/Fresco [Linton and Price, 1993], Object Interface (OI) [Benson and Aitken, 1992], and Tk [Ousterhout and Rowe, 1993], as well as numerous custom toolkits and object libraries.

Parenthetically, we should point out that an X application is an X application. That is, regardless of the toolkit used for development, if X clients and X servers follow the rules set forth in the *Inter-Client Communication and Conventions Manual* (ICCCM) [Rosenthal, 1992], an X application will run (display) properly on any X server, and the choice of window manager is unimportant operationally.

Unfortunately, a minority of commercial vendors have been quite arrogant, essentially thumbing their noses at the conventions adopted by the X community, by designing, for example, a Motif toolkit-based application that assumes that you're running the Motif window manager, *mwm*. Symptoms of poor software design include pop-up dialog boxes that behave properly only when *mwm* is running. This type of "lazy" software development introduces problems for users who like to vary their choice of window managers depending on the nature of their current work environment. Unless users reject these vendor-imposed limitations, specifically, the vendor's noncompliant commercial X software, these developers will continue to ignore established conventions, further limiting users' flexibility and freedom of choice in customizing their X environments.

In terms of the look and feel of the X environment, the window manager makes a substantial contribution. Visually, the user's view of an application is fundamentally influenced by the decoration that a window manager provides for each application's windows. Operationally, the window manager provides the facilities for resizing an application's window(s), terminating an application, rearranging the windows of various applications (the desktop metaphor in action), and so on.

Most window managers provide much of their functionality through one or more menu systems. *twm* and others provide a root menu that can be customized quite easily (see Figure 3.1). (See Chapter 12 for various customizations to *twm* including the addition of a window menu.) If you choose a menu option that, for example, deletes a window, you are then given an opportunity to click on the intended window. As a visual cue, *twm* uses a skull-and-crossbones mouse pointer to signal that it is waiting for you to designate which window it should delete. (Actually, a well-designed window manager sends a delete-window message to the application instead of directly deleting the window. This approach is preferred because the

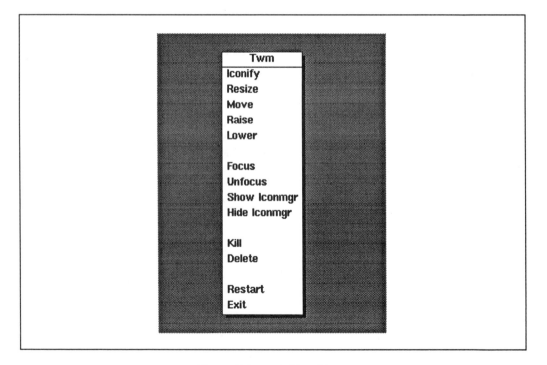

Figure 3.1 *twm*'s Root Menu

application is better able to decide on the proper course of action, such as prompting the user regarding unsaved work, in addition to deleting the window gracefully.)

In their default configurations, *mwm* differs from *twm* in that it provides several operations through its background menu (you can modify the menu entries), plus a pull-down (window) menu that is invoked from the menu button on the left side of the title bar of an application's top-level window(s) (see Figure 3.2). As with many PC GUI products, *mwm* uses mouse button 1 to manipulate the title bar-based menu. Some of the operations in the title bar menu duplicate operations that are more easily done with a mouse, a leftover liability (or feature, depending on your point of view), of Motif having been modeled (ultimately) after the character-based PC interface of the mid-1980s, rather than having been designed from the beginning for today's more powerful computing equipment.

The OPEN LOOK window manager, *olwm*, provides a third type of look and feel. Like *mwm*, it provides a pull-down menu that is activated from the menu button on the left side of the application's title bar; its window menu is invoked with mouse button 3 (see Figure 3.3).

Note that there is no established convention for naming menu entries based on their functionality. For example, most window managers use a "Delete" or "Quit" menu option to terminate an application (or one of its top-level windows). *mwm*, however, names this menu operation "Close", a label that some window managers reserve for the iconify operation and that is more ambiguous than "Quit", and somewhat inappropriate except in the case of pop-up dialog boxes.

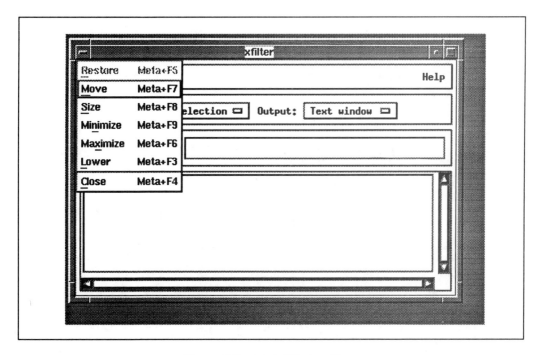

Figure 3.2 *mwm*'s Window Menu

3.2 The Window Manager as a Superapplication

In Chapter 1 we mentioned that the window manager is an X client. That is, like other X applications, the window manager registers an interest in several types of (display) events, related to its window management strategy. When the events of interest occur, the X server passes them along to the window manager. The window manager registers an interest in essentially two categories of events: (1) mouse events occurring in the window manager decoration areas that it adds to each application window, as well as mouse events in the window manager-related menus (root window and application window menus), and (2) keyboard events occurring either within an application's main window, as well as keyboard events occurring when a window manager-related menu is posted.

Events that occur within the window decoration areas (such as title bars) are of no direct interest to an application, because these areas are not strictly part of the application's window hierarchy (hierarchies). That is, "to decorate an application window" is a nontechnical way of saying that the window manager has *reparented* an application window. Reparenting is the process of establishing a new top-level window for the application and making the old top-level window subordinate to (a child of) the new (parent) window. (A top-level window is any window that is a child of the root/background window.) Reparenting an application window packages it and its decoration inside an all-encompassing window, managed by the window manager in a manner that is transparent to the application.

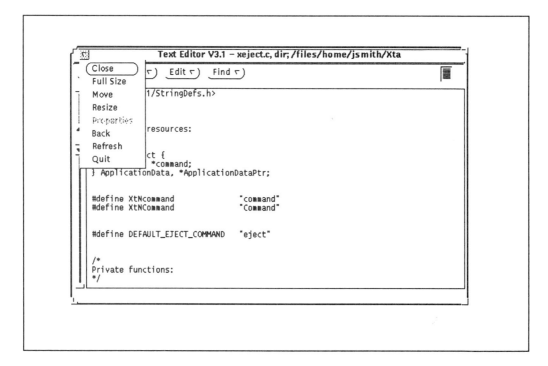

Figure 3.3 *olwm*'s Window Menu

Thus, when you use a window manager in an X environment, each time you start an application the window manager essentially *intercepts* that application's request to create one or more top-level windows, creating it inside an alternate top-level window along with several other small windows that implement that window's decoration. For example, each resize handle would be a tiny window within the (new) top-level window, one that has been designed to perform specific actions in response to specific mouse events.

Consider *mwm*. When you move the mouse pointer over an *mwm* resize handle, the mouse cursor changes to a new shape that signals *mwm*'s readiness to resize the window. Then, when you press mouse button 1 within the resize handle, *mwm* dynamically grows or shrinks the application window so that its corner follows the position of the mouse pointer as you drag it across the screen. Thus, in addition to the application window, there are numerous small windows that are being resized dynamically, for example, the windows that constitute the border for each top-level window.

The point of this low-level description of a resize operation is to illustrate the clear dichotomy of event categories relative to the application. First, many events occur strictly as a result of the services provided by the window manager, and within the confines of the window manager's decoration. Events in this category include those generated by dragging, resizing, and manipulating the stacking order of windows. Second, many events occur within an application window that, depending on the window manager, may be intercepted/usurped by the window manager.

A common example of the latter category is keystrokes that are interpreted as shortcuts for window manager operations. For example, by default, with *mwm* typing <Alt>-<F3> in an application window lowers it in the stacking order, if possible. That is, if you're working in a window that's hiding part of another window, you can bring the partially hidden window to the foreground by typing <Alt>-<F3>. Unfortunately, having many keyboard accelerators dedicated to window manager operations limits the command set for applications. Note that in the X server's eyes the window manager has first priority—that's why we refer to it as a superapplication.

As an aside, keyboard accelerators were important in the old days in PC environments when many users didn't have a mouse, or, because of the inadequacies of the PC GUI environments, they found it more productive to use the keyboard. With modern workstations, however, most users do use the mouse to manipulate the windows "on their desktops." In a sense, it is a GUI design travesty to dedicate some of the most "convenient," or economical, keystrokes to the window manager, because they could be used more productively by applications, especially considering that most users employ the mouse to manipulate their desktop. If users spend most of their time working within the application, does it make sense, in terms of overall economy, to restrict applications' accessibility to keystrokes? In Chapters 11 and 12, we describe how to customize your X environment, including how to suppress the window manager keyboard accelerators. It's ironic that with today's sophisticated and computationally powerful workstations, we're still enduring the legacy of GUIs designed for PCs that had less than 1 percent of the computing power of today's modern workstations.

To reiterate the objective of this section, the window manager is a superapplication that has first priority with respect to workstation events, in particular, keyboard events. Moreover, it has the authority (1) to reparent an application window, making it part of a package that includes window decoration, (2) to manipulate the organization of windows on the desktop, and (3) to delete application windows.

3.3 Levels of Window Decoration

There are three levels of window decoration, or from another perspective, window manager intervention. Top-level windows receive the maximum amount of decoration, typically, with title bars that include iconify buttons in addition to the application title areas. Some window managers, for example, *twm*, provide a resize button in the title area (Figure 3.4.a), whereas other window managers provide resize handles at the window corners, for example, *mwm* (Figure 3.4.b) and *olwm* (see Figure 3.4.c).

Windows at the second level have less decoration than top-level windows, typically referred to as minimal decoration. These windows are sometimes called *transient* windows, because they are implemented via a programming abstraction called a *transientShellWidget*, although this terminology is often confused with that applied to the third type of application window. For this reason, the second level of decoration can be referred to as *minimally-decorated* windows, or simply *pop-up dialogs*. The exact level and style of decoration is up to the window manager; typically, there will be no iconify or maximize buttons with minimally decorated windows. (A maximize button resizes a window so that it fills the entire screen.) Applications typically request top-level decoration for windows that it makes sense to resize, for example, an edit window and minimal decoration for windows that exist on-screen for short durations (hence, the name "transient"), for example, pop-up dialog boxes. Figure 3.5 illustrates minimally-decorated windows.

There is a third level of window decoration—none (see Figure 3.6). The technical name for this type of window is an *override-redirect* window. It is really not important to know this

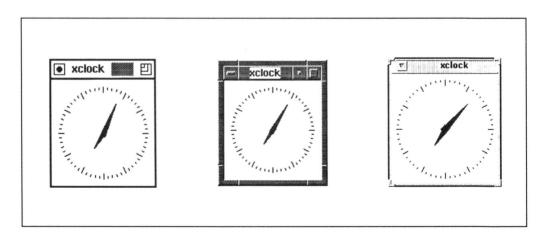

Figure 3.4 Window Decoration

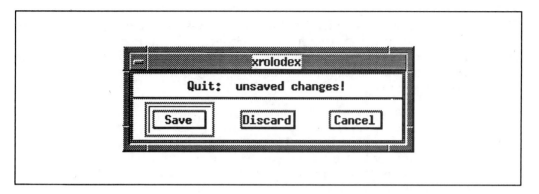

Figure 3.5 Minimal Window Decoration

terminology, and it is more convenient to think of decoration-free windows as *lightweight* windows. The proper use of lightweight windows can greatly increase the efficiency of applications, but they typically are not addressed in style guides so UI designers often consider them taboo. In an X terminal environment, or with heavily loaded workstations or networks, lightweight windows can be much more enjoyable for power users who want instantaneous pop-up windows. Also, an application can provide configuration options that provide the user with some control over the behavior of lightweight window, eliminating potential conflicts with the window manager.

3.4 Window Decoration

The title bar is the most prominent and most often used form of decoration (see Figure 3.4). As mentioned earlier, title bars are actually windows that the window manager attaches to the application window, through which it processes various user-generated mouse events.

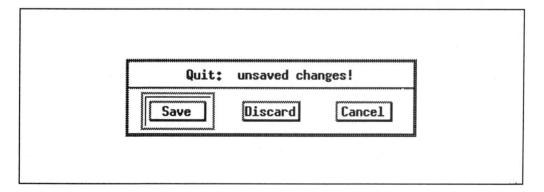

Figure 3.6 No Window Decoration

With standard and simple applications, the title area typically contains the application name, although some programs allow you to change this characteristic with a command-line option or X resource. X clients such as text editors often display application-specific information in this area, for example, the name of the file that's being edited, whether or not there are unsaved changes, and so on.

Beyond the title area, most window managers provide additional, shortcut buttons or handles. *olwm*, for example, provides a combined iconify and menu button, whereas *mwm* provides iconify, menu, and maximize buttons. With *olwm* you can also activate the window menu with mouse button 3 anywhere inside the title area. Because *mwm* is highly customizable, you can add this functionality to *mwm* as well (see Section 12.3.2). (Some versions of *mwm* have this functionality as part of their default button bindings.)

Both *mwm* and *olwm* provide resize handles on an application's window corners, so that you can simply grab the corner with the mouse (pointer) and stretch it. One of the main reasons, however, for *mwm*'s popularity is the additional resize borders that extend along the full length of each side of an application's windows. These resize edges allow you to extend a window in one direction only, without inadvertently varying the other window dimension. Another convenience is that clicking mouse button 1 on a resize corner or resize edge instantly brings that window to the foreground.

With respect to window decoration, *twm* is rather modest. It provides a title bar only, containing the title area, an iconify button, and a single resize button. The practical result of having only a title bar as decoration is that when your desktop is cluttered a window's title bar is often hard to access, making it more difficult to rearrange windows on the desktop. On the other hand, *twm* is considerably smaller than *mwm*, a significant factor when workstation memory is in short supply. (The addition of a window menu to *twm* compensates for many situations in which the iconify and resize buttons are hidden; see Section 12.5.5.)

3.5 Window Manager Menus

There are essentially two types of window manager menus: (1) application window menus, invoked/originating from the application's title area, and (2) root window menus. Window menus provide commands that apply to that window, for example, lowering the window to the bottom of the stack. Menus that pop up from the root window provide commands that apply specifically to the window manager, for example, restarting and terminating the window manager, as well as commands that apply to the user environment in general, for example, executing a specific application and saving a record of the current desktop layout. In Chapter 12 we illustrate how to customize both types of menus.

3.6 Icons

All modern window managers support icons. When you iconify an application, its window is replaced by a small window that represents the application. In terms of the desktop metaphor, you get the illusion that the application window has shrunk "to a mere shell of its former self." In practice, there is no significant reduction in the usage of X system resources. The window manager simply unmaps the application window, which simply means that it still exists but it is now invisible. When you click on the icon, the window manager maps the application window to the screen and unmaps the icon.

All window managers support what can be called primitive icons for which the icon window contains a static bitmap (pixel) image, supplied by either the application or the window manager. Some window managers support more sophisticated icons for which the application can dynamically update the contents of the icon window. Applications such as electronic mail software (mail tools) employ this type of icon window to signal the user that there has been a change in the state of the application, for example, when new mail has arrived.

Some window managers, for example, *mwm*, support an icon box, which is simply a scrolling repository for your applications' icons (see Figure 3.7). If you tend to have, say, 10 or more X clients running concurrently or several X clients with numerous top-level windows, you probably should consider using an icon box; otherwise, the icons occupy too much screen space and are often inconveniently hidden behind application windows.

Lastly, if you prefer that your applications start up in iconic form, note that many X clients support the `-iconic` command-line option and/or the *iconic* X resource.

3.7 Modality

A pointing device such as a mouse in conjunction with a graphical, windowed user environment has provided the enabling technology for concurrent interaction between the user and multiple applications, or between the user and multiple windows of the same application. With modern GUIs, an application can (when the circumstances permit) display messages, prompt for required information, and other tasks in a manner that simply delays execution of that portion of the application until the user responds. In the meantime, the user is free to interact with some other component of the application. In a sense, instead of the application controlling what the user does next, the user controls what the application does next.

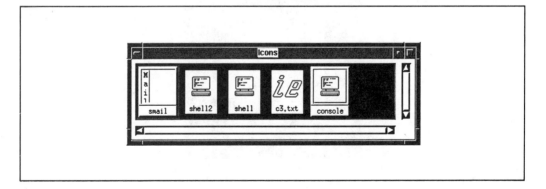

Figure 3.7 *mwm*'s Icon Box

This type of operation is sometimes referred to as *modeless*. *Nonmodal* is perhaps a more appropriate term, primarily because the application still has a user-application interaction mode. The term *modal* has a long history and traditionally has been used to describe applications that have a highly structured style of user interaction. For this reason, in this book we use the term *nonmodal* to describe an application, or application component, that is designed to offer the user greater flexibility in its order of user interaction.

The modality issue often arises in the construction of dialog boxes (see Figure 3.8). With a modal dialog box, the application essentially blocks its execution (and hence its interaction with the user) until the user responds to the dialog box prompt. Based on the user's response, the application conditionally performs one of several possible actions. Although nonmodal dialogs often can be used to provide greater flexibility in user-application inter-action, they typically require mouse usage. That is, if you've moved the mouse pointer to some other window to perform an operation while the application component that presented the nonmodal dialog is suspended, you must move the mouse back to the dialog box and/or click a mouse button to respond to the prompt. In many situations, this type of user interaction is entirely appropriate, if not ideal.

On the other hand, there are at least two circumstances for which nonmodal dialogs can be a liability. First, if an application uses a modal dialog, it "knows" that the user's next response applies to the blocking dialog. This design facilitates the use of keyboard-based responses; that is, no explicit mouse response is required on the user's part to direct keystrokes to that dialog box. It is easy to design nonmodal dialog boxes that accept both keyboard and mouse/button responses; however, by definition, a nonmodal design implies that the user must explicitly direct his or her response to that dialog box.

Second, providing the user with too much flexibility can produce confusion, for the user as well as the programmer(s) designing the application. For example, suppose a user edits a

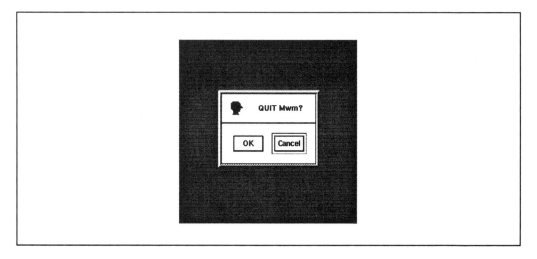

Figure 3.8 *mwm*'s Modal Dialog Box for Window Manager Termination

letter with a word processor, and then attempts to edit another letter in the same workspace without first saving the modified letter. The application could use at least two nonmodal designs. One approach would be to display a dialog box asking if the user wants to save the modified letter first—loading the second letter for editing would be contingent on the user's response. That is, a "Yes" or "No" response to the save-text message would be followed by loading of the second letter, but a "Cancel" response would terminate the pending load operation.

The second approach would be to abandon immediately the load operation for the second letter, because the text hasn't been saved, leaving it up to the user to answer "Yes" or "No" to the save-text message either now or at some point in the future. Because the request to edit the second letter had been abandoned, the user would have to reissue this request as appropriate.

This example provides a realistic, but rather simple, scenario for when an application could be designed to use nonmodal dialog boxes. The nonmodal approach provides flexibility because the user is not forced to respond to the dialog prompt immediately. In particular, when a dialog box is used to warn the user of a potentially dangerous operation, and, hence, requires a confirmation from the user before completing the task, a nonmodal approach allows the user to go to another window to "investigate the situation" before making a decision. On the other hand, if an application overuses the nonmodal approach, the out-of-sight-out-of-mind phenomenon can become an issue, or the user could get into a situation for which there are several pending dialog boxes and it is impossible to remember in which order they should be addressed.

It is clear that both modal and nonmodal user-application interactions have their places among today's relatively crude GUIs. Unfortunately, when technologies such as X and other modern GUIs first appeared, a few zealots quickly proclaimed that modal user interactions were no longer acceptable. It is up to application developers to employ the proper balance of modal and nonmodal user-application interactions.

3.8 Focus Models

A *focus model* is, in effect, a strategy by which the user indicates to the X server which application it should direct keystroke events to (assuming that that X client has registered an interest in keystroke events). Of course, there could be many X clients executing concurrently. Most X environments (window managers) support two common focus models. Following one model, the user *explicitly* indicates that keystrokes should be delivered to a particular window, typically, by clicking mouse button 1 in that window. Following the other model, the user *implicitly* indicates the appropriate window by moving the mouse cursor to the window before typing—keystroke events are delivered to the window containing the mouse cursor.

The explicit focus model is often referred to as *explicit*, or *click-to-type*, keyboard focus (also called input focus). The implicit focus model is often referred to as *real estate–driven* (or *pointer-follows-mouse*) keyboard focus. In either case, when the focus changes some window managers, including *mwm*, highlight the new focus window, making it easy to distinguish which application window receives keystroke events. Typically, highlighting is provided by varying the color(s) of the title bar and window border areas. Chapter 12 addresses the exact configuration options for specifying the focus model for various window managers.

To some extent, the focus model is a look-and-feel component that is provided by the window manager. Although an application can register an interest in focus-change events, and the X server will notify it when the keyboard focus changes from one window to another, managing the change in keyboard focus is primarily *directed* by the window manager. From the user's perspective, you simply set the focus model that you prefer and the window manager, the X server, and the application handle the details. The focus model as a look-and-feel component is not solely a window manager issue because, if you operate without a window manager, the X server will use the real estate–driven focus model.

3.9 Virtual Window Managers

With a traditional window manager, the desktop corresponds to the display screen—what you see is all there is. With a virtual window manager, the desktop can be larger than the physical dimensions of the screen. For example, it could be four times the size of the physical screen, so that at any given moment you could view one-fourth of the desktop. With a virtual desktop you can think of the screen as a viewport onto the desktop.

The freeware window manager *tvtwm* is one example of a virtual window manager (see Figure 3.9). The small window in the top-right portion of the screen is used to manipulate the displayed segment of the virtual desktop. With mouse button 1 you can grab the outline that designates the portion of the desktop that's presently viewable and drag it to another area of the desktop at which point the screen is immediately updated.

Several other virtual window managers are now available. For example, Hewlett-Packard's X environment, VUE, includes a control panel with six buttons for instantly switching among six different segments of a virtual desktop (see Figure 3.10).

3.10 Interclient Communication

There are many forms of interclient communication in an X environment. When a user chooses the "Close" (*mwm*) or "Quit" (*olwm*) option from a window menu, the window manager sends an X client a message indicating that it should terminate that particular window, or the application itself if the target window is the application's primary window. Another example of interclient communication is when the window manager sends a client message to an application each time one of its windows receives or loses the keyboard focus.

Window manager hints are another form of interclient communication. An application can send the window manager various suggestions regarding icon size, the level of window decoration for a specific window, whether or not the application should start up as an icon, and so on. As we've mentioned, they are called hints, or suggestions, because the window manager can simply ignore them.

Another form of interclient communication is copy and paste operations between applications. Most X clients are designed to exchange simple text. Depending on the nature of the application, it may also exchange data in other known formats, for example, integer values, pixmaps, and even windows. Users sometimes *incorrectly* believe that the window manager handles data transfer between applications. Even though the window manager decorates and manages the application windows it does *not* perform, and is not responsible for, copy, cut, and paste operations between X clients.

At this point, we simply want to emphasize that if you're using, say, the word processor ABC and the spreadsheet XYZ, and you have a problem getting them to exchange data (using their prescribed mechanisms), it is not the window manager's fault. There could be several problems: (1) you are performing the data exchange improperly, (2) the clients do not recognize each other's exchange protocols, (3) there is an error in the exchange strategies, or some other incompatibility.

For example, if you are using *mwm* and various Motif-based applications in an Open-Windows environment, it is important to realize that (1) OpenWindows applications such as *cmdtool* use one clipboard for copy and paste operations (the CLIPBOARD selection); (2) other X clients traditionally use a different facility for copy and paste operations (the PRIMARY selection); (3) the official clipboard client, *xclipboard*, uses the CLIPBOARD

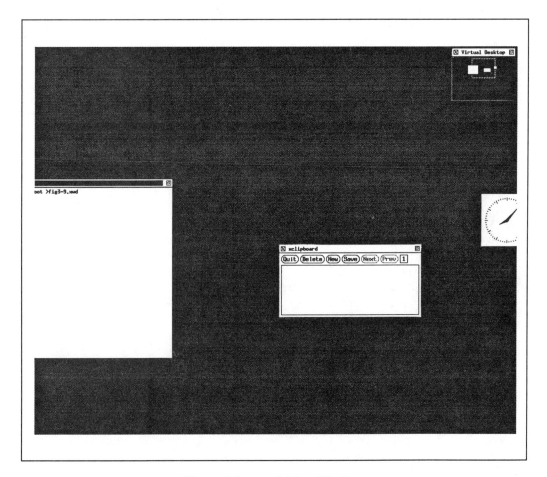

Figure 3.9 *tvtwm*'s Virtual Desktop

selection, following standard conventions; and (4) Motif-based applications typically use Motif primitives that in turn use a slightly different clipboard protocol.

Data exchange between applications is one area where X's virtually infinite flexibility, and its dependence on interclient communication conventions (as opposed to hard-and-fast standards), is conducive to abuse. In particular, the lack of hard standards, and hence, inevitable noncompliance with X's conventions, leads to commercial and freeware applications that simply cannot communicate with each other.

If you experience this problem and your basic requirement is to exchange *text* between applications or files, consider the freeware X application *xfilter* [Smith, 1992] (see Appendix H). In addition to applying UNIX filters to X data stores, *xfilter* can perform simple data exchanges between, say, OpenWindows clients that use one clipboard facility for copy and paste and traditional X clients that use a second facility.

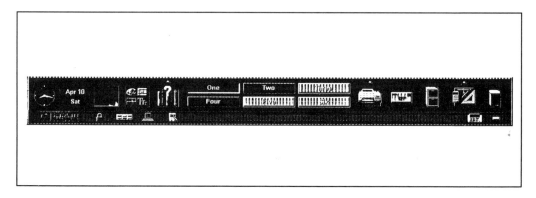

Figure 3.10 The HP VUE Control Panel

4

Using Common X Clients

Although there is considerable variability among vendors, the X distributions shipped by most third-party and workstation vendors include numerous X clients that are especially designed for and useful in an X environment. These applications include basic system utilities plus vendor-specific X clients. In addition, many freeware X clients are available from common network sites. In this chapter we investigate X clients from each of these categories. X clients such as *editres* and *xrdb* that perform tasks discussed in others chapters are described elsewhere.

4.1 X Clients and Nongraceful Termination

Early distributions of X, originating or coordinated from the MIT X Consortium, included a variety of useful X clients. Because X was still evolving, there were numerous little details, such as the proper way to terminate an X client, that went unattended and hence remained unresolved. Because the preponderance of X's early users were UNIX old-timers, there was no real incentive to address this issue; these users were perfectly content to look up the client in the (UNIX) process table and simply kill it from the command line [with *kill(1)*]!

Despite the *many* great features of X, lack of attention to these details led to a certain amount of "bad press." Since those early days, the X community has developed conventions regarding the proper handling of many such details; these conventions are described in the ICCCM. For example, it is now generally accepted that the application menus provided by window managers should contain a menu option for terminating the X client. Most recent software conforms to these conventions including many, but not all, of the X clients in the Consortium X distribution. Although most commercial applications provide for program termination from within the application, they also cooperate with the window manger by processing termination requests initiated by the user from a window menu.

Clients such as a clock application are rather special in that there are no user-controlled operations other than starting and stopping them. Before there were established conventions, such as support for client termination via the window manager, programmers often neglected to provide facilities such as command buttons or menus for graceful program termination. Moreover, even after the appearance of these conventions, several X utilities having this affliction remain unchanged. This semihostile attitude toward the novice X user should be unacceptable among programmers, but unfortunately it persists today among some X programmers. This attitude continues to affect, that is, attenuate, the acceptance of "UNIX on the desktop," which indirectly diminishes the acceptance of X. Despite their many great features, both UNIX and X still suffer from a lack of attention to details.

A few of the X clients that we discuss in this book have no provision for graceful termination. Thus, if you choose the "Close" or "Quit" options from their window menus (depending on the window manager), you should not be too surprised by output such as the following in a console window, in a command window from which you started the X client, or even plastered across the root window:

```
XIO:   fatal IO error 32 (Broken pipe) on X server "unix:0.0"
       after 43 requests (40 known processed) with 0 events remaining.
       The connection was probably broken by a server shutdown or KillClient.
```

These messages do *not* imply that your X environment or workstation has been damaged in any way, but they are still quite annoying.

As a cautionary note, we should mention that there is an X client, *xkill*, that you should be aware of—in most cases, you should avoid it. Your first impression might be that *xkill* is a special X client for (gracefully) terminating X clients, but this is not the case. Depending on how you use *xkill* it has the potential to kill your entire X environment, including applications with unsaved work, so it is best simply to ignore its existence. The situations in which it could be useful are irrelevant in today's X environment (or should be), so it doesn't merit further discussion.

4.2 Using Scrollbars with X Clients

Because X permits multiple UI styles, for example, OPEN LOOK and Motif, there is no single type of scrollbar for all X clients. In addition to the scrollbar styles for applications developed from OPEN LOOK- and Motif-based X toolkits and widget sets, X's standard widget set (the Athena widget set), provides scrollbars with a third type of look and feel. The scrollbar for OpenWindows applications, such as *textedit* in Figure 4.1.a, has an elevator-on-a-cable appearance. This design is very attractive and it is rather powerful, but for many users it is difficult to use the elevators as efficiently as the more traditional scrollbar that accompanies X clients such as *xterm* because the small components of the elevator require a more deliberate placement of the mouse cursor.

To move to the top or bottom of the scrollable text, you simply click on the small rectangles at the top and bottom of the elevator cable, respectively. For panning, that is, dragging the viewport vertically over the entire length of the text, press mouse button 1 with the mouse cursor positioned over the middle partition of the elevator. To scroll a line at a time, click

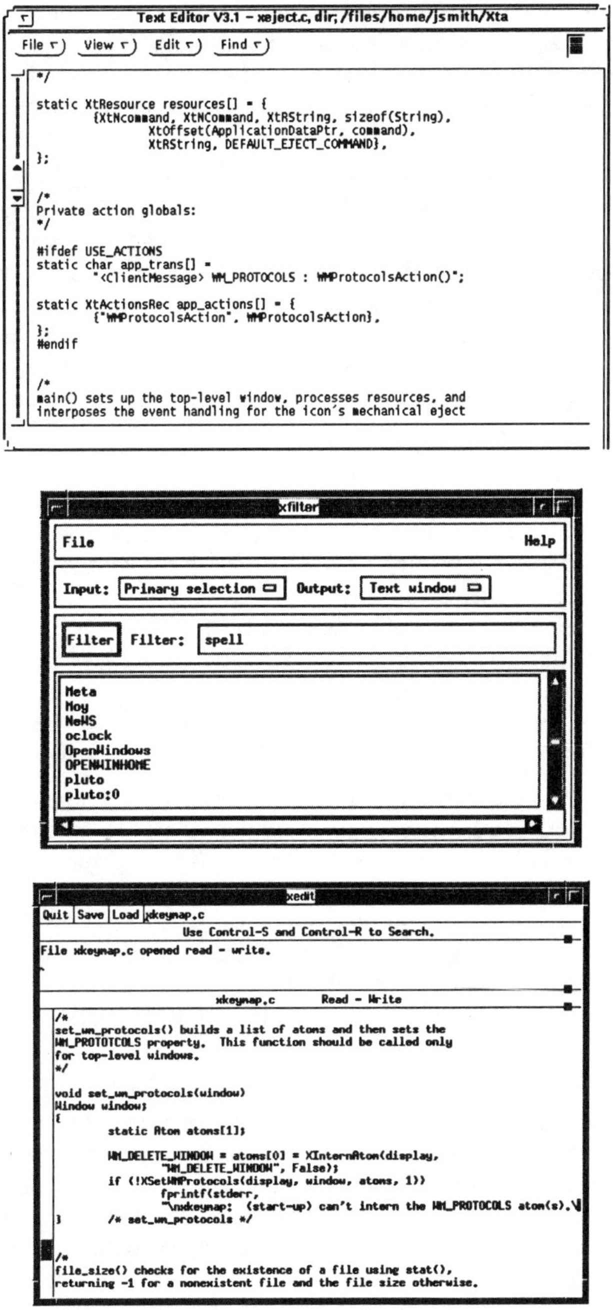

```
 ⊤          Text Editor V3.1 – xeject.c, dir; /files/home/jsmith/Xta
File ⊤)   View ⊤)   Edit ⊤)   Find ⊤)

*/
static XtResource resources[] = {
        {XtNcommand, XtNCommand, XtRString, sizeof(String),
             XtOffset(ApplicationDataPtr, command),
             XtRString, DEFAULT_EJECT_COMMAND},
};

/*
Private action globals:
*/

#ifdef USE_ACTIONS
static char app_trans[] =
        "<ClientMessage> WM_PROTOCOLS : WMProtocolsAction()";

static XtActionsRec app_actions[] = {
        {"WMProtocolsAction", WMProtocolsAction},
};
#endif

/*
main() sets up the top-level window, processes resources, and
interposes the event handling for the icon's mechanical eject
```

```
                              xfilter

 File                                                    Help

 Input: [Primary selection ▭]  Output: [Text window ▭]

 [Filter]  Filter: [spell                              ]

 ┌──────────────────────────────────────────────────┐
 │ Meta                                               │
 │ Moy                                                │
 │ NeWS                                               │
 │ oclock                                             │
 │ OpenWindows                                        │
 │ OPENWINHOME                                        │
 │ pluto                                              │
 │ pluto:0                                            │
 └──────────────────────────────────────────────────┘
```

```
                              xedit
 Quit  Save  Load  xkeymap.c
               Use Control-S and Control-R to Search.
 File xkeymap.c opened read - write.

                  xkeymap.c      Read - Write

 /*
 set_wm_protocols() builds a list of atoms and then sets the
 WM_PROTOTCOLS property.  This function should be called only
 for top-level windows.
 */

 void set_wm_protocols(window)
 Window window;
 {
         static Atom atoms[1];

         WM_DELETE_WINDOW = atoms[0] = XInternAtom(display,
             "WM_DELETE_WINDOW", False);
         if (!XSetWMProtocols(display, window, atoms, 1))
                 fprintf(stderr,
                 "\nxkeymap:  (start-up) can't intern the WM_PROTOCOLS atom(s).\
         /* set_wm_protocols */
 }

 /*
 file_size() checks for the existence of a file using stat(),
 returning -1 for a nonexistent file and the file size otherwise.
```

Figure 4.1 Three Scrollbar Designs

mouse button 1 (with the mouse cursor) over the small arrows in the elevator. Or, you can *press* mouse button 1 for autoscrolling (automatic, continual scrolling as you hold down the mouse button). Scrolling a page at a time is handled similarly, except that you click/press mouse button 1 (with the mouse cursor) above or below the elevator in the elevator cable area. There is no provision for scrolling in partial-page increments, as with traditional X scrollbars.

Figure 4.1.b shows a Motif application's scrollbar, in this case, with the freeware application *xfilter*. The Motif toolkit-based scrollbar is more similar to that of traditional X clients than the OpenWindows scrollbar. Even so, some of the traditional functionality has been abandoned to produce a simpler PC-like scrollbar. The scrollbar contains an area of alternate color, relative to the scrollbar background, that moves vertically within the scrollbar area to indicate the relative distance of the viewable text from the top or bottom of the scrollable text—a viewable-area handle. Also, the size of this handle relative to the length of the scrollbar indicates the percentage of the scrollable text that is currently viewable.

To move to the top, middle, or bottom of the scrollable text, you simply click mouse button 2 near the top, middle, or bottom of the scrollbar, respectively. That is, to position the text cursor one-third of the way through the scrollable text, simply position the mouse cursor one-third of the way down the scrollbar as you click mouse button 2. For panning, press mouse button 1 on the viewable-area handle and drag it up or down, as with the elevator of the OpenWindows scrollbar. To scroll a line at a time, click mouse button 1 on the small arrows. To scroll a page at a time, click in the scrollbar area above or below the viewable-area handle. Motif toolkit-based scrollbars are problematic for page-level scrolling because the paging terminates when the viewable-area handle overtakes the mouse cursor. As with OpenWindows scrollbars, there is no provision for scrolling in partial-page increments.

The scrollbars available with traditional X clients are simpler in appearance than those of OpenWindows and Motif-based clients, yet more powerful; see the *xedit* session in Figure 4.1.c. Traditional X scrollbars are similar to Motif toolkit-based scrollbars, except that (1) there are no up and down arrows for scrolling a line at a time and (2) the viewable-area handle is dark on light instead of light on dark. Instead, of using one-line-at-a-time scroll arrows, traditional X scrollbars employ a more powerful approach. Specifically, with *xedit*, to scroll a line at a time you position the mouse cursor adjacent to the second line of text; to scroll three lines at a time, you position the mouse cursor adjacent to the fourth line in the scrollable text window, and so on.

The direction of the scroll is indicated by using mouse button 1 to scroll down (toward the botton of the scrollable text) and mouse button 3 to scroll up. If this approach were used with Motif, (1) it would differ from the traditional PC approach after which Motif's GUI is modeled and (2) traditionally, the PC GUI environments have not assumed the presence of a third mouse button. For power users, the traditional X scrollbars are infinitely more desirable because you can, in effect, vary the scrolling speed dynamically based on how far down the scrollbar you position the mouse cursor while scrolling—you can vary the scroll increment. We should point out that many traditional X scrollbars do not provide autoscrolling. There are, however, X clients that use a traditional X scrollbar design, but with an autoscrolling provision, in particular, the X text editor *ie* [Iris Computing Laboratories, 1993].

4.3 Getting Help on Utilities and Other X Clients

Most X clients that are distributed by vendors, as well as freeware X programs, recognize the -help command-line option:

```
{your system prompt} xclock -help
Usage: xclock [-analog] [-bw <pixels>] [-digital]
        [-fg <color>] [-bg <color>] [-hd <color>]
        [-hl <color>] [-bd <color>]
        [-fn <font_name>] [-help] [-padding <pixels>]
        [-rv] [-update <seconds>] [-display displayname]
        [-geometry geom]
```

Typically, the output is restricted to information regarding the available command-line options. To get additional information, for example, a list of an X client's application resources, you typically have to consult either printed documentation or the man-page command *man(1)*. The following output indicates that your system has not been configured properly for X; that is, the X-related man-pages have not been added to the standard man-page locations:

```
{your system prompt} man xclock
No manual entry for xclock.
```

If your vendor didn't configure the man-pages properly, ask your system administrator to install the man-pages.

If the man-page directories have been configured properly, you should get output similar to the following:

```
{your system prompt} man xclock
Reformatting page.  Wait... done

XCLOCK(1)               USER COMMANDS                 XCLOCK(1)

NAME
     xclock - analog / digital clock for X

SYNOPSIS
     xclock  [-toolkitoption ...]   [-help]  [-analog]  [-digital]
     [-chime] [-hd color]
               [-hl color] [-update seconds] [-padding number]

DESCRIPTION
     The xclock program displays the time in  analog  or  digital
     form.  The time is continuously updated at a frequency which
     may be specified by the user.  This program is nothing  more
```

```
     than a wrapper around the Athena Clock widget.

OPTIONS
     Xclock accepts all of the standard X  Toolkit  command  line
     options along with the additional options listed below:

     -help   This option indicates that a brief  summary  of  the
             allowed  options  should  be printed on the standard
             error.
 . . .
 . . .
AUTHORS
     Tony Della Fera (MIT-Athena, DEC)
     Dave Mankins (MIT-Athena, BBN)
     Ed Moy (UC Berkeley)

X Version 11         Last change: Release 5                        3
```

If you prefer a higher level approach to getting help for X clients, or you do not know the exact name of an X client, you can use the X client *xman* (see Figure 4.2.a). This application provides menu-based access to each man-page category through the "Sections" menu. Many X distributions install their man-page files in the "n" man-page directory. Thus, if you choose the "n" section ("n" for New) from the "Sections" menu of the "Manual Page" window, the available topics are listed in the "Manual Page" window (see Figure 4.2.b). If you click mouse button 1 on a topic, for example, *xclock*, its information replaces the list of topics (see Figure 4.2.c). To return to the index, simply choose the "n" section from the "Sections" menu as before.

xman is quite sophisticated, so you should explore its capabilities with its "Help" menu option (in the "Options" menu). In particular, there are numerous keyboard accelerators, such as <Ctrl>-S, which is quite useful in searching for a man-page topic when the list of topics is large and the one you're looking for is difficult to spot. Also, with <Ctrl>-S you can avoid altogether the two stage process of (1) displaying a listing of topics for a particular section and (2) clicking on a specific topic. Instead, simply use <Ctrl>-S from a "Manual Page" window to specify the name of an application or utility, for example, *xterm*, and *xman* will automatically search all man-page directories.

xman has three characteristics that you should note. First, *xman* has no provision to guard against accidental double-clicks, so if you double-click (instead of single-click) a topic, you will have to wait for the man-page to be built twice, which is annoying with lengthy man-page topics. Second, with a few implementations of *xman*, there is no provision for graceful termination; in these cases, you should terminate *xman* with its "Quit" button. Third, don't overlook the fact that you can start up multiple "Manual Page" windows, which is an especially useful feature of *xman*.

4.4 Clock Applications

The two most common clock applications are *oclock* and *xclock*, primarily because both are shipped with most X distributions. Figure 4.3.a demonstrates *oclock*, an analog clock that

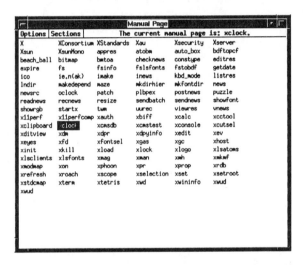

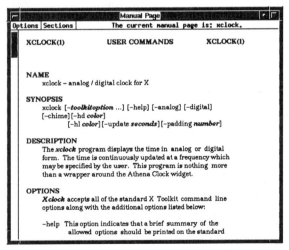

Figure 4.2 *xman*'s Top-level and Man-page Windows

is designed in part to demonstrate a particular feature of X, called the shape extension, which is involved in implementing windows with nonstandard shapes. In some X distributions, *oclock* provides no mechanism for graceful termination. You can install it as a default desktop application, one that is there for the duration of your X session, or you can start and terminate it manually.

xclock is shown in Figure 4.3.b. You can start *xclock* in either analog or digital mode. Analog mode is the default, although, of course, it is possible that this configuration option has been set in a system-wide resource file to request digital output.

Both of these applications have numerous command-line options (and X resources) that control their appearance, for example, the color of the clock's hands, background color, and so on. *xclock* provides an `-update` command-line option that controls the interval (in seconds) between updates. You can increase this interval if you are concerned about the use of system resources (or avoid the application altogether and use the watch on your wrist).

4.5 Controlling Display Access Privileges

We mentioned *xhost* in Section 2.8 in our discussion of the various ways in which you can start X clients on one workstation and work with them from a remote display. For X's existing minimal security system, *xhost* is the utility for modifying one workstation's receptivity to accepting display connections from another workstation. For example, suppose your colleague's workstation has the hostname "pluto", and you have been given access to pluto, possibly for cooperative work between the two of you:

```
{the system prompt from pluto} xhost +saturn
saturn being added to access control list
```

You can now execute any X client and have it display on pluto. For example, to make sure your colleague is alert, you could redirect the program *xeyes* to pluto; for maximum effect, use a very large window:

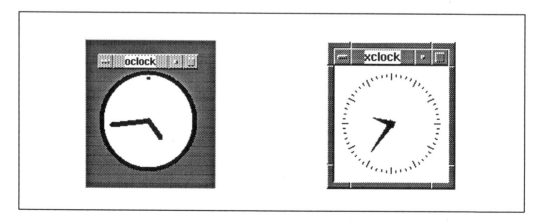

Figure 4.3 Clock Applications

```
{your system prompt on saturn} xeyes -g 750x750 -display pluto:0 &
```

If you attempt this maneuver when you do not have access to the requested display, you will probably be "discovered." If your colleague has an active console window, this security breach will be reported with a statement such as

```
X11/NeWS Network security violation
Rejected connection from: saturn (<network address>)
For more information, see the xhost(1) and xauth(1) man pages
```

You'll also know that your surprise operation failed because your system will report a message such as

```
Xlib:  connection to "pluto:0.0" refused by server
Xlib:  Client is not authorized to connect to server
Error: Can't open display: pluto:0
```

On the other hand, if your surprise is successful, you will more than likely hear about it via some communication medium other than the local network.

Of course, the exact message depends on the X server. In this case, pluto is running OpenWindows with Sun's X11/NeWS server, *xnews*, which is reflected in the message. In contrast, saturn is running the sample X server for Sun workstations that's part of the Consortium X11R5 distribution.

Note that if you and your colleague are working from X terminals connected to the same file server, you may not have to take any explicit steps to gain access to each other's displays. *xhost* is a component of X's host-based access control facilities; see Section 13.15 for more information on *xhost* as well as user-based access control, which offer a more selective form of protecting your display from intruders.

4.6 *xcalc*

xcalc is a very handy calculator program. By default, it is configured for traditional (infix) operation, common with Texas Instruments® and many other calculators. With the -rpn command-line option you can request RPN (reverse Polish notation) operation (also known as postfix operation), which is used for Hewlett-Packard® scientific calculators. Figure 4.4.a shows *xcalc* configured for TI-30 emulation and Figure 4.4.b demonstrates HP-10C emulation.

With *xcalc* you can use mouse button 1 to "press" the calculator keys, and in most cases, the keyboard works as well. Although it is not immediately apparent (unless you check the documentation), you can terminate *xcalc* directly from the calculator keypad by pressing mouse button 3 over the "AC" key in TI mode, or over the "ON" key in HP mode.

Note that you can click mouse button 1 in the display area to select a computed value for pasting into another application. The behavior is slightly nonstandard in that clicking mouse button 1 toggles between selecting and deselecting the calculator's display output; you cannot drag select part of the output. Also, you cannot paste a number from another X client into the calculator's display as part of a calculation, which can be a significant limitation. In contrast, *calctool*, which is part of the OpenWindows DeskSet™ [Sun Microsystems, 1992], fully supports copy and paste operations.

4.7 *xclipboard*

In this section and in Section 4.8, we discuss *xclipboard* and *xterm*, respectively, without specifically focusing on their copy and paste operations. In Section 4.9, however, we use both of these X clients in our discussion of X clients' support for copy, cut, and paste operations.

xclipboard is just one of many X clients that use a formal X clipboard, known technically as the CLIPBOARD selection. For example, with OpenWindows on a Sun workstation, if you use the <**Copy**>, <**Cut**>, and <**Paste**> keys within OpenWindows applications such as *calctool* and *cmdtool*, the X clipboard manages the text behind the scenes. That is, normally, the contents of the X clipboard are invisible. If, however, *xclipboard* is running, you can see the X clipboard's contents as it is updated during OpenWindows' cut and copy operations.

Not all applications use the formal X clipboard, even though they provide clipboard operations. An X client may use an X-based clipboard of its own design, that is, one that is implemented with X system resources, or an internal (private) clipboard allocated directly from the computer's main memory. For the user, these variations on clipboard implementations mean that interapplication data transfer via clipboards can be problematic, depending on the working set of X clients that you use daily.

Another point is that, typically, the X clipboard is not employed for copy and paste operations with the mouse. With traditional X clients such as *xterm*, when you select text

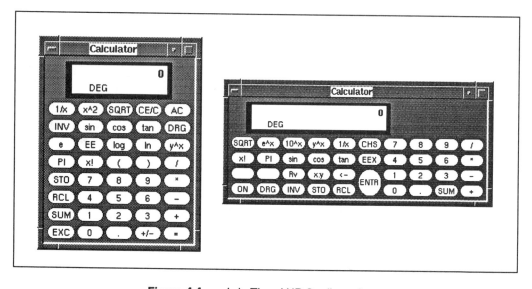

Figure 4.4 *xcalc* in TI and HP Configurations

using a drag, or sweep, operation with mouse button 1, and then paste it with mouse button 2, the selections are handled by another type of "clipboard," known technically as the `PRIMARY` selection. The advantage of using different X selections (`PRIMARY` and `SEC-ONDARY`) for mouse- and menu-based text selection is that you can retain a large text segment on the formal X clipboard for periodic pasting operations without overwriting it each time you select a small text segment. You should not be concerned about the technical aspects of X's selections; simply think of them as invisible data repositories. The primary selection, for example, can be thought of as a quick-copy facility.

For whatever reasons, *xclipboard*'s implementation varies more than most standard X clients from one X distribution to the next. Figure 4.5 shows *xclipboard* as distributed with the Consortium's X11R5 distribution. Earlier *xclipboard*s typically had fewer features; for example, the "Save", "Next", and "Previous" operations were absent for MIT's X11R4 distribution.

Suppose you mark the first eight words of this sentence with a text editor. If you then copy the text to the X clipboard, *xclipboard* appears as shown in Figure 4.6. To provide visual feedback for the user, *xclipboard* displays its contents in a small, scrollable text window. *xclipboard* provides horizontal and vertical scrollbars automatically. That is, if you resize its viewport so that the entire text is visible, in either dimension, *xclipboard* removes the scrollbar(s). Any time that part of the text is hidden, *xclipboard* automatically provides a scrollbar so that you can scroll the hidden text into view.

Normally, you do not really need to see the contents of the X clipboard, and we should emphasize that it is not necessary to have *xclipboard* running for an X application to use the X clipboard. On the other hand, there are occasions when some users might need to manipulate several text segments simultaneously. In this case, a recent release of *xclipboard* is useful because it provides "Next" and "Previous" buttons for "paging" through recent X clipboard postings. Also, *xclipboard* now provides a "Save" button so that you can save its contents to a text file. Thus, for X clients that allow you to copy text to the X clipboard, but provide no mechanism for saving small segments of text, *xclipboard* can serve as an

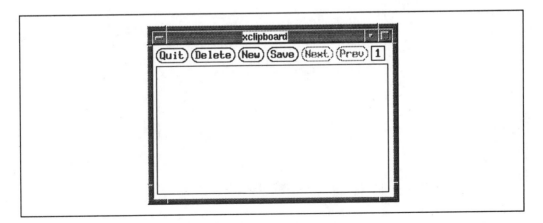

Figure 4.5 *xclipboard* Displaying the X Clipboard (Currently Empty)

intermediary agent. If you need to read the contents of a file and store it on the X clipboard, you should obtain the the freeware program *xfilter*, mentioned in Section 3.10.

4.8 *xterm*

As described in earlier chapters, *xterm* is a terminal emulator, or command window, that runs a command shell. Within an *xterm* window you can run traditional character-oriented applications that occupy the entire *xterm* window, as they would with a character terminal. In addition, however, you can launch X clients that execute in their own (X) windows.

Every GUI-based environment has advantages and disadvantages relative to its competitors. In some cases the user environment is quite restrictive, but with the advantage of greater conformity and consistency across applications. X is quite the opposite; it is very flexible in many ways, and this flexibility is reflected in its support for traditional command-line computing. The capability for handling both character- and X-oriented software is a tremendous advantage for X users. This flexibility has allowed users to migrate gradually to new-generation, more powerful software that takes advantage of X, while continuing to use selected character-based applications as well as numerous utilities that longtime users have collected over the years.

If you are using DESQview/X, *xterm* is not an issue because you would most likely prefer a DOS-like command window, which DESQview/X already provides. The disadvantage of using a DOS command window within a DESQview/X environment is that the command window does not support X-oriented, interclient communication, for example, copy and paste operations between the DOS command window and other X clients. On the other hand, for DESQview/X users who primarily operate from a higher level application manager, a DOS command window is not especially important.

xterm is somewhat like an iceberg—there is more beneath the surface than you first realize. What first appears to be a simple window for entering shell commands is in reality a very sophisticated program. *xterm*, for example, emulates a VT102 terminal *and* a Tektronix 4014 terminal, each emulation in itself being a significant accomplishment. Terminal emulation

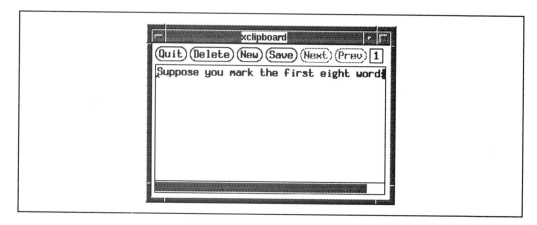

Figure 4.6 *xclipboard* Displaying the Contents of the X Clipboard

and other options can be set from X application resource files, from the command line, as well as on the fly from one of *xterm*'s menus, accessed by pressing mouse button 1, 2, or 3 while the **<Ctrl>** key is down. *xterm* has a dizzying number of command-line options, which you can peruse from the *xterm* man-page with *xman*.

Many of *xterm*'s configuration options are terminal- and UNIX-related, for example, its relationship with *termcap(5)*, and these topics are beyond the scope of this book. Because our focus is X, we must limit our discussion to the X-related aspects of *xterm*. First, we should reiterate that *xterm* is an X application that, by default, executes the user's preferred UNIX shell (as configured for the user's account). For many users, the C shell, *csh(1)*, is the default command interpreter; for others, the Bourne shell, *sh(1)*, is the default. More generally, however, *xterm* can execute any character-oriented application, as requested via the -e command-line option. For example, the following command starts an *xterm* that executes *more(1)* against the text file *c4.txt*:

```
{your system prompt} xterm -e more c4.txt
```

When the application completes, in this case, after *more(1)* has displayed the last page of the file, *xterm* automatically terminates. If you intend to start an *xterm* solely to host a character application, it is more efficient to do so with the -e command-line option than to start an *xterm* session first (with a running shell) and then launch the character application. Note that -e must be the last *xterm* option because all trailing options are passed to the program executing in the *xterm* window.

One convenient feature of *xterm* is its logging facility, which captures all output to an *xterm* window in a logfile. If you are having problems with a character application, or an X application that reports errors in the *xterm* window from which it was launched, you can use the logging facility to build a record of your interaction with the application that includes error messages, unexplainable output, and so on.

You can enable logging dynamically with the "Main Options" menu. Press and hold **<Ctrl>** and then press mouse button 1 in the *xterm* window. Without releasing the mouse button, slide the mouse cursor down to the menu option "Log to File" and release mouse button 1. (You can release **<Ctrl>** at any time after the menu is displayed.) You can also enable logging with the command-line option -l. A companion option, -lf <filename>, allows you to specify the name of the logfile. If -lf <filename> is omitted, the logfile is created in the directory from which the *xterm* session *originated*, *not* the current directory for the command shell running in the *xterm* window. The default name for the logfile begins with "XtermLog."; system-generated characters are appended to the filename that minimize name conflicts with previous logfiles.

You should explore the menus associated with the other two mouse buttons as well. They allow you to modify dynamically certain *xterm* characteristics, such as the presence or absence of a scrollbar, as well as choose fonts other than the font selected when *xterm* started executing.

xterm is truly a great program because of its inherent capabilities and the fact that it provides an X environment in which the user can mix modern X clients with traditional character applications. On the other hand, it is a mistake for users to expect *xterm*, combined with a character application, to provide the X-related functionality that can be achieved from a similar application that has been designed from the beginning as an X client. Some longtime UNIX users scoff at all modern X applications, for example, GUI-based text editors, because they have been dissatisfied with certain poorly performing X clients. There are, however, many X clients that execute very efficiently with a level of X integration that supports efficient (for the user) cooperation among applications well beyond what can be accomplished by using an older character-based application in an *xterm* window.

One problematic aspect of using *xterm* to host character-based applications is that in an X environment it is only natural to want to grab the resize corner and change the size of an *xterm* window. With almost any character application other than a command shell, resizing the *xterm* window does not translate into updated display dimensions for the character application. In fact, many character applications will work properly only with an 80-column *xterm* window.

Other character applications, such as the text editor *vi(1)*, can adapt to terminal windows of varying dimensions, but you have to exit and restart these applications following a resize operation, because they cannot dynamically recognize changes in dimensions of their host *xterm* windows. In addition, in some cases, you must run a UNIX command, *resize(1)*, that updates various system variables and table entries that are important to character applications. For additional information on *resize(1)* consult its man-page information using *xman*. If you frequently resize your text editor windows, you probably should consider a text editor designed for X.

Lastly, *xterm* provides an opportunity to discuss the issue of a hardware versus a software cursor. Users migrating to UNIX from a PC environment are often accustomed to character-based applications that are launched directly from the DOS interpreter and that write to "the screen" (by writing directly to video memory). In this type of environment it is possible to have a cursor that is, essentially, managed by the computer's microprocessor. This type of low-level programming and dependence on specific hardware characteristics is neither possible nor desirable with modern GUI-based environments, regardless of the operating system or hardware platform.

Because GUI environments are built on top of existing operating-system and graphics-processor primitives, the mouse cursor and other cursors displayed within application windows are implemented by the software. In other words, instead of having a micropro-cessor that manages a single cursor on a PC monitor, GUI environments must support multiple cursors within application windows, which are in turn implemented via the windowing system (software). For this reason, it is often impractical to manage flashing cursors, especially with X's network-oriented design. Each flash (for each cursor) would generate network activity; this overhead would be prohibitive in many multiuser environ-ments. On the other hand, given the tendency toward use of color monitors in the X world, users can increase a cursor's visibility by setting it to a bright color such as magenta.

4.9 Copy, Cut, and Paste Operations with X Clients

To the user, X's data transfer operations are the most visible manifestations of interclient communication. For example, transferring data between a spreadsheet and a word processor is a common situation. Suppose you have just generated a small table with a spreadsheet application. In many cases, the most straightforward way to incorporate this table into a report is simply to select the appropriate table with mouse button 1 and then paste it into the word-processor document by first positioning the text cursor and then clicking mouse button 2 to paste the table at the text cursor.

For this scenario to work properly, both applications must be X clients that follow the guidelines established by the ICCCM (see Section 3.1). The ICCCM outlines several mechanisms and conventions by which X clients can transfer data. With most text-oriented applications, for example, word processors, editors, desktop publishing software, command tools, and so on, data transfer is straightforward and intuitive. On the other hand, with applications that manipulate other types of data such as bitmaps, you should not assume that X clients will be able to perform conversions from one data type to another during the data transfer. Even if the conversion makes sense and is outlined in the ICCCM, one X client or the other may not support it.

To understand why some form of data conversion is typically required, consider an X-based text editor. X is a graphical window system; the characters that you see in an edit window are represented internally in a format that is purely a function of the developer's text editor implementation. An edit window presents a graphical interpretation of characters that you have typed into your text file via the editor. One of the editor's many duties is to update the edit window (continually) with an *image* that *represents* the characters that exist at the corresponding offset in your text file.

Another text editor, however, may use a completely different *internal* representation of the contents of the text file. For these two X clients to interchange data, they both must be capable of accepting and delivering the data in a standard format, one of which is ICCCM's TEXT format. This process involves more than simply delivering the characters that represent the text segment; there are numerous conventions, for example, reporting the length of the text segment so that the requesting X client has the opportunity to abandon its request. Suppose, for example, that the requesting X client has an arbitrary upper limit on the amount of data that it can manage and the requested data exceeds that length. That is, when a user performs a paste operation for a text segment in another application, that X client must request the data, but it has no prior knowledge of the length of the incoming text segment.

Having outlined how transferring even the simplest type of data, namely, text, involves multiple communications, it is clear that X clients must closely adhere to specific conventions and that not all X clients will properly do so, especially for less straightforward data exchanges. In some circumstances when X users have described certain applications as having "incompatible cut and paste strategies" the problem has been something as trivial as whether or not the X clients report and expect the end-of-text marker to be part of the length count. Hereafter, we confine our discussion to data transfer for simple text.

With most X clients (those in the OpenWindows environment being an exception), you select text by dragging/sweeping the relevant text with mouse button 1 down, and then releasing mouse button 1. This text is highlighted by the application and established as the PRIMARY selection, which simply means the text is available to other X clients that request it via a simple paste operation (see Figure 4.7). To paste the highlighted text into another

X client (or within the same application), you first position the text cursor at the appropriate location in that client's text window and then click mouse button 2. These copy and paste operations are supported by X clients built from common toolkits and widget sets, such as the X toolkit (Xt) and the Athena and Motif widget sets. Most Xlib-based X clients that manipulate text also support primary selection-based copy and paste.

To cut a text segment, typically, you select the text as described, and then press either **<Delete>** or **<Backspace>**. Depending on the X client, the cut operation may not be supported. For example, within an editable text window a cut operation makes sense; *xterm*, on the other hand, does not allow you to cut the selected text.

OpenWindows applications use a data repository called the `CLIPBOARD` selection for data transfer, and the method of selecting text differs. Specifically, to select the text (in the marked block sense), you highlight the text segment by dragging it with mouse button 1. Then, to complete the selection (or copy the text, depending on your preferred terminology), you press **<Copy>**. You can then paste data from the `CLIPBOARD` selection by pressing **<Paste>**.

4.10 Copy and Paste among OpenWindows and Other X Clients

We've mentioned that Motif toolkit-based and standard X clients use the `PRIMARY` selection for simple data transfer (and typically the `CLIPBOARD` selection for data transfer via a formal clipboard), whereas OpenWindows applications such as *cmdtool* and *textedit* employ the `CLIPBOARD` selection for simple data transfer. For users who regularly work with both types of X clients, these differences can be a real hassle. There are essentially two approaches that you can take to circumvent these differences.

First, you can modify non-OpenWindows X clients so that they use the `CLIPBOARD` selection instead of the `PRIMARY` selection. This modification is not a trivial operation because (1) not all X clients allow you to modify/reconfigure their selection behavior and (2) you must modify X clients on a one-by-one basis. In Chapter 5, we investigate X's application resource database facility, but, for now, simply note that adding the following

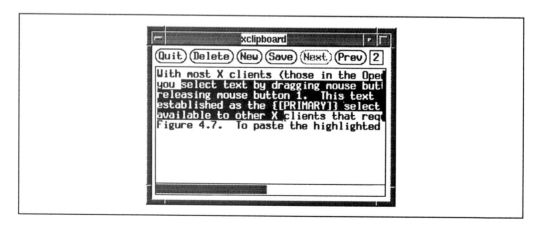

Figure 4.7 *xclipboard* Managing (Primary) Selected Text

lines to the file *$OPENWINHOME/lib/app-defaults/XTerm* will request that *xterm* use the
`CLIPBOARD` selection in lieu of the `PRIMARY` selection:

```
xterm*vt100*translations: #override\n\
    Shift <KeyPress> Select: select-cursor-start() \
        select-cursor-end(CLIPBOARD, CUT_BUFFER0) \n\
    Shift <KeyPress> Insert: insert-selection(CLIPBOARD, CUT_BUFFER0) \n\
    ~Ctrl ~Meta <Btn2Up>: insert-selection(CLIPBOARD, CUT_BUFFER0) \n\
    <BtnUp>: select-end(CLIPBOARD, CUT_BUFFER0)
```

Depending on your OpenWindows configuration, you may need to exit and restart Open-Windows before these changes take effect. These statements modify existing *xterm* operations so that the `CLIPBOARD` selection is substituted for the `PRIMARY` selection. To see the original translations, use *xman* to locate them in the *xterm* man-page topic (near the end of the discussion); we simply substituted "CLIPBOARD" for "PRIMARY".

After this substitution, you can transfer text easily among *xterm* and OpenWindows clients because they use a common data repository. On the other hand, with this substitution *xterm* no longer sends text to the `PRIMARY` selection, which may introduce problems in transferring data to X clients. Chapter 7 provides a more complete discussion of these and related issues.

Instead of modifying non-OpenWindows applications to use the `CLIPBOARD` selection, a second approach to handling these clipboard differences is to use an intermediary X client during copy and paste operations. For example, with *xclipboard* running, text copied to the X clipboard from a *cmdtool* window will appear in *xclipboard*'s text window, because it displays the current contents of the X clipboard. From *xclipboard*, you can (1) select this text with mouse button 1, which establishes it as the primary selection, and (2) paste it into an *xterm* window with mouse button 2.

To copy text in the opposite direction, (1) select the text in an *xterm* window, (2) select "New" in *xclipboard* to empty the X clipboard, (3) click mouse button 2 in *xclipboard*'s text window to add the primary selection to the X clipboard, and (4) use <**Paste**> to paste the X clipboard's contents into a *cmdtool* window.

xfilter is similar in some ways to *xclipboard*, except that it has menus for setting various input and output targets and it can apply a filter during a data transfer. With *xfilter*, for example, you can transfer text directly from a text file to the X clipboard. From the X clipboard, you can then deliver it to most X clients.

4.11 *xedit*

The Consortium X distribution includes *xedit*, a simple X text editor. Typically, the X distributions provided by hardware vendors, for example, OpenWindows, include *xedit* as well, even though they also provide more powerful, and more user-friendly, text editors.

xedit is a nice X client to have around, and you can pretty much count on it being there across X environments (see Figure 4.8). On the other hand, it has an incredibly dangerous characteristic. Specifically, there is a single text field that is used to enter filenames for both the "Load" and "Save" commands. Thus, if you (1) edit the file *xyz* without saving your work, (2) enter the filename *abc* in the text field, in preparation for editing *abc*, and (3) select the "Load" command, *xedit* warns you that you have unsaved changes with the prompt "Unsaved changes. Save them, or press Load again."

The knee-jerk reaction that even veteran users will make under stress is simply to select "Save" at this point. Unfortunately, the "Save" operation writes the unsaved text to the file specified in the text field (*abc*), which, of course, is the file you intended to load, not the file in which the unsaved text should be stored (*xyz*). You have just overwritten a file for which you may not have a recent back-up copy! Except for this "small" UI design glitch, *xedit* is a handy X client.

With *xedit* you can edit files one at a time in its lower text window. In addition to the text field in which you specify filenames, it provides one text field for messages and prompts and two label areas. *xedit* has a rather powerful and elegant pop-up window for search and replace operations, which is invoked with either **<Ctrl>-S** or **<Ctrl>-R**.

We should note that *xedit*'s edit window is implemented with the Athena text widget, as is the text window for *xclipboard*. Athena widget set-based scrollbars differ slightly from *xterm*'s scrollbar. Specifically, with *xterm* you place the mouse cursor adjacent to the first line of text to scroll one line, next to the second line of text to scroll two lines, and so on; this design is intuitive. With X clients that employ Athena widget set-based scrollbars, you place the mouse cursor adjacent to the second line to scroll one line, next to the third line to scroll two lines, and so on. That is, the height (in lines) of the scrollbar area *above* the mouse

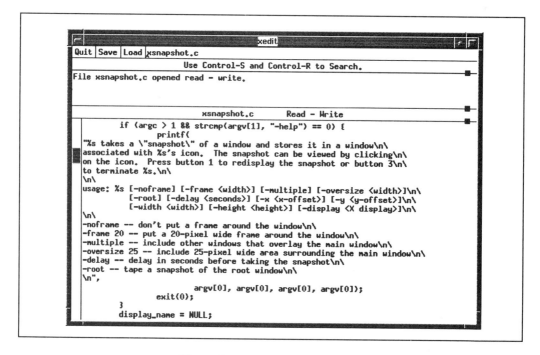

Figure 4.8 *xedit* Editing a Text File

cursor determines the number of lines for the scroll increment.

4.12 Vendor-supplied Application Suites

Many hardware vendors provide their own set of X utilities, sometimes geared for system administrators, as well as X clients that perform traditional tasks such as electronic mail handling, appointment scheduling, capturing screen shots, file management, and many others. In this section we mention several vendor-supplied application suites.

4.12.1 Hewlett-Packard Visual User Environment

Hewlett-Packard's X environment, VUE, [Hewlett-Packard, 1992] includes a control panel with embedded executing applications, such as a clock and system-load performance meter, plus icons for its configuration facility, help system, command window (*hpterm* by default), notepad, and other tools (see Figure 4.9). This control panel provides many conveniences, although, if you prefer, you can iconify it and work primarily from command windows. Figure 4.10 illustrates several tools from the VUE X environment.

There are several other tools that are integrated very well with the HP X environment. For example, the man-page facility pops up from the control panel. Aesthetically, it is quite pleasing; also, it does not suffer from the ICCCM inadequacies of some *xman* implementations. The recent initiative among vendors to establish a common X desktop environment borrows extensively from VUE (see Section 4.13).

4.12.2 OpenWindows DeskSet

One of the more well-known application suites is the OpenWindows DeskSet [Sun Microsystems, 1992]. DeskSet includes a broad range of X clients, some of which are variations on traditional X clients; for example, the clock application is similar to *xclock*, but with the capability for displaying the time based on numerous time zones, with stop-watch capabilities and so on (see Figure 4.11). The more powerful X clients include a calendar manager, a text editor an X interface to UNIX printing, a calculator, a command tool, an electronic mail tool, an audio tool, an icon editor, and others. Figure 4.12 shows the text editor, *textedit*.

The most sophisticated X client is the DeskSet file manager (see Figure 4.13). For users who prefer a higher level interface than, say, the X root window populated with several *xterm* or *cmdtool* windows, the file manager has a rudimentary capability for managing the

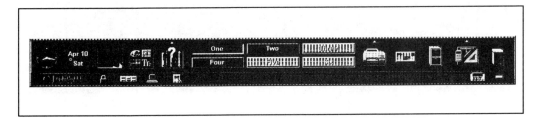

Figure 4.9 Hewlett-Packard VUE Control Panel

entire X environment. In addition to performing a number of file-management operations, the file manager allows you to launch X applications. The DeskSet application suite represents an early approach to desktop interoperablity. Software vendors must use what is, in effect, a proprietary form of interclient communication for their applications to participate fully in the loosely organized DeskSet environment. More recently, Sun's participation in the initiative among major UNIX workstation vendors to establish a common X desktop environment will eventually lead to greater interoperability among X clients (see Section 4.13).

4.12.3 Silicon Graphics Toolchest

Silicon Graphics workstations provide several applications through their Toolchest facility [Silicon Graphics, 1992], which complements the X user environment very nicely. As with other *mwm*-like environments, the window manager provides a root menu. The Silicon Graphics window manager is *4Dwm*, a variation on *mwm*. (You can configure Silicon

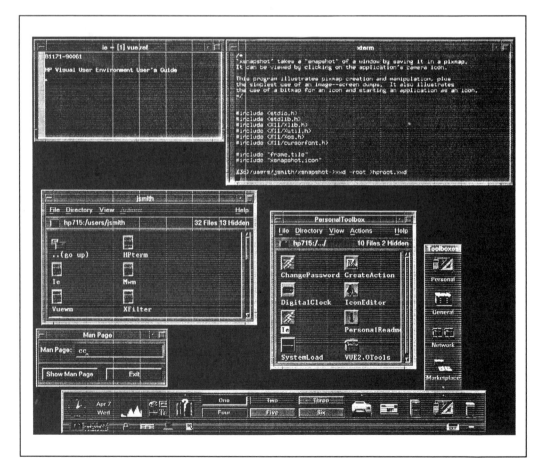

Figure 4.10 Hewlett-Packard X Environment, VUE

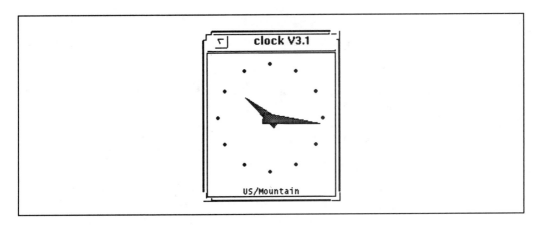

Figure 4.11 OpenWindows DeskSet Clock Application

Graphics workstations to use *mwm* instead of *4Dwm*.)

Toolchest's small, main menu (see Figure 4.14) exists nonobstrusively as part of the desktop (see Figure 4.15). From this top-level window you can access a wide range of desktop tools including a workspace manager, a text editor, customization facilities, clocks, and others

```
                     Text Editor V3.1 – xeject.c, dir; /files/home/jsmith/Xta

     File ⊽)   View ⊽)   Edit ⊽)   Find ⊽)                                ▤

      */
      static XtResource resources[] = {
              {XtNcommand, XtNCommand, XtRString, sizeof(String),
                  XtOffset(ApplicationDataPtr, command),
                  XtRString, DEFAULT_EJECT_COMMAND},
      };


      /*
      Private action globals:
      */

      #ifdef USE_ACTIONS
      static char app_trans[] =
          "<ClientMessage> WM_PROTOCOLS : WMProtocolsAction()";

      static XtActionsRec app_actions[] = {
          {"WMProtocolsAction", WMProtocolsAction},
      };
      #endif


      /*
      main() sets up the top-level window, processes resources, and
      interposes the event handling for the icon's mechanical eject
```

Figure 4.12 OpenWindows Deskset Text Editor

including Silicon Graphics' notepad application. Figure 4.16 shows two posted notes.

Recently, Silicon Graphics began shipping workstations with their new Indigo Magic™ user environment [Silicon Graphics, 1993]. The Indigo Magic X environment presents a higher level desktop environment than the familiar Toolchest-based application suite. The Indigo Magic desktop manager is considerably more sophisticated than earlier third-party desktop managers, and it integrates network and digital media support. Like the HP VUE desktop, the Indigo Magic environment supports multiple desktops (which is an extension of the virtual window manager concept described in Section 3.9).

4.12.4 Solbourne Applications

Solbourne Computer is another vendor that early on provided a small suite of applications as part of its X environment [Solbourne Computer, 1991]. In comparison, the Solbourne file manager is less sophisticated than the OpenWindows application; in fact, it is designed primarily as a directory browser. Both X clients, however, have relative advantages and disadvantages (see Figure 4.17). In addition to the directory browser, the Solbourne application suite includes an appointment book, a font viewer, an electronic mail tool, and an electronic news reader/manager. Figure 4.18 demonstrates the mail tool, *smail*. Because Solbourne computers are SPARC workstations, users can also install Sun's OpenWindows environment and its Deskset tools as described in Section 4.12.2.

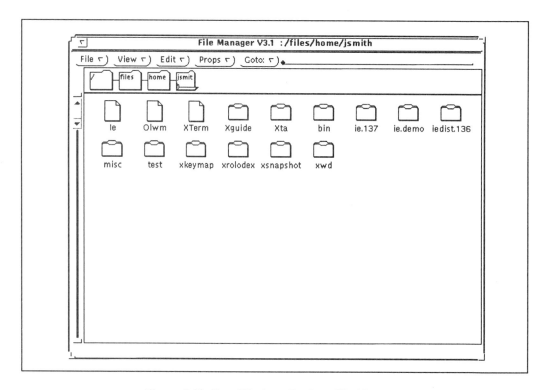

Figure 4.13 OpenWindows Deskset File Manager

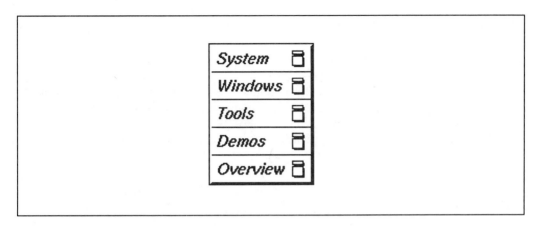

Figure 4.14 Silicon Graphics Toolchest Menu

4.13 High-level Desktop Applications

There now are numerous third-party desktop managers for X. Also, with Sun Microsystems acceptance of Motif and its participation in the common open software environment (COSE) initiative, a common desktop environment (CDE) is expected across all of the major UNIX

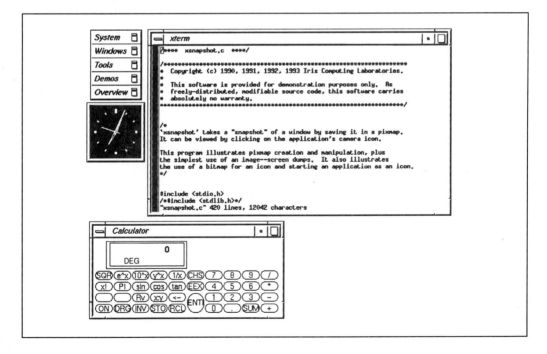

Figure 4.15 Silicon Graphics Toolchest Applications

workstation platforms [X/Open, 1993].

Although current third-party desktop managers vary greatly in terms of look and feel (even those that follow a common style guide), their basic objective is to provide a higher level UI for X. In doing so, current desktop managers essentially use an application-and-file orientation. For example, they typically provide a directory browsing tool that supports drag-and-drop operations across directories for file management operations such as copy, move, and delete, as well as drag-and-drop support for associating an application with a file. With this design, desktop managers typically manage icons for each application that the user may activate during the course of the user session.

Drag-and-drop is a technique whereby a user can apply an operation to an object by dragging the icon that represents an object to the icon that represents the operation. For example, to print a file, you could drag the icon for a particular file over the icon for a print tool and drop/release it (assuming the software supports this particular drag-and-drop operation).

Most UNIX old-timers would prefer to type a print command in an *xterm* window. Their preference has more to do with the *way* they work than their like or dislike for high-level features such as drag-and-drop. In isolation, dragging a file icon to a print tool icon and dropping it is a quick operation, probably quicker than typing a print command with a filename argument. On the other hand, for users who are involved in many types of tasks on a daily basis, the high-level approach implies that they must have many, many applica-

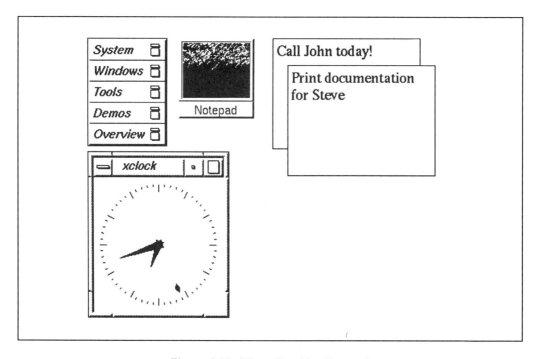

Figure 4.16 Silicon Graphics Notepad

tions active concurrently. Notwithstanding the power of modern UNIX workstations, it is somewhat nonproductive to have many concurrently executing applications when you use each one only occasionally, for example, a print tool. This sometimes leads to a desktop that is quite cluttered.

Another issue is whether or not applications must be executing to support a high-level user interface. With an application suite that exists as a loosely integrated collection of X clients, each application must be executing. That is, you have to execute the print tool to have access to its icon, so that you can drag and drop a file icon "at the printer." There must be a significant level of cooperation among the components of a particular application suite; otherwise, the print tool would not understand how to "receive" the file as an object of its operation. If, however, the workstation community can agree on one drag-and-drop protocol, as opposed to two or three, the possibility for interoperability across applications and application suites will become a reality.

We're using the print tool as an example of an application that might participate in a drag-and-drop scheme, and, of course, there are many others. We should point out that application suites take steps to minimize the number of applications that are executing concurrently, such as by including a print option in the file menu for a file manager. It is clear, however, that this scheme breaks down when there are several loosely integrated applications and when the user can dynamically add new participants.

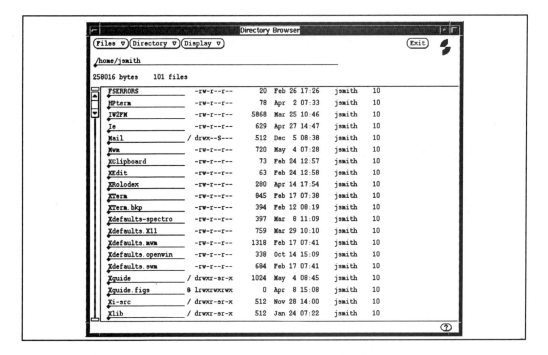

Figure 4.17 Solbourne Directory Browser

Some desktop managers attempt to maximize the overall efficiency of the user interface by using a design wherein the desktop manager provides icons that represent various applications; typically, the user can modify this collection of icons. In this case, the desktop manager's icon for, say, a print tool, is not the icon of an executing application. That is, the desktop manager interjects an additional level of indirection in the application-and-file scheme. Thus, if you drop an object's icon on an application's icon within the desktop manager's window, the desktop manager then associates the object with the operation using lower level operations that are transparent to the user. For example, the desktop manager would handle the tasks involved in (1) starting/executing an application, (2) submitting the object to the application, and (3) terminating the application-and-file association.

Desktop managers can provide an intuitive high-level interface to sophisticated operating systems and user environments, such as a UNIX workstation running X. This type of interface can be useful to secretaries, engineers, and others whose objectives in life do not include a command-line understanding of UNIX, or of the many facets of X.

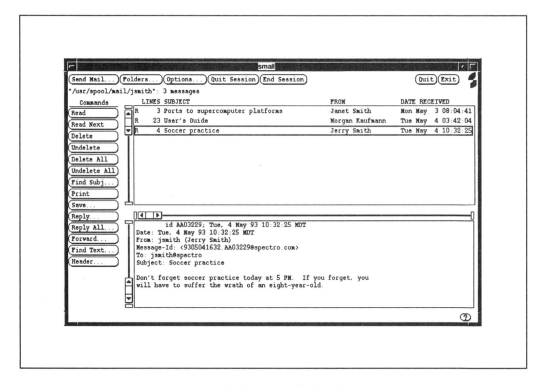

Figure 4.18 Solbourne Mail Application

5

Configuring X Clients
with X Resources

In this chapter we address X's facility for configuring X clients, commonly referred to as the X resource database, or the resource manager. This chapter includes background information for the perceived variances in X resource handling that are due to an X client's method of implementation. The primary objective is to provide general guidelines and suggestions that are useful in the day-to-day configuration of X applications.

In this chapter and others we use common X clients such as *xterm* in our example. In your environment, however, it is likely that you will use these guidelines to customize your word-processor or spreadsheet software, not *xterm*.

5.1 Application Conformance

It is ironic that the largest, or at least the most visible, debate in the X world focuses on look-and-feel issues. In many ways, the look and feel of an application is a less critical issue than whether or not it follows the recommendations of the ICCCM and supports configuration via X resources (or via higher level facilities).

In this chapter we focus on another X "feature" that is rather open-ended in terms of whether or not software developers must comply. X provides a facility, the X resource manager, that is the preferred mechanism for supporting application configuration. On the other hand, because X leans toward flexibility instead of imposed compliance to a formal standard, there is nothing to prevent developers from continuing to use more traditional configuration facilities.

With UNIX systems, the tradition has been to configure applications via ".*rc" configuration files in the user's home directory, for example, the configuration file for *csh(1)* is *.cshrc*.

With DOS systems, many applications support "*.cfg" configuration files that record color settings, menu organizations, and so on. In both DOS and UNIX environments, many applications also process environment variables for configuration options. Configuring software with environment variables can be rather messy, in terms of the potential for confusion over where and when each global variable is modified. Also, setting environment variables here and there is inherently low level compared with the more structured approach in which resources (configuration variables) are maintained in specific, common locations.

It may appear that X perpetuates this continuing tradition; for example, *xinit* reads the file *.xinitrc*. *xinitrc*, however, is really a special situation because it sets up the X environment. That is, because *xinit* starts the X server, the X resource manager cannot possibly be available to *xinit*. In contrast, with *xdm*, which presents a log-in window *after* the X server is "up and running," X resources are processed from a special file, */usr/lib/X11/-xdm/Xresources*.

For traditional applications such as word processors and typesetting software, developers can ease the user's burden significantly by implementing *all* configuration options as X resource settings. This strategy also applies to configuration data for a user's default, or start-up, work environment. Many applications still save this type of information in an application-specific file; thus, for the curious user, the challenge is to unravel the meaning of numerous data fields, which vary in significant ways for each application. Fortunately, the number of applications and environments that take the X approach is increasing. For example, with OpenWindows when you modify your workspace properties (see Figure 5.1) and then commit the changes, these settings are stored in your *.Xdefaults* file.

5.2 X Resource Format

X resources settings with the following formats are common:

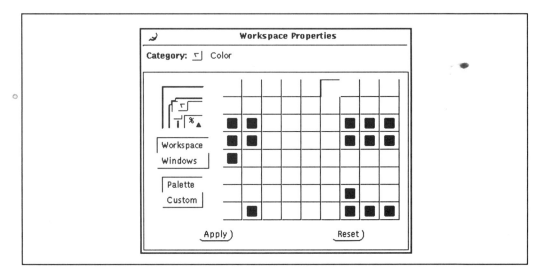

Figure 5.1 OpenWindows Properties Window

```
<application>*<UI component>*<UI subcomponent>...*<UI attribute>:   <value>
```

```
<application>*<feature>:   <value>
```

Consider several concrete examples for a hypothetical X word processor, *xwp*:

```
*background:  SkyBlue
xwp*background:   AntiqueWhite
xwp*mainWindow*popupMenu*background:   MintCream
xwp*scrollbarLocation:   left
xwp*scrollbar:   true
xwp*autoBackup:   on
xwp*deleteHistory:   50
xwp*readOnly:   no
```

From these examples you can see that each UI component in a resource specification is optional, except the resource attribute, for example, *background* or *readOnly*.

Note that resource names are case sensitive. For example, *xwp*'s scrollbar resources expect lowercase letters, for example, "scrollbar", whereas *xterm*'s scrollbar resource uses mixed-case letters, for example, "scrollBar":

```
xterm*scrollBar:   on
```

Most applications are quite flexible in their interpretation of resource values, allowing you to use various Boolean values interchangeably, for example, "on", "yes", and "true". Other X resources expect specific numeric- and string-style values such as 50 and "red". In many cases, applications specify the type of resource value that they expect for each resource by providing examples via a help system and printed documentation.

As implied by the previous generic resource formats, most X clients support configuration options for their UI components as well as for non-UI components, for example, application "behaviors" such as whether or not automatic backups are enabled. In the latter case, there is (typically) no hierarchy in the resource specification:

```
xwp*autoBackup:   on
```

Here, automatic back-ups are enabled for *xwp*.

When an application requires a more specific resource setting, based on software components, it will provide the additional specificity as part of the resource name(s), or it will introduce a resource hierarchy. For example, suppose a word processor makes a distinction between primary and secondary edit windows with respect to how it handles automatic backup operations. The following resources encode the type of edit-window environment in the resource name itself:

```
xwp*autoBackupPrimaryWindow:   on
xwp*autoBackupSecondaryWindow:   off
```

A different text processor might provide this distinction between windows with a UI component hierarchy:

```
xeditor*primaryWindow*autoBackup:   on
xeditor*secondaryWindow*autoBackup:   off
```

With OpenWindows, for example, the location of the scrollbar is specified within a single resource name rather than via a hierarchy:

```
OpenWindows.ScrollbarPlacement:   left
```

If there were many categories of scrollbar configuration, for example, scrollbar location, behavior/style, and so on, they could be categorized using specific resource names, falling under the "scrollbar" resource.

5.3 Resource Instances and Classes

First, consider the resource naming convention that has been adopted by most X clients. If the resource name is derived from multiple words, for readability, X clients use a mixed-case naming convention, as opposed to separating words with underscore characters, hyphens, or some other delimiter.

```
OpenWindows.ScrollbarPlacement:   left
```

The X resource manager supports both resource instances and resource classes. By convention, if the first character in a resource name is lowercase, it is a resource instance, for example, *background* and *cursorColor*; otherwise, it is a resource class, for example, *Background*:

```
xterm*background:   SkyBlue
```

versus

```
xterm*Background:   SkyBlue
```

Resource instances "belong to," or are associated with, resource classes—a class can have multiple instances. Note that a resource instance can have a different name than its class. For example, with *xterm*, *cursorColor* is an instance of the class *Foreground*. Interpretation: the text cursor is part of the window's foreground.

What does this imply in terms of specific resource settings? Suppose that you make the following setting:

```
xterm*foreground:   PapayaWhip
```

In this case, because you've specified the color for the foreground text using the *foreground* instance, it will not affect the cursor color, even though both *foreground* and *cursorColor* are instances of the same class, *Foreground*. On the other hand, the following setting affects both the foreground text and cursor colors because both *foreground* and *cursorColor* are instances of the *Foreground* class:

```
xterm*Foreground:   Magenta
```

Note, however, that with both settings active simultaneously, the color will be PapayaWhip for the foreground text and Magenta for the text cursor:

```
xterm*foreground:   PapayaWhip
xterm*Foreground:   Magenta
```

That is, setting a resource instance is a more specific, or more fine-grained, approach to application configuration.

Setting resources with both instances and classes can be confusing if you view classes as somehow being more powerful than instances (because a class can encompass multiple instances)—this view is incorrect. Instead, think of an instance as being *more specific* than a class. Thus, you can set a resource class to provide a broad level of configuration and then supplement the class specification with resource-instance specifications, as necessary, to override the class-level settings.

Another point is that with many applications there is a one-to-one correspondence between resource instances and classes. In this case, specifying the configuration option with either an instance or a class setting will yield the same result.

Lastly, instance and class conventions apply to applications as well. For example, in Section 2.7.1 we mentioned the class *XTerm*. There can be multiple X clients belonging to the class *XTerm*, the most common *XTerm* application being *xterm*. This convention allows developers to introduce applications that are variations of other applications, and that support the same or similar X resources. Thus, resource settings for *XTerm* would apply to both *xterm* and the hypothetical X client *myterm*. Users could then provide instance-level *xterm* and *myterm* resource settings to override the more general settings provided for the class *XTerm*.

5.4 User-interface Objects and Resources

In Section 1.4 we mentioned that applications are often built from a common toolkit and object set. The most common X toolkit is *the* X toolkit, or Xt; it is part of the Consortium X distribution. Although the Athena widget set is part of the Consortium X distribution, the Motif widget set is the most common widget set for implementing commercial applications. As mentioned in Chapter 1, a toolkit provides the software routines that implement the generic functionality of an application's user interface, whereas widgets implement the UI objects that allow a user to interact with and control an application, for example, command buttons, toggle buttons, menus, scrollbars, and so on.

The facilities that we refer to as the X resource manager are actually implemented in a basic form as part of X's low-level programming interface (library), Xlib. Toolkits such as Xt provide higher level routines (from a programmer's perspective) for setting and retrieving values from the resource database, typically, dependent on the object/widget hierarchy of the application. For the user, the higher level support for resources by toolkits means that most toolkit-based applications will support these facilities. Many applications built directly with Xlib, or with Xlib-based custom toolkits provide less sophisticated, but often quite adequate, resource handling.

For X clients built from the X toolkit and a common widget set, the organization (specifically, hierarchy) that is inherent in the application's UI objects determines the set of all possible, valid resource specifications. The organization is hierarchical because, for example, there can be command buttons within dialog boxes, control panels, and other higher level UI objects; higher level objects such as control panels can exist as components of other higher level objects such as primary and secondary application windows.

For simplicity, suppose our hypothetical X word processor, *xwp*, consists of one top-level edit window plus a menu bar. In this case, the object hierarchy would be similar to the one outlined in Figure 5.2.

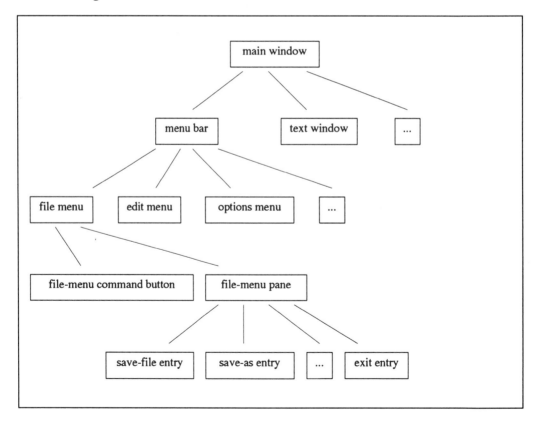

Figure 5.2 A Hypothetical *xwp* Object Hierarchy

Note that the developer chooses the resource instance names for each UI component and, typically, informs the user of these names somewhere in the documentation or in the help system. On the other hand, toolkits are designed such that the resource classes in the application are derived from the class names provided by the widget set. For example, with Motif widget set-based applications, the class for text windows is *XmText*; with applications based on the Athena widget set, the class for text windows is *Text*.

To some extent, these issues are of little concern to users, because an application should document its resource instances as well as resource classes (unless, of course, there is a one-to-one correspondence between instances and classes). Nevertheless, this explanation is still useful because it provides a user with an insight into the resource naming conventions that exist within and across X clients.

Figure 5.3 provides a hypothetical widget hierarchy for a Motif widget set-based implementation of *xwp*. (For brevity, we often say Motif-based implementation, Motif-based application, or even Motif application, even though we recognize that Motif is a user-interface style specification that provides guidelines for various window manager and toolkit implementations.) In Figure 5.3, for simplicity, several miscellaneous components of the exact widget hierarchy have been omitted.

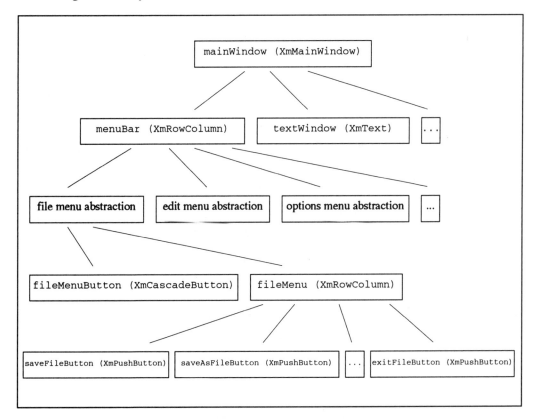

Figure 5.3 A Hypothetical *xwp* Motif Widget Hierarchy

Consider the menu bar. You might not expect a menu bar to belong to the class *XmRowColumn*, whatever that is, but the class names are really just a by-product of numerous implementation and programming details that are largely irrelevant to the user. You simply need to know the class name if you intend to configure UI components with class-level resource settings.

For this reason, it is often helpful to have a minimal understanding of specific widget sets, especially if you are interested in class-level resource settings. Unfortunately, if you use applications based on the Athena, Motif, and OLIT widget sets, developing a minimal understanding of various widgets becomes a significant task—part of the price we pay for user-interface flexibility.

For example, with Motif-based applications it is useful to know that many different types of UI components belong to the *XmRowColumn* class including menu bars, pull-down menus, pop-up menus, and other application-specific UI objects that require a row or column organization. If you are using a large Motif-based X client, such as a word processor, you can verify this fact with a resource specification such as

```
*XmRowColumn*background:   HotPink
```

Note that this will work only if your X client does *not* provide more specific resource settings elsewhere. For example, if your word processor is *xwp* and you have a resource specification such as

```
xwp*background:   Gray
```

the *XmRowColumn* specification will not affect *xwp* because the latter resource setting overrules the HotPink background (for *xwp*). General guideline: More specific resource settings overrule less specific resource settings.

As an aside, if you are using an application that does not document which UI components belong to which classes, you can experiment with various resource class names to determine their relationships by trial and error. Of course, you must know the toolkit and widget set used to implement the X client in order to make intelligent guesses at the class names. On the other hand, there is virtually no way to guess the instances names for each UI component, simply because the developer chooses these names. If an application is compatible with the X utility *editres*, you can explore its widget hierarchy dynamically (see Section 7.6).

Again using Figure 5.3 as an example, consider the following resource specifications, each one in isolation:

```
xwp*XmRowColumn:   HotPink                            (1. error!)
xwp*background:   HotPink                             (2.)
xwp*XmRowColumn*background:   HotPink                 (3.)
xwp*menuBar*background:   Purple                      (4.)
xwp*fileMenu*XmPushButton*background:   HotPink       (5.)
```

(Note that the numbers in parentheses are for references here; they are not part of the specification.) Specification 1 illustrates a common mistake; specifically, we provide a resource class, *XmRowColumn*, that may match multiple UI components, but no specific attribute for that component. This specification is invalid because it would require the system to make a guess as to whether you meant to request HotPink foreground text, background text, or even something ridiculous such as menu buttons with a margin width of HotPink pixels.

Specification 2, assuming there are no other conflicting or overriding resource specifications, requests a HotPink background for everything in *xwp*: the menu bar, the menus, the text window, and so on. Specification 3 differs from specification 2 in that it requests a HotPink background for any UI component that belongs to (is an instance of) the *XmRowColumn* class.

Compare resource specifications 3 and 4. The former applies to any instance of the *XmRowColumn* class, whereas the latter targets a specific UI component by its instance name, *menuBar*. Specification 5 differs in another way; it makes a class-level specification but only within the specific UI component *fileMenu*. *fileMenu*, of course, is a composite object that includes menu entries (implemented from *XmPushButton* objects), as well as menu-entry margins and menu-entry separators. (Specification 5 is intended as an example only; with the Motif look and feel, menu entries and the surrounding margins really should have a consistent background color.)

5.5 Resource Bindings

So far, in our examples we've mostly used a "*" to bind together UI components and attributes in resource specifications, for example:

```
xwp*mainWindow*popupMenu*background:   MintCream
```

This form of connecting the resource names for UI objects is called a *loose binding* because it is an *inexact* specification of an application's UI object hierarchy. In most cases, an inexact specification is a good thing. That is, the resource database's support for loose bindings allows much-needed flexibility in resource specifications.

Except for trivial applications such as our *xwp* example, the true widget hierarchy for a Motif-based X client can be incredibly complicated. For example, the object (sub)hierarchy for a straightforward pull-down menu includes numerous objects that virtually defy explanation. From the user's perspective, a menu is a rectangular object with several entries; from the toolkit's perspective, there are many other components including the top-level shell (window), the menu pane (background area), visual separators between menu entries, the actual menu entries, and so on.

If, however, your goal is to set the background color of all the menus of a particular application, you probably don't want to have to specify the background color for the many miscellaneous UI components. When you use a loose binding, you are requesting that the resource database process each "*" as a wildcard, similar to a wildcard in UNIX or DOS file specifications (but at the component, not character, level). Also, beginning with X11R5, a "?" serves as a wildcard for a single level in the widget hierarchy.

In essence, when you start an X client, the X resource manager formulates an exact representation of the complete object hierarchy. It compares this hierarchy against a merged list of resource specifications from various standard locations and configuration files. Wherever there is a match, the application honors the configuration request. Thus, if you have included a resource specification such as

```
xwp*mainWindow*background:   MintCream
```

in a configuration file, *xwp* will provide a MintCream background color for all UI objects in its main window (assuming that the documentation states that the main window's instance name is *mainWindow*, and that there are no overriding resource settings elsewhere).

Sometimes the configuration files provided by vendors, or generated by their software, include a "." to bind together UI objects and attributes. A "." separator is called a *tight binding*. Tight bindings apply (1) when there is an *exact* match between a resource specification and the actual object hierarchy, for example,

```
*mainMenu.Label:   Main Options
```

or (2) when an application provides resources that transcend specific UI objects, for example,

```
OpenWindows.ScrollbarPlacement:   left
```

The example for tight bindings for category 1 is taken from the standard resource file for the class *XTerm*, typically located in the file */usr/lib/X11/app-defaults/XTerm*. It includes many other resource settings with a combination of loose and tight bindings:

```
*SimpleMenu*BackingStore: NotUseful
...
*SimpleMenu*Cursor: left_ptr
*mainMenu.Label:   Main Options
...
*mainMenu*quit*Label:   Quit
...
*vtMenu.Label:   VT Options
*vtMenu*scrollbar*Label:   Enable Scrollbar
...
*fontMenu.Label:   VT Fonts
*fontMenu*fontdefault*Label:     Default
...
```

Note that the resource specifications do not have to begin with *xterm...* or *XTerm...* because they are located in a file that bears the class name. This type of file provides default configuration settings for all X clients (such as *xterm*) that are instances of the class *XTerm*;

for this reason, it is often called a *class resource file*. Another common name is *application defaults file*, hence, the name of the subdirectory in which these files reside: */usr/lib/X11/app-defaults* for Consortium X distributions, *$OPENWINHOME/lib/app-defaults* for OpenWindows, and ... *dvx**app-defa* for DESQview/X.

Consider category 2. OpenWindows has a specific resource, *ScrollbarPlacement*, that allows you to configure the scrollbar location, independent of any particular UI object hierarchy:

```
OpenWindows.ScrollbarPlacement:  left
```

Because OpenWindows is a vendor-specific X implementation, this type of resource makes sense. All OpenWindows applications are designed to honor these object hierarchy-independent resources.

You should be careful if you decide to use tight bindings in resource specifications because (1) it is easy to leave out a component when attempting a complete specification and (2) X does not provide any specific feedback when a resource specification doesn't match what you intended it to match.

By design, X supports both loose and tight bindings, allowing you total flexibility in how you formulate your resource specifications—only you know your intentions. Some users and writers have been quick to criticize X because they perceive that X simply ignores "errors" in resource specifications with loose bindings. After a little reflection, however, it is obvious that in many cases X cannot anticipate when a specification is "wrong." This situation is somewhat analogous to using wildcards in filename specifications:

```
{your system prompt} ls -l *.txt
```

Of course, DOS and UNIX command shells and high-level file selection boxes do not warn you as to the potentially many files that do not match a particular file specification.

5.6 Resource Precedence

For several of the examples in previous sections we mentioned that one resource specification might override, or be overridden by, another resource specification. The resource manager has straightforward rules that govern the matching of resource specifications, as well as their entry, management, and replacement in the resource database. In this section we number our precedence rules for easy reference, but otherwise the numbers are not significant.

1. More recent specifications override/replace less recent specifications. If you include the following configuration settings in the same resource file, the latter setting will override the former setting:

```
*foreground:  black
...
*foreground:  red
```

Be careful, however, in making assumptions regarding the order of identical resource specifications across configuration files, because not all configuration files are processed in certain X environments (see Section 5.7). Because this type of conflict in resource settings is typically an error on the user's part, you may get a warning message that the latter setting overrides the former setting.

2. Instance specifications take precedence over class specifications. Our previous *xterm* example illustrates this rule. For example, suppose a configuration file includes

```
xterm*foreground:   PapayaWhip
xterm*Foreground:   Magenta
```

In this case, the foreground text color will be PapayaWhip. Because there are no instance specifications for *cursorColor* and *pointerColor* to override the *Foreground* class specification, both the text and pointer cursor would be Magenta.

As another example, consider the following resource settings:

```
*vtMenu*Background:    SkyBlue
*SimpleMenu*Background:  HotPink
```

xterm's VT100 menu (**<Ctrl>-<MouseButton2>**) is an instance of the *SimpleMenu* class, so the menu will be blue, not pink.

3. More complete, or explicit, specifications take precedence over less complete specifications. This rule makes perfect sense. In general, you should use loose bindings because it is very tedious and quite easy to make a mistake with a resource setting that must exactly match the UI object hierarchy. The following example is often given as an example of a situation in which loose bindings can be problematic:

```
xterm*geometry:   80x30
```

The probable intent with this setting is to configure *xterm*'s main VT100 window to have 80 columns and 30 rows. The mistake is that this specification ignores the fact that *xterm* has other windows that will be affected, in particular, the windows housing the pop-up menus. The result is that the windows that implement the menus are reduced to 80 by 30 pixels, obscuring the menu entries.

An often-cited remedy for this mistake is the specification:

```
xterm.vt100.geometry:   80x30
```

Actually, however, the problem is not one of loose versus tight bindings but rather a UI object specification that is simply too incomplete. Our suggestion to use loose bindings whenever possible is still valid because the following resource setting is equally successful in overcoming the ambiguity:

```
xterm*vt100*geometry:   80x30
```

4. Tight bindings take precedence over loose bindings. According to our general guideline in Section 5.4, which is restated as precedence rule 3, a more specific setting takes precedence over a less-specific setting. A tight binding is more specific than a loose one, so this often-stated precedence rule is actually redundant, but, perhaps, important to include anyway. The irony is that in almost every situation in which you have enough knowledge of the object/class hierarchy to formulate a resource specification with a tight binding, a loose binding would have worked just as well!

First, if you have exactly/completely identified an object in an application's object hierarchy, replacing "." with "*" is not likely to match any other object, for example,

```
xwp.mainWindow.mainPanel.menuBar.fileButton:   Blue
```

versus

```
xwp*mainWindow*mainPanel*menuBar*fileButton:   Blue
```

That is, the wildcarding has no effect because of the complete specification of all objects in the hierarchy.

Second, consider the following subset of the resource specifications contained in the class file *XTerm*:

```
...
*vtMenu.Label:  VT Options
*vtMenu*scrollbar*Label:   Enable Scrollbar
*vtMenu*jumpscroll*Label:   Enable Jump Scroll
...
*vtMenu*tekshow*Label:   Show Tek Window
*vtMenu*tekmode*Label:   Switch to Tek Mode
*vtMenu*vthide*Label:   Hide VT Window
...
```

These settings specify the labels for the VT100 menu entries (accessed by pressing mouse button 2 while <Ctrl> is down). The first setting provides the label for the menu itself. (On your system, the class name may be prepended to each of the resource settings, that is, "XTerm*vtMenu...".)

In general, if you replace

```
*vtMenu.Label:  VT Options
```

with

```
*vtMenu*Label:  VT Options
```

nothing will change, even given the current precedence rule. The effect is the same because both "*vtMenu*Label" and "*vtMenu*scrollbar*Label" match the object that implements the "Enable Scrollbar" menu entry (an Athena *Label* widget), but because of precedence rule 3 the latter settings are *not* overridden by the more general setting.

5. Including a level/component to the left in the object hierarchy yields a resource specification with higher precedence. For example, consider the following resource settings:

```
*Background:  SkyBlue
*SimpleMenu*Background:  HotPink
```

Except for objects that are instances of the *SimpleMenu* class, the background will be SkyBlue. Adding otherwise equivalent levels to the left of the hierarchy does not change the level of specificity:

```
xterm*Background:  SkyBlue
xterm*SimpleMenu*Background:  HotPink
```

6. Other things being equal, specifying an object that is higher in the object hierarchy (further to the left in a complete object hierarchy specification) yields higher precedence than specifying an object that is lower in the hierarchy. This rule is really a restatement of precedence rule 5 but nevertheless useful for clarity. This rule is easily illustrated by the following resource settings:

```
*vtMenu*Background:  HotPink
xterm*Background:  SkyBlue
```

Users are sometimes surprised that these settings do *not* produce a pink VT100 menu in *xterm*, because a "specific" component of an *xterm* client is specified in the first setting. This interpretation of "specific" is incorrect—including an object further to the left in the object hierarchy is considered being "more specific." With these settings, *xterm*'s VT100 menu, the resource instance *vtMenu*, is blue because *xterm* is more specific than *vtMenu*. You must keep in mind that you know that a VT100 menu is a specific component of an *xterm* client, but to the resource manager *vtMenu* is just a name for a resource instance.

5.7 Other Resource-related Issues

So far we have not really given any reasons for using tight bindings, but in certain situations, they can be quite useful. Consider the menu labels for X clients of the class *XTerm*:

```
. . .
*vtMenu.Label:  VT Options
*vtMenu*scrollbar*Label:  Enable Scrollbar
*vtMenu*jumpscroll*Label:  Enable Jump Scroll
. . .
*vtMenu*tekshow*Label:  Show Tek Window
*vtMenu*tekmode*Label:  Switch to Tek Mode
*vtMenu*vthide*Label:  Hide VT Window
. . .
```

Suppose you want to change the label for the menu (but not its entries) from "VT Options" to "VT100 Menu". If you add the following resource setting to a file and then merge it with X's existing resource database, it will change the label for the menu as well as the menu entries:

```
xterm*vtMenu*Label:   VT100 Menu
```

Consider a more specific resource setting such as

```
xterm*vtMenu.Label:   VT100 Menu
```

This specification cannot possibly match the menu-entry objects with resource instance names *scrollbar*, *jumpscroll*, and so on (because of the tight binding); thus, it has no unintended side effects.

At this point, you may be thinking that "*vtMenu*scrollbar*Label" is more specific than "xterm*vtMenu*Label" because the former setting includes the instance name for each menu entry, in this case, *scrollbar*—based on precedence rules 2 and 3. In fact, however, the reason that all the menu labels are set to "VT100 Menu" is precedence rule 6. The presence of "xterm*..." causes this resource setting to override those that begin with "*vtMenu*...".

Our main objective with this example is to illustrate that there are often many resource settings that will achieve the same result. In this example, for which the goal is to set the menu label, you can use either a tight binding ("xterm*vtMenu.Label") to overrule the presence of "xterm*..." or eliminate the "xterm*..." ("*vtMenu*Label").

Despite the many precedence rules, specifying resources is typically quite easy. For example, you may want to request, say, MintCream menus for the "Send Mail" secondary window in your mail tool application, but you aren't sure exactly, or don't really care, where the menus occur in the UI hierarchy. The resource manager will scan all possible UI subhierarchies and find each situation that matches your request for MintCream menus:

```
xwp*sendMailWindow*Menu*background:   MintCream
```

This type of specification is quite easy with toolkits and widget sets that have a one-to-one correspondence between widget classes and UI objects. For the user, one of the most annoying aspects of Motif-based applications is that the Motif widget set includes various generic widget classes, such as *XmRowColumn*, that are used to implement a variety of UI objects including tables, pop-up menus, option menus, pull-down menus, and menu bars. Because there is no *Menu* class per se, you frequently have to set menu colors by determining the exact instance names and providing multiple resource settings.

In contrast, the Athena widget set provides a widget class called *SimpleMenu* that implements a basic menu. A programmer can, of course, build higher level menu systems from *SimpleMenu* instances. For the user, having a class specifically for menus means that in many cases you can use a class resource setting to achieve the intended effect:

```
*SimpleMenu*background:   HotPink
```

Because common X clients such as *xterm* and *xman* are implemented with the Athena widget set, this *single* specification should change the color of their menus (unless it is overridden by other resource specifications).

The resource manager is one component of X for which flexibility and power supports and encourages simple, not complex, statements from the user.

In Section 2.7.4 we suggested the use of the -n command-line option with many traditional X clients for setting the application and icon name, plus -title for setting the name in the title area only. We also briefly mentioned the existence of -name with many X clients. At this point, we can clarify the differences. In essence, -n and -title have "cosmetic" effects only; that is, they change the on-screen appearance of the application and icon names, for X clients that supports them. In contrast, -name instructs an X client to use an alternate instance name during start-up operations when it evaluates X resource settings.

Suppose that you add the following resource settings to a configuration file:

```
myterm*background:   Ivory
myterm*foreground:   SteelBlue
```

If you then start an *xterm* session with the -name command-line option and the value "myterm", it will honor these color requests:

```
{your system prompt} xterm -name myterm &
```

Without the -name option, *xterm* clients would honor the "xterm" instance and "XTerm" class resource specifications.

5.8 Specifying X Resources from a File or the Command Line

Typically, when users go through the effort of customizing an X client, they want to use those resource settings again and again. For this reason, the resource manager is designed to read resource specifications from a variety of files, as described in Chapter 6.

A resource file is a standard text file, typically created with a text editor such as *xedit* or with a word processor (in text mode). Each resource setting should be specified on a separate line, for example:

```
!
! Potpourri of X resource specifications:
!
*SimpleMenu*background:   HotPink
xterm*background:   SkyBlue
xedit*background:   Ivory
*iconic:   on
xrolodex*fontList:   7x13bold
xterm*vt100*geometry:   80x36
xterm*saveLines:   255
```

```
Mwm*resizeBorderWidth:   8
Mwm*keyboardFocusPolicy:   pointer
```

The resource file does not require any other text/lines beyond the X resource specifications. For clarity, however, you can include comment lines (or comment out certain resource settings); any line beginning with a "!" is ignored by the resource manager. Note that the font resource for Motif applications (*xrolodex* in the previous example) is *fontList*, not *font*.

With certain resource files, you can mix together resources for different X clients; in class-oriented resource files, however, you should include resource settings for one particular X client class only, for example, the class *XTerm*. These issues are also addressed in Chapter 6.

You can also make temporary resource settings, for example, when you're experimenting with colors, font sizes, and other attributes from the command line. Most X clients honor the -xrm (X resource manager) command-line option. The following example shows how it works:

```
{your system prompt} xterm -xrm '*background:  AquaMarine' &
```

Lastly, we should mention that X clients (and the resource manager) traditionally do *not* ignore trailing blanks. That is, the following command should produce an error/warning on your system:

```
{your system prompt} xterm -xrm '*background:  AquaMarine ' &

Warning: Color name "AquaMarine " is not defined in server database
```

This characteristic becomes important with, for example, commercial X software that expects a password:

```
xwp*password:   ABCDEFGHIJ
```

If there are blanks on the line after the password (in the resource file), you could get a "wrong password" error message, even though to your eyes the password appears correct.

6

Managing X Resource Specifications

Chapter 5 focuses on X resources per se including precedence-related issues. The precedence rules describe the pattern matching strategies and interactions of multiple X resources, when considered as a unit without regard for other contributing factors.

X, however, must be sufficiently flexible to accommodate sophisticated user environments, for example, UNIX workstations operating in a client-server relationship. For this reason, X clients must provide configuration mechanisms that support system-wide as well as user-, display-, and host-specific X resource specifications. This chapter describes the rules that X clients employ, in conjunction with the precedence rules described in Chapter 5, to combine/process resource settings from multiple locations. We also provide several guidelines for specifying X resources.

6.1 Merging X Resource Specifications

During start-up operations, X clients use resource-management routines that are commonly referred to as the *resource manager* to merge resource specifications from files in several locations. In the DESQview/X environment, describing these locations is simple, because the DOS environment is simple. In a UNIX environment, X supports several different locations for resource files to accommodate the many different client-server environments. After consulting these files for X resources, X clients consider X resources specified via the -xrm command-line option and then application-specific, command-line options such as -autoBackup. Sections 6.2 through 6.4 describe the order in which X clients consult these various X resource repositories. Appendix C provides a quick reference for these various resource locations.

6.2 DESQview/X Resource Files

With DESQview/X, resource files have the extension ".res" appended to their client name; for example, the resource file for *xeyes* is *xeyes.res*. Regardless of the class name for an X client, for example, *Mwm, Xedit, XLogo,* and *XTerm,* there is no lowercase/uppercase distinction because the DOS filesystem does not support mixed-case filenames. The location for resource files that contain standard, or default, configuration options is in the subdirectory ...\dvx\app-defa. (The term *application defaults* is commonly used to refer to these default application-configuration options, hence, the directory names *app-defa* and *app-defaults* for DESQview/X and UNIX environments, respectively.) Thus, if you were to install the hypothetical X word processor *xwp,* its application-defaults file would be ...\dvx\app-defa\xwp.res.

Quite often, users prefer to modify the configuration options for X clients without disturbing the default, system-wide resource file. Because DOS is a single-user environment, DESQview/X X clients look for user-supplied resource settings in the DESQview/X installation directory ...\dvx, unless the user has defined the environment variable HOME to specify an alternate directory. The user-defaults filename is *xdefault.res*.

6.3 X/UNIX Resource Files

UNIX users, especially in workstation environments, often work within multiple client-server situations. For example, one user might have multiple user accounts (with the same or different user names) across several workstations. In some cases users work from stand-alone workstations; in other cases they depend on file servers located elsewhere on the network. And, as we've mentioned, X offers many possibilities for remote client-server computing.

For these reasons, X implementations for UNIX are designed to accommodate application-, host-, and X server-specific resource files. Also, because UNIX is a multiuser operating system with both user-level and system-wide accounts and filesystems, X clients support user-defined and system-wide resource files.

A third factor that must be considered is that X clients are developed using a variety of toolkits, as well as the low-level programming interface, Xlib. Beyond the traditional locations for resource files, beginning with X11R4 Xt-based applications support *additional* resource file locations based on the environment variables XFILESEARCHPATH and XUSERFILESEARCHPATH. In this section we focus on traditional locations for resource files; Chapter 7 and Appendix C address X toolkit-specific issues.

With these issues in mind, let's consider the order in which X clients such as our hypothetical word processor *xwp* merge X resource specifications.

1. Application-related locations. The process begins by loading resources from a system-wide file with the same filename as the X client's class name. For *xwp,* this file would be *XWp.* The class name for an X client is determined by the developer. By convention, however, the class name is the same as the application name except that the first character is uppercase, and if the application name begins with an "x", the first two characters are uppercase: *Bitmap, EditRes, Ie, XTerm, XWp,* and so on. Class resource files include resource settings for X clients belonging to that class only. For example, *XWp* contains resource specifications for *xwp*, but not for *xterm* and *xedit*.

The directory designated for class, or application-defaults, files varies from one X implementation and workstation vendor to the next, with the most common location being */usr/lib/X11/app-defaults*. With OpenWindows, for example, this location is *$OPEN-WINHOME/lib/app-defaults*, where $OPENWINHOME is the value of the OPENWINHOME environment variable, typically, "/usr/openwin". With Xt-based applications, the environment variable XFILESEARCHPATH overrides this default location (see Section 7.3).

Application-defaults files in this type of system-wide location are typically managed and accessible only by the system administrator. The advantage of putting X resource settings in a system-wide directory is that a system administrator can do it once, and it applies to all users—it is not necessary to go around to each user's workstation to set up configuration options that are common to all users.

Despite the (welcomed) presence of a system-wide file with common resource settings, users often have personal preferences, for example, background and foreground colors, font selection, whether or not automatic backup is enabled, and others depending on the application. For user-level, application-specific resource specifications X clients next consult the directory specified by the environment variable XAPPLRESDIR. Users can configure their workstation to set this variable automatically during log-in operations. With Xt-based applications, the environment variable XUSERFILESEARCHPATH overrides XAPPL-RESDIR (see Section 7.3).

If XAPPLRESDIR has *not* been defined, an X client looks for resources in the user's home directory. In both cases, it searches for a resource file with the application's class name. Thus, to configure *xwp* to use your personal preferences for background and foreground colors, you could simply create the file *XWp* in your home directory containing the following resource settings:

```
xwp*foreground:   black
xwp*background:   AntiqueWhite
```

2. Server-related locations. Because X users often work from remote displays, as described in Chapter 2, an X client also consults two server-related locations: (1) the RESOURCE_MANAGER property of the root window, and, if this property does *not* exist, (2) a file with the name *.Xdefaults* in the user's home directory. Server-related resource settings affect all X clients displaying on that X server, regardless of where they are executing.

We haven't mentioned properties; for a discussion of the property concept see Appendix B. You can simply think of a property as global data, similar to an environment variable, except that instead of being defined in a user's "log-in space" it is associated with a particular window, in this case, the root window. Typically, the RESOURCE_MANAGER property is set by the X client *xrdb* (X resource database) (see Section 6.6). Some X environments execute *xrdb* during X server start-up operations. Of course, you can execute *xrdb* manually to set the RESOURCE_MANAGER property.

Users are sometimes confused over the relationship between these two X resource repositories. Note that an *X client* merges X resource settings from *.Xdefaults* if and only if the
RESOURCE_MANAGER property is not defined. In contrast, some X environments, for
example, OpenWindows, use the resource settings in your *.Xdefaults* to define the value of
the RESOURCE_MANAGER property. With OpenWindows, there are two other points to
note.

First, when you customize your X environment with the OpenWindows "Properties" pop-up
window (see Figure 6.1), it stores this information in your *.Xdefaults* file as X resources. If
you have also placed resource settings in this file with nicely written comments, your
comments will be lost when the "Properties" pop-up window updates *.Xdefaults*. With
OpenWindows, you should consider *.Xdefaults* to be a computer-generated file—use an
alternate X resource file for personal customizations.

Second, OpenWindows runs *xrdb* from the *openwin* start-up script in the file *$OPEN-
WINHOME/lib/Xinitrc*, loading *.Xdefaults* as the value for the RESOURCE_MANAGER
property:

```
# .xinitrc - OpenWindows startup script.

if [ -f $HOME/.Xdefaults ]; then
    xrdb $HOME/.Xdefaults        # Load Users X11 resource database
else
    xrdb $OPENWINHOME/lib/Xdefaults # Load Default X11 resource database
fi
...
```

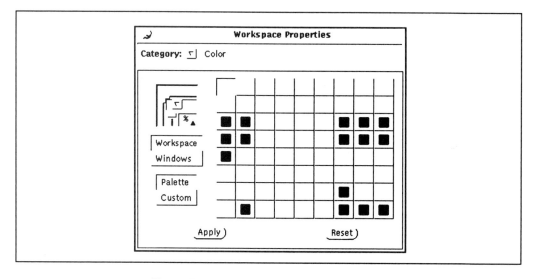

Figure 6.1 OpenWindows Properties Window

The point is that you cannot place resource settings in *.Xdefaults* and expect them to take place immediately. Because of the rule given for stage 2 in the resource merging process, an X client does not consult *.Xdefaults* because the RESOURCE_MANAGER property exists. Moreover, the RESOURCE_MANAGER property still has the contents of your *.Xdefaults* file when OpenWindows started. Section 6.6 describes how to use *xrdb* to reset the value of the RESOURCE_MANAGER property.

3. Host-related locations. Lastly, an X client honors host-related resource settings from two locations: (1) the *file* (not directory) named by the environment variable XENVIRON-MENT, and, if this variable does *not* exist, (2) a file with the name *.Xdefaults-<hostname>* in the user's home directory. In the latter case, *<hostname>* is the hostname (not hostid) of the workstation. X terminal users should note that *<hostname>* is *not* the network name for their X terminals (see Section 6.7).

XENVIRONMENT is a complete path specification for a file, for example, */home/mary/my-host-resources*. There are no restrictions on the filename—X loads resources from whatever file you specify. Thus, you could use a class file in your home directory or a file from anywhere on the system for which you have read access. It is important to note that the name has nominal value. That is, even if you specify a system-wide application-related class file, its contents are merged as host-related resources.

Host-related resource files provide a mechanism for configuring an application based on the host where the application is executing, regardless of the X server (display) where the client is currently displaying (supporting user interaction). Some users regularly execute applications on remote workstations, controlling them from their personal workstations. In this case, it may be helpful to configure the remote X clients to use different colors as a visual reminder of which X clients are executing on which workstations.

Also, this approach allows you to maintain multiple *.Xdefaults-<hostname>* files in your home directory, which may exist on a remote workstation (file server). Suppose, for example, you regularly work from two diskless workstations that mount (access) your home directory over the network. Also, suppose one workstation, pluto, is monochrome and the other workstation, saturn, has a color monitor. This facility allows you to set up configuration files named *.Xdefaults-pluto* and *.Xdefaults-saturn* that are tailored to each workstation.

6.4 Resource Specification from the Command Line

As mentioned, in addition to file-related resource specifications, X clients also support (transient) configuration using (1) the -xrm command-line option and (2) client-specific command-line options. Note that we've described the various resource repositories in the order in which an X client consults them. Likewise, command-line resource specifications and options are merged *after* those provided through resource files.

From the command line, an X client first merges resources, if any, associated with the -xrm keyword. If, for example, you want to experiment with an alternative background color, you can override an existing *background* resource setting in one or more resource files with the following:

```
{your system prompt} xterm -xrm '*background:  AquaMarine' &
```

Having this feature is especially nice when you have installed a new X client and you would like to test various configuration options. Once you decide on your preferred settings, you would, of course, permanently locate them in a resource file. Note that you can use `-xrm` for any X resource that an X client honors—if it works in a resource file, it should work with `-xrm`. Also, don't forget the single quotes; otherwise, the UNIX shell will attempt to interpret any "*"s in the resource setting as a file specification.

After merging resources provided via `-xrm` with those from resource files, an X client processes command-line options. Most X clients support common command-line options such as `-background`, `-bg`, `-foreground`, and others. In addition, however, they often support application-specific command-line options such as whether or not to perform automatic backups:

```
{your system prompt} xwp text.file -autoBackup off &
```

These client-specific X resources and command-line options should be described in the X client's documentation, or help system, along with information on the traditional X resources that it honors. Typically, the documentation will also provide default values and examples using each resource.

Novice X users often overlook the importance of being able to configure X clients from the command line. Suppose you (or your system administrator) have just installed a new product, say, our now-famous word processor *xwp*. Further, suppose that it requires a proper password; otherwise, it exits immediately with the error message "xwp: wrong password". Suppose you are supplying the password in a resource file, as the documentation describes, but you are still getting the message "xwp: wrong password". There are two likely errors: (1) the password resource name or its value is incorrect or (2) *xwp* is not processing the intended resource file. You can quickly diagnose where the problem lies by submitting a command-line resource specification via `-xrm`:

```
{your system prompt} xwp text.file -xrm '*password:  ABCDEFGHIJ' &
```

or by using the equivalent command-line option given in the documentation:

```
{your system prompt} xwp text.file -password ABCDEFGHIJ &
```

If you continue to get the message "xwp: wrong password", it is likely that the problem is with the resource value (assuming you have specified the resource name and command-line option properly), not with the resource file that you are using.

We should mention that there is a rumor circulating among some X sites and users, as well as in multiple written sources of information on X, that `-xrm` only works with X toolkit-based applications. This rumor is incorrect! The source of the rumor is X clients, developed with alternate toolkits or Xlib, that simply fail to consult, that is, "merge in" `-xrm` resource settings. Any X-compliant application should support the resource repositories described here, and possibly more; consult the documentation for alternatives, if any.

A final point is that many users work in computing environments where changes to system-wide files are handled exclusively by a system administrator—who always seems to be incredibly busy, out to lunch, on vacation, or in a bad mood. (In their defense, there are, of course, many *excellent* system administrators!) If you are in this unfortunate situation, simply abandon this approach to setting resources and use one of the user-oriented resource files that we've described.

6.5 Using a Shell Script for Application Configuration

An inferior, alternate approach to setting resources in user-oriented resource files is to build a script that invokes the X client with the proper command-line options. The following is a Bourne shell script for our hypothetical *xwp*:

```
#! /bin/sh
# Shell script to start xwp with a specific configuration
#

xwp $* -background Gray -foreground black -password ABCDEFGHIJ \
   -iconic &

# end of script
```

After you create a shell script with a text editor, you must designate it as an executable file. There is more than one way to change its mode, but the following should work:

```
{your system prompt} chmod 755 my.xwp
```

And, you must (possibly) copy the script to a "bin" directory and, with *csh(1)*, make it known to the shell from which you are submitting commands:

```
{your system prompt} rehash
```

Now, you can use *my.xwp* instead of invoking *xwp* directly, and it will supply the proper start-up options:

```
{your system prompt} my.xwp text.file
```

Note that you do not need the "&" to start the client as a background process, because it is included in the script. Also, the "$*" includes arguments that accompany the *my.exp* command as additional arguments to *xwp*.

6.6 Using *xrdb*

xrdb is an X client that simply manipulates the RESOURCE_MANAGER property of the root window. As mentioned in Section 6.3, X clients consult this resource repository in (our) stage 2 of the resource merging process.

You can view the value of the RESOURCE_MANAGER property by executing the X client *xprop* in a command window. When you click mouse button 1 over the root window, *xprop* displays all properties attached to the root window. Depending on your X environment, RESOURCE_MANAGER may or may not be defined.

The easiest way to define RESOURCE_MANAGER with specific resource settings is to create a text file containing the resource specifications, say, a file named *test.res*:

```
*background:   gray
*foreground:   black
*font:   8x13bold
```

(For Motif applications, use the resource *fontList* instead of *font*.)

xrdb's -load option will set RESOURCE_MANAGER to those values given in *test.res*:

```
{your system prompt} xrdb -load test.res
```

Then, you can use *xprop* to see the results:

```
{your system prompt} xprop   (then click mouse button 1 over the root window)

CUT_BUFFER0(STRING) = "The easiest way to define"
WM_ICON_SIZE(WM_ICON_SIZE):
        minimum icon size: 1 by 1
        maximum icon size: 160 by 160
        incremental size change: 1 by 1
. . .
RESOURCE_MANAGER(STRING) = "*background:\tgray\n*foreground:\tblack\n
*font:\t8x13bold\n"
. . .
```

You can also use *xrdb* with the -query option to examine the value of this property:

```
{your system prompt} xrdb -query

*background:   gray
*foreground:   black
*font:   8x13bold
```

Warning: The -load option *replaces* any existing value for the RESOURCE_MANAGER property. If your system depends on resource settings associated with RESOURCE_MAN-AGER, they will be overwritten!

Typically, however, *xrdb* is used with -merge, as opposed -load to add resource settings from a specific file to those that already exist as part of the RESOURCE_MANAGER property:

```
{your system prompt} xrdb -merge test.res
```

Another important point is that if you omit both -load and -merge, *and* supply a filename, *xrdb* substitutes/assumes -load *not* -merge. That is, -load is the default operation. We saw this earlier with the OpenWindows start-up script *$OPEN-WINHOME/lib/Xinitrc*, which loads *.Xdefaults* as the value for the RESOURCE_MANAGER property:

```
# .xinitrc - OpenWindows startup script.

if [ -f $HOME/.Xdefaults ]; then
    xrdb $HOME/.Xdefaults        # Load Users X11 resource database
else
    xrdb $OPENWINHOME/lib/Xdefaults # Load Default X11 resource database
fi
...
```

If you want to modify the RESOURCE_MANAGER property (add or remove one or more resources), a common technique is first to query the current value, redirecting the output to a file:

```
{your system prompt} xrdb -query > current.res
```

Then, you can edit this file with your favorite text editor and resubmit it as a replacement:

```
{your system prompt} xrdb -load current.res
```

Note that you can also use the -edit command-line to accomplish these types of updates. *xrdb* is a handy utility, and we suggest that you consult its man-page with *xman* for a complete explanation of its capabilities.

6.7 X Resources with X Terminals

Suppose you are operating from an X terminal network connected to a UNIX workstation. For the sake of illustration, let's say the workstation has the hostname solar and the X terminals have the network node names, mercury, mars, ..., uranus, and pluto. Next, suppose that you frequently work from the X terminals at nodes jupiter and saturn. In this environment, the configuration file *.Xdefaults-jupiter* or *.Xdefaults-saturn* will not be merged by X clients during (our) stage 3 of the resource merging process as described in Section 6.3.

That is, it is true that X clients consult the file *.Xdefaults-<hostname>* in the user's home directory, but *<hostname>* is the hostname for the workstation, not the X terminal's network node name. In this situation, one common approach to loading X terminal-specific resources is to set up your *.xsession* file in your home directory so that it reads a special resource file for each X terminal that you use, loading these resources with *xrdb*. In this case, the resource filenames are totally arbitrary, but for consistency you might want to name them something similar to *.Xdefaults-jupiter*, *.Xdefaults-saturn*, and so on. One technique is to examine the DISPLAY variable to determine which resource file to load.

The following statements are from an *.xsession* file that uses this technique:

```
...
if expr $DISPLAY : "saturn*"
then
  xsetroot -bitmap /home/jsmith/icon/graytile.bit
  ...
  xrdb -merge .Xdefaults-saturn
elif expr $DISPLAY : "jupiter*"
then
  xsetroot -solid "SlateGray"
  ...
  xrdb -merge .Xdefaults-jupiter
elif expr $DISPLAY : "earth*"
then
  xsetroot -solid "Plum"
  ...
  xrdb -merge .Xdefaults-earth
else
#
# workstation-related, xdm configuration
#
  ...
fi

xterm -sb -geometry 60x30-1-1 -fn 8x13bold -n shell -iconic  &
exec xterm -sb -geometry 66x8+2+2 -fn 6x10 -C -n console -iconic &
exec mwm
```

With this approach you can tailor your log-in environment based on a number of issues including color versus monochrome screen, font selection for X clients based on the size of the X terminal or workstation screen, and others.

7

Working with X Toolkit-based Applications

Many X clients are implemented with the X toolkit. All Xt-based applications share certain characteristics that are significant for users. For example, Xt-based applications support: (1) additional mechanisms for specifying X resource files, such as the environment variable XFILESEARCHPATH, and (2) a translation facility for customizing keyboard and mouse bindings.

Although there are other X toolkits, we limit our discussion to Xt because it is the most popular. For X clients implemented with an alternate toolkit, there are similar toolkit-related characteristics that lead to common user-interface functionality in the applications.

We also mention widget sets. There are several full-scale widget sets for the X toolkit, plus numerous special-purpose widget sets designed to complement one of the more complete widget sets. In this book, we focus on the Athena widget set, which is part of the Consortium X distribution, and the Motif widget set, the most popular widget set for implementing commercial Xt-based software.

7.1 The X Toolkit

In Section 1.4 we described a widget as the programming-equivalent of a user-interface object. Specifically, a widget is a system of data structures and routines that supports application components such as menus, scrollbars, text-entry fields, and others. The X toolkit supplies a larger system of routines that manages the entire user-interface side of an X client, for example, creating and deleting widgets, activating and deactivating dialog boxes, processing X resources via the resource manager, and so on (see Figure 7.1).

In this book, it is important to clarify the difference between Xt and the various widget sets to distinguish between those application characteristics that exist with all Xt-based applications and those that vary from one widget set to the next. For example, all Xt-based applications support the X resource *translations*, which is often useful in configuring an application's keyboard and mouse support. On the other hand, the widgets from a *particular* widget set share common resource naming conventions, idiosyncrasies with respect to clipboard support, and so on.

7.2 Recognizing Static versus Dynamic X Clients

Character-based applications, X clients implemented with the low-level X library (Xlib), and Xt applications are provided by a vendor in static or dynamic format. A statically linked Xt-based application includes *all* of the data structures and routines necessary for execution. A dynamically linked application, in the interest of saving space on disk and in computer memory, omits common routines. These common code segments are available to all dynamically linked applications from *shared* libraries. X clients, with the help of OS utilities, then access this code on the fly (dynamically) from the appropriate libraries.

Although the issue of static versus dynamic executables is independent of X, it is common for users to encounter problems in this area because (1) GUI applications are inherently large in static format and (2) X and X-related software originates from a variety of vendors. The amount of code required to implement the user interface for a significant commercial X client is really quite large, especially relative to character-based applications. To reduce

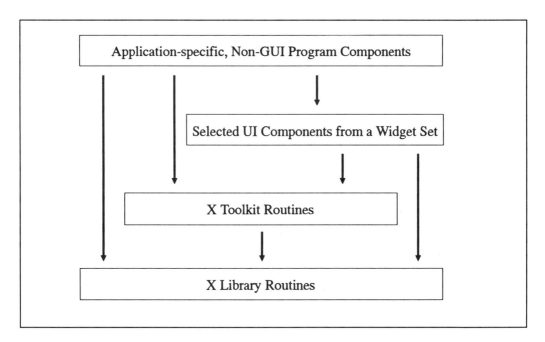

Figure 7.1 Components of an X Toolkit-based Application

the disk and memory demands for their applications, many software developers are now shipping dynamic executables for their X software.

Essentially, a dynamically linked X client executes until it discovers that a required routine is missing. At this point, it requests the missing routine (via the operating system) from a specific library—this library-related information is stored in the executable. On Sun workstations, for example, the names for shared libraries include "so" or "sa" plus a revision number. For example, there are two shared libraries for Xt on a Sun workstation with a Consortium X implementation of X11R4:

```
/usr/lib/libXt.sa.4.0
/usr/lib/libXt.so.4.0
```

Typically, static libraries do not have revisions numbers; the static-library analog is

```
/usr/lib/libXt.a
```

If an X client is built with the static library, it is complete in the sense that it includes all of the code from the library that is required for subsequent execution. Hence, if a vendor provides you with a static executable, it doesn't matter whether or not you have these X libraries on your system. The disadvantage of static executables, as mentioned (especially with GUI applications), is the relatively large size of the application. Static X clients usually require a large amount of disk storage space. More important, perhaps, they often exhaust workstation memory very quickly, leading to frequent page swapping when you run several X clients concurrently.

Because dynamic executables are smaller, they require less space on disk and in memory; moreover, they load (begin execution) more quickly. The disadvantage of shared executables is that you may encounter problems when you upgrade part or all of your X system software, but not your X clients. Suppose, for example, that you start an X client and get a message to the effect that a particular library was expected, but not found, and the X client then terminates.

There are several conditions that can produce this, or related, problems. For example, your system may require that you specify the locations for shared libraries in an environment variable such as LD_LIBRARY_PATH, and this variable may not have been updated for the current software. The following library path specification comes from the *csh(1)* configuration file, *.cshrc*, on a Sun workstation running OpenWindows:

```
setenv LD_LIBRARY_PATH /opt/SUNWspro/SC2.0.1:/usr/ccs/lib:$OPENWINHOME/lib
```

Note that each relevant directory that contains required libraries is specified in this colon-delimited list. In this particular X environment, the X libraries are stored in *$OPEN-WINHOME/lib*:

```
{your system prompt} ls $OPENWINHOME/lib/libX*
/usr/openwin/lib/libX.a          /usr/openwin/lib/libXinput.a
```

```
/usr/openwin/lib/libX.so              /usr/openwin/lib/libXinput.so
/usr/openwin/lib/libX.so.1            /usr/openwin/lib/libXinput.so.0
/usr/openwin/lib/libX11.a             /usr/openwin/lib/libXmu.a
/usr/openwin/lib/libX11.so            /usr/openwin/lib/libXmu.so
/usr/openwin/lib/libX11.so.4          /usr/openwin/lib/libXmu.so.4
/usr/openwin/lib/libXau.a             /usr/openwin/lib/libXol.a
/usr/openwin/lib/libXaw.a             /usr/openwin/lib/libXol.so
/usr/openwin/lib/libXaw.so            /usr/openwin/lib/libXol.so.3
/usr/openwin/lib/libXaw.so.4          /usr/openwin/lib/libXt.a
/usr/openwin/lib/libXext.a            /usr/openwin/lib/libXt.so
/usr/openwin/lib/libXext.so           /usr/openwin/lib/libXt.so.4
/usr/openwin/lib/libXext.so.0
```

If your library path is set properly, and you still get a missing-library message, the required library may actually be missing. Or, some other condition may be present that prevents your system from recognizing that the appropriate libraries exist.

We've used the X toolkit libraries, *libXt**, for our examples, but these issues arise with other X-related and non-X libraries as well. The previous output from *ls* illustrates that there are numerous X-related libraries, so the potential for encountering this problem is significant, especially if you acquire X software regularly from a variety of sources. It is important to recognize this type of problem immediately to short-cut the accompanying frustration. For this type of problem, it is important to consult your system administrator because it should be taken care of on a system-wide basis.

7.3 Toolkit-specific X Resource Locations

All Xt-based software developed since X11R4, as well as selected non-Xt applications, recognize the environment variables XFILESEARCHPATH and XUSERFILESEARCH-PATH. In Section 6.3 we described the traditional strategy that all X-compliant software uses to load X resources. This scheme for merging resources includes two environment variables: XAPPLRESDIR, for specifying the directory for user-level application-related resources (in each application's class file), and XENVIRONMENT, for specifying the complete path for a host-related resource file. XFILESEARCHPATH and XUSERFILE-SEARCHPATH have five significant characteristics: (1) they specify application-related resources; (2) they override the traditional locations for application-related resources; (3) they are composite variables; (4) they specify the complete path for a resource file; and (5) they accept various symbolic variables that apply to all X clients.

Characteristic 1 implies that XFILESEARCHPATH and XUSERFILESEARCHPATH are not directly useful for server- and host-specific client configuration. To set up resource files that differentiate between executing and displaying on a local workstation versus executing remotely and displaying locally, it is still necessary to use *xrdb* to load the appropriate resources for the local display.

Characteristic 2 implies that if XFILESEARCHPATH is set, a system-wide resource file, for example, */usr/lib/X11/app-defaults/XWp*, is *not* consulted. And, for user-level customizations, if XUSERFILESEARCHPATH is set, the X client does *not* process resources from class files in the directory XAPPLRESDIR (or the user's home directory if

XAPPLRESDIR is not set).   Note that these precedence rules are true even if XFILESEARCHPATH and XUSERFILESEARCHPATH are set to improper values, for example, empty/null values.

Characteristic 3 means that you can specify colon-separated lists of resource locations, for example,

```
setenv XFILESEARCHPATH /usr/lib/X11/app-defaults/XWp:\
$OPENWINHOME/lib/app-defaults/XWp

setenv XUSERFILESEARCHPATH /home/mary/config/XWp:/home/mary/config/XTerm
```

[The "\" allows the first assignment to continue onto a second line. Also, our example is based on *csh(1)*; use set instead of setenv with *sh(1)*.] Each location in the list is processed in sequential order. As soon as an X client locates an appropriate resource file (in this example, when *xwp* locates class file *XWp*), the search terminates. For example, based on the previous value of XFILESEARCHPATH, if *xwp* finds the file */usr/lib/X11/app-defaults/XWp*, it will *not* search for additional resources in *$OPENWINHOME/lib/app-defaults/XWp*, even if the first file is empty.

According to characteristic 4, the specification must include a filename (that is why XFILESEARCHPATH and XUSERFILESEARCHPATH have "FILE" in their names). Thus, if you use 100 different X clients, each with its own class resource file, must you provide 100 different path specifications (or merge the contents of all resource files into one huge file to specify a single filename)? No.

Because the path specification must include a filename, X clients that honor XFILESEARCHPATH and XUSERFILESEARCHPATH also honor several predefined symbols that function as variables. Otherwise, you really would have to create long lists of path specifications. These symbols and what they represent are

   %N — the application's class name
   %T — the directory *app-defaults*
   %C — a customization resource (available beginning with X11R5)
   %S — a suffix
   %L — a language, locale, and codeset customization
   %l — the language portion of %L (lowercase "L")
   %t — the territory portion of %L
   %c — the codeset portion of %L

For engineers, scientists, and writers who have more to do than study the intricacies of X, this mechanism is somewhat ridiculous. Without question, application customization by setting resources is another aspect of X in which the programming-oriented background of X's designers and early users is clearly evident. The flexibility provided by this complexity is enormous, and it allows an X environment to support multiple language environments, among other things, but more should be done to isolate regular users from an overly complicated configuration process. Currently, regular users depend on system administrators who are often either very busy or nonexistent.

X programmers might counter our complaint with the argument that you do not have to use these environment variables. But, the fact that they override the (sufficiently complicated) traditional X repositories implies that you must have at least minimal understanding of this mechanism, or your other resource settings could be ignored.

Briefly, we should consider the rationale behind this syntax and its origin. Xt provides two programming functions, `XtFindFile()` and `XtResolvePathname()`, that are very useful within Xt-based applications for manipulating filenames. Because they support (variable) substitutions for these predefined symbols, applications can use them in a variety of ways to process filenames; that is, their use is not restricted to resource processing. The convention, as established with X clients distributed by current X vendors, is to pass this syntax directly through to the user.

The general-purpose design behind these functions is critical in understanding the relevance of these symbols for specifying resource files with `XFILESEARCHPATH` and `XUSERFILESEARCHPATH`. Specifically, the use of these symbols is restricted and sim- plified with resource files. For example, the suffix parameter `%S` often appears in the default pathnames for `XFILESEARCHPATH` and `XUSERFILESEARCHPATH`. Many workstation vendors now define these variables as part of their standard user environment; for example, OpenWindows 3.1 makes the following definitions:

```
XFILESEARCHPATH=/usr/openwin/lib/locale/%L/%T/%N%S:/usr/openwin/lib/%T/%N%S
```

In any case, in formulating resource filenames `%S` is typically null (empty). That is, when an application builds a pathname, if it contains "%S", it is simply stripped out.

You can determine the values for `XFILESEARCHPATH` and `XUSERFILESEARCHPATH` in your X environment by entering the command *setenv* (set environment variable) with no arguments, if your command window employs the *csh(1)* command interpreter. In this case, *setenv* lists the values of each defined environment variable. If your command window executes a Bourne shell, *sh(1)*, use *set* instead of *setenv*. You can also use the *echo(1)* to display the value of a single environment variable:

```
{your system prompt} echo $XFILESEARCHPATH
```

Another point is that even though this wide range of symbols is recognized, it is typical in practice to use only a subset of the symbols. For example, `%L`, `%l`, `%t`, and `%c` allow a vendor to set up directory hierarchies containing customization files for different written languages. With this facility, for example, French- and Spanish-speaking users (or their system administrators) can customize an application to their preferred language. Because the language symbol incorporates language, territory, and codeset subparts, it is possible to customize applications to distinguish between English-speaking users in Canada, England, the United States, and other countries.

The syntax for `%L` is

language[_territory][.codeset]

(The square brackets indicate that a particular component is optional, but the square brackets are not part of that component.) Suppose one or more X clients establish the convention that the language value "French_Belgium" represents the French language as spoken in Belgium (the territory component), ignoring the codeset component. Or, that "English_US" and "English_Canada" represent the English language as spoken in the United States and Canada, respectively.

Then, if the *xnlLanguage* (server) resource is set to, for example,

```
*xnlLanguage:   English_Canada
```

an X client would substitute "English_Canada" for "%L", "English" for "%l" (lowercase "L", not the numeral for the quantity one), and/or "Canada" for "%t" in a path specification provided by XFILESEARCHPATH or XUSERFILESEARCHPATH.

The customization symbol, %C, is used in a manner similar to %L except that it represents a single value, as defined by the X resource *customization*. (If they are defined, *xnlLanguage* and *customization* should be set during system start-up operations as part of the RESOURCE_MANAGER property of the root window by the X client *xrdb*.)

In most cases, however, users primarily encounter and use the symbols %T and %N, which represent the *app-defaults* directory and class name, respectively. Suppose a user sets XFILESEARCHPATH as follows in *.cshrc*, the configuration file for *csh(1)*:

```
setenv XFILESEARCHPATH /usr/lib/X11/%T/%N:$OPENWINHOME/lib/%T/%N
```

With this setting, Xt-based applications first consult the directory */usr/lib/X11/app-defaults* for a file bearing their respective class names; for example, *xwp* would load resources from */usr/lib/X11/app-defaults/XWp* and *xterm* would load resources from */usr/lib/X11/app-defaults/XTerm*. For each X client, if the appropriate resource file is found in the first path specification in the colon-separated list of paths, the remaining path specifications are ignored. If not, the second path specification is expanded and the X client attempts to load resources from this file. This process continues until a matching file is located, or the list of pathnames is exhausted.

If XFILESEARCHPATH is not defined, the search for system-wide application-related resources follows the strategy provided in Section 6.3. As mentioned, in many X environments, the default location for system-wide application-related resources is */usr/lib/X11/app-defaults*. Many X environments now include this default location as the final path specification in their (default) settings for XFILESEARCHPATH, a practice that is somewhat confusing.

Note that for users whose systems are configured to support dynamic switching among multiple X environments, for example, Consortium X and OpenWindows, this support for multiple path specifications is quite convenient. That is, for X clients that will execute in both environments, but have class files defined in only one environment, setting XFILESEARCHPATH to include each X environment's application-defaults directory

allows one XFILESEARCHPATH setting to service all X environments without the neces-
sity of duplicating class files across multiple application-defaults directories:

```
setenv XFILESEARCHPATH /usr/lib/X11/%T/%N:$OPENWINHOME/lib/%T/%N
```

For user-level customizations, simply set XUSERFILESEARCHPATH to include the appropriate path specifications, for example,

```
setenv XUSERFILESEARCHPATH /home/mary/config/%N
```

In this case, because XUSERFILESEARCHPATH is defined, X clients will consult the
config directory within Mary's home directory for class files containing her preferred
private customizations. This approach allows users to avoid littering their home directories
with numerous class files; instead, all class files are located in a common subdirectory. Of
course, the directory name *config* is arbitrary; you could even use the name *app-defaults* to
be consistent with the naming convention for the system-wide directory.

As described in Section 6.3, if XUSERFILESEARCHPATH is not defined, X clients first
consult the environment variable XAPPLRESDIR for the user's directory of class files.
And, if XAPPLRESDIR is not defined, X clients look for class resource files in the user's
home directory. Appendix C provides a quick reference for resource file processing.

7.4 Application Resources

In Appendix A.3 we make a distinction between X system resources, such as windows and
fonts, and the X resources used for configuring X clients, as described in Chapters 5 and 6.
In making this distinction, it is convenient and common to refer to the latter as "application
resources," because user's set these resources to configure X applications. The application-
defaults directory, .../app-defaults, bears a name that is consistent with this terminology.

Xt programmers, however, often use the term *application resources* in a specific way—to
refer to application-specific X resources. That is, most X clients, including all Xt-based
applications, support common UI-related resources such as *background*, *foreground*, *font*,
and many others, plus application-specific resources such as *autoBackup*, *directoryMask*,
licenseServer, and others. Xt programmers often refer to the latter as application resources.

This distinction could be important when you are reading the documentation that accompanies X software, but, otherwise, application-specific resources should follow the same
precedence and syntax rules as common resources. One important point is that application
resources often pertain to non-UI functionality; in this case, they are not part of the widget
hierarchy. For this reason, they will not be visible with utilities such as *editres*, which
examines an Xt-based application's widget hierarchy (see Section 7.6).

7.5 Translations

In Chapter 1 we described X as an event-oriented environment. X's event-driven nature is
not especially apparent, nor should it be. When you use a word processor or spreadsheet,
you automatically move the mouse cursor to the appropriate window, pressing keys and
mouse buttons without really thinking about the many events that occur. For example, when

you press a key, the X server sends a key-press event; when you move the mouse cursor across a window boundary, enter-window and leave-window events are generated; and so on. The operation that potentially generates the largest flurry of events is simply moving the mouse cursor; each pixel-level movement generates a motion event. (Not all X clients, or windows, solicit all events, in particular, motion events, because of the potential network overhead.)

X clients, on the other hand, perform a variety of high-level operations, or *actions*. Examples of actions include the back-space and page-down operations (in a text editor), highlighting a command button when it is selected, displaying a menu, ringing the console "bell," exiting the program, and so on. With many applications, you initiate program actions via UI objects; for example, selecting the "Save..." entry in the "File" menu causes the application to perform certain save operations. In other cases, you initiate program actions directly with a mouse- or key-based command, for example, sweeping text with mouse button 1 to select it or pressing **<Alt>-S** to save your work.

Of the many high-level operations present in a typical Xt-based application, a developer will formally designate a specific subset as external, or public, actions. These actions can be associated with event sequences via the *translation* resource; for example, Section 4.10 describes how to modify copy-and-paste behavior with *translation*. In particular, (1) the documentation will include names and descriptions for these actions and (2) the user can customize the X client so that specific event sequences are associated with specific actions.

This association, or mapping, of events to program actions is specified by an event-action pair:

```
<event>, <event>, ... : <action>, <action>, ...
```

This event-action mapping is commonly called an *event translation*. In essence, an event translation describes a sequence of events and a set of publicly defined actions that the application executes if this event sequence occurs. Appendix D provides reference information related to events and translations.

All Xt-based applications support the resource instance *translation* and the class *Translation*. The *translation* resource can, and typically does, represent multiple event translations. In other words, the *translation* resource represents a table, or list, of translations.

Translations exist at the widget level. Thus, the process of setting the *translation* resource for a text widget is similar in principle to setting its background and foreground colors. Instead, however, of setting a single application characteristic such as background color, with a translation resource, you set one or more event translations from a table of many translations.

7.5.1 Syntax for the Value Field

When a *translation* resource is provided at the widget level, you can often use a class- or widget-level resource specification to configure multiple X clients. For example, Motif-based applications (at the time of this writing) interpret **<Delete>** and **<Backspace>** differently; **<Delete>** deletes the character under the cursor and **<Backspace>** deletes the character to the left of the cursor. These mappings, or key bindings, make sense because workstations often have both keys; hence, both actions are available from the keyboard. Many users, however, expect **<Delete>** to perform the same operation (action) as **<Backspace>**. If you have this preference, one solution (although not the preferred solution) is simply to add the following resource to the appropriate X resource file:

```
*XmText.translations:  #override <Key>osfDelete: delete-previous-character()
```

(Note the use of `osfDelete`, not `Delete`, for Motif applications. `osfDelete` is a *virtual keysym*; see Appendix F.)

In contrast, Athena-based applications map **<Delete>** and **<Backspace>** to the same action, namely, deleting the character to the left of the cursor (because **<Ctrl>-D** deletes the character under the cursor). If your preference is for **<Delete>** to delete the character under the cursor, simply add the following resource to the appropriate X resource file:

```
*Text.translations:  #override <Key>Delete: delete-next-character()
```

We're using the phrase "appropriate X resource file" because, as we discussed in Chapter 6, there are many ways to specify X resources in a network (client-server) environment.

Another point is that, initially, this type of resource specification appears more complicated than, say,

```
*Text.background:  HotPink
```

Note, however, that *translation* resources follow the same rules as other resources with respect to describing the widget hierarchy (as discussed in Chapter 5). The added complication is within the value field, which contains multiple subfields that are parsed (broken apart) by a translation processing facility provided by Xt, specifically, the *translation manager*.

To understand these translation examples, first consider how they differ. The class name for Motif text widgets is *XmText*, whereas the class name for Athena text widgets is *Text*. In both cases, we specify the resource at the class level, to have the translations apply to all X clients that use these text objects. If we wanted to restrict these translations to a particular X client, we could prepend its name (plus a "*") to the left of the resource specification:

```
xrolodex*XmText.translations:  #override\n\
   <Key>osfDelete: delete-previous-character()
```

Also, we could make distinctions *within* an X client containing multiple text widgets by specifying instance names instead of a class name.

Next, consider the value field of the resource specification. The directive `#override` instructs Xt to override/replace the corresponding event-action pair in the translation table; that is, to override the matching event, if any. As mentioned, a translation value is actually a table of many event-action pairs. If you were to omit the `#override` directive, the translation value in each of the previous examples (which describes only one event, would replace *all* existing event-action pairs. Generally, you want to include the #override directive because you do *not* want to disturb other, existing event mappings. In particular, general event mappings should not be disturbed, such as the one that associates the insert-char() action with a key-press event for regular keys (for example, "A", "B", and others).

Following the #override directive, you can specify multiple event-action pairs. In the example for the Athena text widget, we specify one event-action mapping:

```
<Key>Delete: delete-next-character()
```

Here, the event is a key-press, formally specified as <Key>, and the action is delete-next-character(). Events, designated in angle brackets, may be followed by *qualifiers*, in this case, Delete, which represents the key <Delete>. Specifically, in this case key symbols, or *keysyms*, qualify the key event; common key symbols are given in Appendix E.

If we were to omit the qualifier, we would be requesting that *any* key-press event should be translated by the application into the delete-next-character() action:

```
<Key>: delete-next-character()            !! wrong !!
```

This type of translation would disable every other program action that is normally initiated from the keyboard.

Note: In this section it is convenient to use the <Delete> versus <Backspace> issue to illustrate the translation mechanism; moreover, this approach to key reconfiguration transcends differences in applications because of widget sets such as Motif versus Athena. With respect to Motif applications, however, Motif's virtual key binding concept allows users to accomplish this key translation at a higher level; see Appendix F for further information and the preferred method for remapping <Delete>.

7.5.2 Actions and Their Arguments

Did you notice that the action specification includes parentheses following the name of the action? Some actions require data, that is, one or more arguments. When you execute a command from the UNIX shell, arguments are separated by spaces:

```
{your system prompt} xwp chapter1.txt -autoBackup off &
```

In this case, the application is designed to interpret the arguments in a particular way.

The same situation applies with actions, except that the arguments, if any, are separated by commas. For example, *xterm* supports the action string(), which requests that *xterm* "artificially type" the argument to string() in the command window. Suppose that you regularly execute a command such as

```
{your system prompt} ls -l
```

Unless you really need the typing exercise, it makes sense to associate this action with a key-press event:

```
xterm*vt100.translations:  #override <Key>F1: string("ls -l\n")
```

In this example, we've instructed *xterm* to insert the string "ls -l" followed by a carriage return character into the command window when we press **<F1>**. (Xt is heavily influenced by the programming language C. "\n" is a special, logical escape sequence that represents the newline control character, as described subsequently.) Once you have used this command short-cut several times, you may want to add others. For example, if your workstation provides no mechanical eject button for the floppy disk drive, the following could be useful:

```
xterm*vt100.translations:  #override <Key>F10: string("eject\n")
```

As an example of multiple arguments to an action, recall our discussion in Section 4.10 regarding how to substitute the X clipboard for the primary selection with *xterm*:

```
xterm*vt100*translations: #override\n\
    Shift <KeyPress> Select: select-cursor-start() \
        select-cursor-end(CLIPBOARD, CUT_BUFFER0) \n\
    Shift <KeyPress> Insert: insert-selection(CLIPBOARD, CUT_BUFFER0) \n\
    ~Ctrl ~Meta <Btn2Up>: insert-selection(CLIPBOARD, CUT_BUFFER0) \n\
    <BtnUp>: select-end(CLIPBOARD, CUT_BUFFER0)
```

Several of these event-action translations are rather complicated, and they will be addressed subsequently. For now, `select-end()` is one of many actions that *xterm* associates with one or more events. `select-end()` is mapped to the event <BtnUp>. That is, when you release the mouse button, *xterm* interprets this event as a command/signal to end the (drag) selection process. The arguments to `select-end()`, `CLIPBOARD` and `CUT_BUFFER0`, request that *xterm* copy the designated text to the X clipboard and to cut-buffer 0. Actions with more than two arguments are handled in an analogous manner.

As an aside, the event specification `<BtnUp>` does not require an explicit button number because, according to *xterm*'s event-action translations, only one button can initiate the selection process, namely, `<Btn1Down>`. For a complete list of *xterm*'s actions and their default event-action bindings, refer to the *xterm* man-page with *xman* (near the end in the "ACTIONS" section). Appendix D provides event-related information.

7.5.3 Combining Event-action Mappings

The previous *xterm* translation examples provide a motivation and a solution for the common situation in which you would like to specify a series of event-action mappings with one resource specification. Suppose you would like to map function keys **<F1>** through **<F10>** to common commands. In this case, you could simply provide a `string()` action for each key event in the file *XTerm* in your home directory. The easiest way to combine them is to place each event-action mapping on a separate line, linked by a logical newline character:

```
xterm*vt100.translations:  #override\n\
 <Key>F1:  string("cd\n")\n\
 <Key>F2:  string("ls\n")\n\
 <Key>F3:  string("ls -l\n")\n\
 <Key>F4:  string("ls ")\n\
 <Key>F5:  string("df\n")\n\
 <Key>F6:  string("du -s\n")\n\
 <Key>F7:  string("cal\n")\n\
 <Key>F8:  string("xman &\n")\n\
 <Key>F9:  string("tar cvf /dev/rfd0 *\n")\n\
 <Key>F10: string("eject\n")
```

In certain areas, both UNIX and X have a C-like flavor. The character strings that you provide as arguments to `string()` may contain standard printable characters, as well as special characters that designate carriage returns, tabs, and so on. In the C programming language, you designate these special characters in this manner: "\f" for a formfeed, "\n" for a newline, and "\t" for a tab. The "\", or backslash, character is interpreted as a "logical escape" character. That is, its presence signals that the next character, say, "f", should be interpreted as a formfeed character, not as the character "f". There are other special characters, but these three are the most common in nonprogramming environments.

In our previous example, we used "\n" at the end of most of the strings, for example, "cd\n", to simulate the carriage return that a user types to submit a command for processing. Note that with **<F4>**, we omitted the newline, as an example of how you can use a function key to paste the common part of a frequent command into a command window. This approach allows you to complete the command "manually" with specific arguments before pressing **<Return>**.

Next, consider the use of "\n\" at the end of each line that separates the event-action pairs. In many UNIX and X contexts, "\" *at the end of a line* indicates that a long character string is being broken across several lines. Software that recognizes this usage of "\" will *logically* undo the line breaks. "\" is necessary for resource values that span multiple lines because the *resource manager* expects all resource values to occupy a single (logical) line. The *translation manager*, on the other hand, expects each event-action mapping to be separated by a newline character ("\n"). Thus, placing "\n\" at the end of each line between event-action pairs satisfies both the resource and translation managers. That is, it inserts a newline character between each event-action pair while requesting that the physically distinct lines be interpreted logically as one (long) line.

Warning: There should be nothing following "\n\" at the end of a line—not even spaces or tabs.

Another important point is that either side of an event-action pair may have multiple components. For example, with our earlier translation example we used one `string()` action to insert a command plus the simulated carriage return:

```
xterm*vt100.translations:   #override <Key>F1: string("ls -l\n")
```

We could have achieved the same effect with the following translation:

```
xterm*vt100.translations:   #override <Key>F1: string("ls -l") string("\n")
```

And, of course, the multiple actions do not have to be the same; that is, you can specify whatever actions you choose for a given X client and they will be processed in sequential order. As an example of an event-action mapping with multiple events, consider the translation for *xclipboard*'s "Quit" button:

```
*quit.translations: #override \n\
   <Btn1Down>,<Btn1Up>:Quit() unset()
```

The interpretation is that when the user presses and releases mouse button 1 in the "Quit" button (instance name "quit"), the `Quit()` and `unset()` actions are executed in sequence. The `Quit()` action terminates *xclipboard* and the `unset()` action restores the command button to its normal state (before the mouse cursor entered the "Quit" button).

In a sense, the translation facility is a good thing; it provides users with a powerful capability for customizing X clients. On the other hand, an Xt-based application typically employs many actions, most of which are rather low level and nonintuitive from the user's perspective. Actions such as `unset()` raise the issue that it is very easy for a user to disable the functionality of an X client by accident. The translation facility is most useful for X programmers who have an intimate understanding of Xt-based applications. Be careful with translations. If you intend to modify translations that many Xt applications make public in their application-defaults (class) files, you should first make a backup of the original file, so that you can restore the original functionality if you accidentally disable certain operations.

We've used a variety of commands in our *xterm* example, but you would, of course, substitute your preferred command short-cuts. Keep in mind also that an X client may already have an action mapped to a particular event, for example, pressing the "A" key when the <Ctrl> key is down. If so, your event-action mapping will override whatever functionality the documentation describes for that event.

Lastly, Xt-based applications should provide a section in their documentation that describes event-action translations, so that you can override all or part of these mappings with your preferred customizations. Use *xman* to examine the man-page for *xterm* and other standard X clients. In some cases, the documentation may only describe event-action mappings that differ from or supplement the standard Xt event-action translations. For example, if an application is based on the Motif widget set, the developer may assume that you already have Motif documentation describing the event translations for the *XmText* widget class (which is typically used to implement text entry areas).

7.5.4 Modifier States

It is important for X and the translation manager to recognize various keyboard- and mouse-based modifiers. For example, with *xterm* you press mouse button 1 to select text. If, however, **<Ctrl>** is down when you press mouse button 1, *xterm* invokes the "Main Options" menu. That is, the modifier concept supports a variety of useful key and mouse combinations for interpretation as commands.

A modifier is different from what we've called a qualifier. A qualifier *qualifies*, that is, restricts, the more general interpretation. For example, consider our earlier example for the Athena-based `Delete` qualifier:

```
<Key>Delete: delete-next-character()
```

`<Key>` requests any key-press, but the trailing `Delete` immediately restricts the event specification so that it applies to only one key.

In contrast, the modifier concept applies to specific keys designated by X as so-called modifier keys. The (logical) modifier names used *in translation tables* include `Ctrl`, `Shift`, `Lock`, `Meta`, `Any`, `Mod1`, ..., `Mod5`, `Button1`, ..., `Button5` (see Appendix D). Note that X interprets a key as a modifier key *only when it is used in conjunction with some other key.* For example, if you press **<Caps Lock>** in an X client's edit window, the X server sends the key symbol `Caps_Lock` to the application—no key is being modified in this key-press event. After you have pressed **<Caps Lock>** to enable uppercase translations of alphabetic keys, if you press the "J" key, the X server sends the key symbol `J` to the application, and the modifier field in the event message is set to `lock`. That is, the key-press event for the "J" key has been modified by the presence of the modifier state `lock`.

You can reassign logical modifier keys to any physical keys as described in Chapter 11. Also, modifier key bindings differ from one workstation and X terminal environment to the next. For example, with Sun workstations running Consortium X and with OpenWindows, the diamond keys (assigned the key symbols `Meta_L` and `Meta_R`) generate the modifier `Mod1` when combined with a regular key such as the "A" key. These X environments differ, however, with respect to the **<Alt>**. With Consortium X on a Sun workstation, pressing **<Alt>** with the "A" key, sets the modifier field to a null value—the X server does not interpret **<Alt>** as a modifier key. With Openwindows, when you combine **<Alt>** with a regular key, the modifier field is set to `mod4`.

Consider two examples that illustrate the use of modifiers. In Section 4.3 we described *xman*, the graphical man-page reader. *xman*'s translations are publicly available in its class resource file *Xman*. (*xman* violates the class naming convention that we described earlier; its class name is *Xman*, not *XMan*.) *xman* uses the following translation resource for its "Manual Page" window:

```
*manualBrowser*directory.translations:    #override \
            Ctrl<Btn1Down>: \
               XawPositionSimpleMenu(optionMenu) \
               MenuPopup(optionMenu) \n\
```

```
Ctrl<Btn2Down>: \
    XawPositionSimpleMenu(sectionMenu) \
    MenuPopup(sectionMenu) \n\
Shift<Btn2Down>,<Btn2Up>: GotoPage(Manpage) \n\
Ctrl<Key>q: Quit() \n\
Ctrl<Key>c: Quit() \n\
Ctrl<Key>r: RemoveThisManpage() \n\
Ctrl<Key>n: CreateNewManpage() \n\
Ctrl<Key>h: PopupHelp() \n\
Ctrl<Key>d: GotoPage(Directory) \n\
Ctrl<Key>m: GotoPage(ManualPage) \n\
Ctrl<Key>v: ShowVersion() \n\
Ctrl<Key>s: PopupSearch()
```

If you press mouse button 1 while **<Ctrl>** is down, the button-press event's modifier field is set to `control`, which corresponds to "Ctrl<Btn1Down>" in translation manager syntax. Because there is a match, *xedit* executes two actions: `XawPositionSimple-Menu(optionMenu)` followed by `MenuPopup(optionMenu)`. Both of these actions accept an instance of a *Menu* widget as an argument, in this case, the instance `optionMenu`, which is the instance name for the menu with the title "Xman Options".

There are several **<Ctrl>** commands. In Section 4.3 we stated that **<Ctrl>-S** invokes *xman*'s search window. You can see this event-action mapping here in the line containing

```
Ctrl<Key>s: PopupSearch()
```

Thus, if there is a key-press event for the "S" key and the `Ctrl` modifier is present, *xman* performs the action `PopupSearch()`.

For the second example, recall our nonstandard *xterm* translation:

```
xterm*vt100*translations: #override\n\
    Shift <KeyPress> Select: select-cursor-start() \
        select-cursor-end(CLIPBOARD, CUT_BUFFER0) \n\
    Shift <KeyPress> Insert: insert-selection(CLIPBOARD, CUT_BUFFER0) \n\
    ~Ctrl ~Meta <Btn2Up>: insert-selection(CLIPBOARD, CUT_BUFFER0) \n\
    <BtnUp>: select-end(CLIPBOARD, CUT_BUFFER0)
```

With this background, *xterm*'s event-action mappings should be clear. Note that the first event-action mapping spans two physical lines. Because the translation manager expects this mapping on one (logical) line, "\" is required to "connect" them.

Let's interpret each of the four event translations. According to the first event-action mapping, if *xterm* receives a key-press event for the `Select` key, and the `Shift` modifier is active, it executes two actions: `select-cursor-start()` and `select-cursor-end()`. This particular key binding is not practical for most users because most keyboards do not assign the logical key symbol `Select` to a specific physical key. (This example uses the event name `<KeyPress>`, whereas the previous example used the abbreviated name `<Key>`. To the translation manager, they are equivalent.)

The second event translation is, perhaps, more useful than the first because virtually all keyboards support `Insert`. In this case, if the user presses **<Shift>-<Insert>**, *xterm* pastes the text from the X clipboard in the command window. If there is no `CLIPBOARD` selection, *xterm* pastes the text from cut-buffer 0, if any.

The third translation is only slightly more complicated. The symbol "~" is interpreted as "not" by the translation manager. The event interpretation is: if *xterm* receives a button-release event for mouse button 2, and if the `Ctrl` and `Meta` modifiers are not present, insert the selection in the manner described for the **<Shift>-<Insert>** key combination.

The fourth translation is the simplest. If *xterm* receives a button-release event for any button, it ends the text selection process and copies the highlighted text to the X clipboard and cut-buffer 0. As mentioned in Section 7.5.2, there is no need for a specific reference to mouse button 1 because, given *xterm*'s other translations, mouse button 1 is the only one that can initiate the text selection process. You can verify this condition by studying *xterm*'s event-action mappings in the "ACTIONS" section of *xterm*'s man-page.

7.5.5 Translation Ordering

The translation manager applies a straightforward matching scheme when you customize an existing translation table by overriding one or more of its event translations. Specifically, if the specified event sequence matches an existing entry in the table, that entry is replaced with the new event-action mapping. If the event does not match an existing entry, there is nothing to override so it is simply appended to the end of the translation table.

Subsequently, when you use an Xt-based application incoming event sequences are compared with translation table entries for that application/widget. The table is searched from top to bottom and the first translation with a matching event sequence is selected. This top-to-bottom table search is particularly significant when there are several similar event sequences differing primarily in their modifiers and qualifiers.

For example, suppose you were to override the default event translations for an Athena *Text* widget with the following, ignoring the fact that this combination of event translations is illogical because they all map to the same action:

```
*Text.translations:  #override\n\
  <Key>: delete-next-character()\n\
  <Key>Delete: delete-next-character()\n\
  Ctrl<Key>Delete: delete-next-character()
```

(For the record, the default event-action binding for **<Delete>** is `delete-previous-character()`). The point of our odd example is that the first entry matches *any* keypress event, so there is no way that the second and third event translations could ever be selected.

Now omit the first entry:

```
*Text.translations:  #override\n\
  <Key>Delete: delete-next-character()\n\
  Ctrl<Key>Delete: delete-next-character()
```

Again, the first entry is more general than the second; its interpretation is if the user presses <**Delete**>, execute the action `delete-next-character()`.

In other words, *not* specifying a modifier implies that it does not matter what modifiers are present. For this reason, the event translation requiring `Ctrl` as a modifier could never be selected from the translation table. The implication is that more specific event sequences must be added to the translation table before more general event sequences.

Now consider a subset of the actual translation table for *xedit*, the Athena-based text editor distributed with Consortium X. For consistency with the user's point of view of translations, we show selected entries from the translation table in *translation* resource format, that is, as if the default translations didn't already exist, or we were overriding some other translation table. Here are several entries:

```
*Text.translations:   #override\n\
  Ctrl <Key>F: forward-character()\n\
  Ctrl <Key>B: backward-character()\n\
  Ctrl <Key>D: delete-next-character()\n\
  ...
  Shift Meta <Key>Delete: backward-kill-word()\n\
  ...
  <Key>Delete: delete-previous-character()\n\
  ...
```

Consider the deletion actions. The entry for <**Shift**>-<**Meta**>-<**Delete**> must occur before the entry for <**Delete**> because it is a more specialized entry. Only if <**Shift**> and <**Meta**> are not pressed along with <**Delete**> will the event dispatching scheme proceed to the subsequent, more generic entry.

Our examples reflect the range of customizations that most users should attempt: from relatively simple rebindings such as changing the behavior of <**Delete**> for the Athena and Motif text widgets to changing arguments in more complex entries such as *xterm*'s text selection actions. The translation idea is a good one, in principle, but the potential for introducing errors when you customize complex translations is great. Moreover, it is very difficult to diagnose errors because both the resource and translation managers largely ignore what is perceived by the user in hindsight as an error.

Also, most users restrict their customization to button- and key-related events. It is unusual for an end-user to delve into the inner workings for an X client to the point of rebinding events such as a mouse entering or leaving a widget, for example, a command button. For completeness, Appendix D includes other translation-related information, such as a list of valid event names for event-action pairs. If you intend to modify translations to the point of specifying a distinction between lower- and uppercase characters in key-press events, you should consult a programming or reference manual for the X toolkit [Nye and O'Reilly, 1992; O'Reilly & Associates, 1992].

Another irony is that while you are free to modify the event translations for most Xt-based applications, they are not always fully documented in their man-page files or in the printed documentation [Quercia and O'Reilly, 1992]. For additional documentation, you can consult class resource files in the system-wide *.../app-defaults* directory, but be careful. In many cases, Xt-based applications *depend* on translations in their class files. That is, if you remove these public translations, or more likely, disable the translations by accident, you could disable the application, or worse, introduce unpredictable behavior. You should always make backups of the original class files, or restrict your customizations to resource files in your home directory as described in the next section.

7.5.6 Resource Files for User-specific Translations

As a review of the material in Chapter 6, consider where you might define the translations we've mentioned so far, assuming you want these configurations to be restricted to your log-in account only. (We're not suggesting that you should modify the existing behavior for **<Delete>**; these translations are provided as practical examples only.) Key mappings for **<Delete>** are not specific to a particular application, so they are good candidates for entry in a general-purpose resource file such as *.Xdefaults*, or a file that's loaded by *xrdb* during start-up operations to define the RESOURCE_MANAGER property for the root window.

If, however, you always execute applications from your host (your workstation), you could also put the **<Delete>**-related translations in *.Xdefaults-saturn*, assuming that your workstation's hostname is "saturn". You could also put the *xterm* translation from Section 7.5.2 and 7.5.3 in this file. On the other hand, because it is *xterm* specific and you may want to configure other *xterm* characteristics to match your personal preferences, you could place this translation in the file *XTerm* in your home directory.

Even if you have superuser capability for your workstation, it is a good idea *not* to modify the class files in the system-wide *.../app-defaults* directory, especially for X clients distributed with your X implementation, or other X clients that have very complicated class resource files. In contrast, if an X client is designed so that its class file is not overly complicated, it may be convenient for a system administrator to add system-wide, common resource settings to this file. For example, for commercial software such as our hypothetical *xwp*, a system administrator could add password- and license server-related resources to the class file *XWp* in *.../app-defaults*. Users could then customize *xwp* from the home directories in their personal *XWp* class resource files.

7.6 Using *editres*

To configure an X client to match your personal preferences, you must set the appropriate resources. As we've indicated in several of our examples, you can sometimes achieve the desired effect by setting class resources. In many cases, the widget hierarchy is described in the software's documentation. If not, the class names are sometimes obvious: the class name for text-entry areas with Athena-based X clients is *Text*; for Motif-based X clients it is *XmText*. With recently developed X clients, however, you can also use *editres* to determine an application's widget hierarchy. In particular, *editres* graphically depicts the hierarchy of UI components in an Xt-based client by instance name and class (see Figure 7.2).

In general, within the same application you can sometimes use class resource settings to achieve different resource settings for two instances of the same class, such as two menus, provided they belong to different widget subhierarchies. For example, the following resource specifications from *.../app-defaults/Editres* set the command button shape differently for the buttons in *editres*:

```
*ShapeStyle:               Oval
*Tree*ShapeStyle:          Rectangle
```

ShapeStyle is a resource class that controls the shape of command buttons in Athena-based Xt applications. In this case, the command buttons will be oval, unless they belong to the *Tree* class, which identifies a particular widget subhierarchy within *editres*.

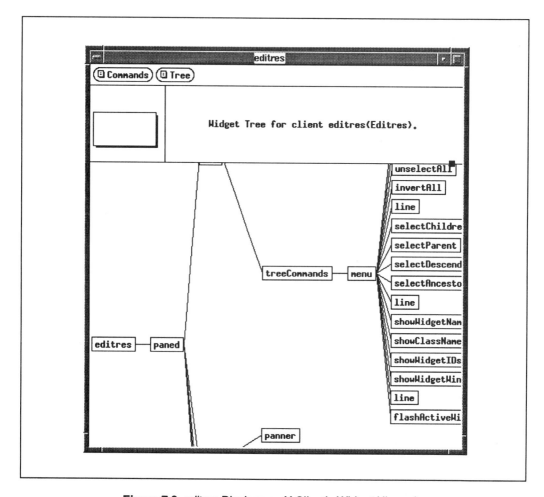

Figure 7.2 *editres* Displays an X Client's Widget Hierarchy

In contrast, configuring individual widget instances, for example, two menus from the same menu bar, requires an instance-level specification. If the documentation provides instance names for each widget contributing to the user interface, you can set the resource manually by adding an entry in the appropriate resource file.

Even when instance and resource names are documented, however, it can be useful to view an application's components graphically. *editres* is distributed as part of the Consortium X distribution and it can be quite useful for automating the sometimes cumbersome process of configuring an X client. Even if you prefer to configure X clients manually, *editres* is useful because it allows you to view the hierarchy from different perspectives: instance names, class names, widget IDs, and the low-level window ID for each widget. Figure 7.2 shows *editres*'s main window. In this example, we use *editres* for "self-examination," that is, to report its own widget hierarchy.

The menu bar manages two menus: "Commands" and "Tree". *editres* uses a convenient point-and-click approach to choosing the target X client. From the "Commands" you choose "Get Widget Tree" to select an X client. The mouse cursor changes to a cross-hair and when you click on an X client's window, *editres* sends a message to the application requesting widget information. If the X client supports the *editres* protocol, *editres* displays its widget tree in the main window. If not, *editres* displays a message to this effect.

From the "Commands" menu you can dump the widget hierarchy to a text file, activate a resource box for directly setting an X client's resources, refresh the widget tree, and so on. The latter option is important because many X clients modify their widget hierarchy dynamically (by creating and deleting widgets as you use the application). Thus, you can update the displayed widget hierarchy at selected intervals during the target client's execution.

Immediately below the menu bar and to the left of the message window, *editres* provides a panning object. That is, widget trees tend to be much larger than *editres*'s main window. You can resize the window up to a point, but, in most cases, you simply use the lower pane of the main window as a viewport for navigating over the entire widget tree. Specifically, the panning object represents the relationship between the underlying widget tree and the typically smaller viewport. You simply drag the small rectangle around inside the panning object to view the corresponding subset of the widget hierarchy.

Once you zero-in on the UI component of interest, you can use the mouse to select a specific widget(s). The "Tree" menu allows you to refine the selection to include the selected widget's parent and sibling widgets. Then, you can dynamically modify the client's resources.

Note that *editres* does not work with all X clients. It will probably work as expected with most standard X clients distributed with Consortium X, but only those that are implemented with Xt—there are several Xlib-based utilities. Also, *editres* typically does not work with Motif-based applications, especially in an X11R4 environment. We cannot be definitive in specifying when it will work with Motif-based applications because Motif applications do not automatically support the *editres* protocol. With X11R4, a significant amount of optional work must be done to the X environment for *editres* and Motif applications to communicate.

With X11R5 and the more recent Motif widget set releases; however, it's likely that the developer built the X client so that it supports the *editres* protocol.

In any case, *editres* is a very nice utility. Future releases of X and Xt-based applications are likely to provide additional facilities for automatically configuring X clients on the fly. For more information see the *editres* man-page.

8

Fonts

In this chapter we focus on fonts from the perspective of a typical user. Fonts are important to users because they allow us to choose the most visually appealing font, given the physical size, resolution, and color characteristics of a particular X environment. In contrast, the many tasks inherent in making fonts available to users is largely a concern for system administrators, not users.

8.1 Bitmapped versus Outline Fonts

There are essentially two types of fonts: bitmapped and outline. With bitmapped fonts, each displayable character is defined by a distinct bitmap, that is, a "little picture" formed from a matrix of dots. Thus, for each character or symbol, in every size and slant, there must be a separate bitmap that describes that character's image. With outline fonts, on the other hand, each character is described by a mathematical formula; thus, a font can be generated in virtually any point size.

Although there are numerous techniques for rendering characters, a character outline is often generated, or described, by a series of line segments, hence, the term outline font. Outline fonts are sometimes called *scalable fonts*; technically, however, the outline approach is not the only way of providing scalable fonts.

With a limited set of fonts, the bitmapped approach may require less disk space to store the font information. Also, the characters may display more quickly because in some circumstances it's faster to display a bitmap than to calculate the image from a mathematical description of a character. But, as the number of typefaces—for example, Times Roman® and Helvetica®—becomes large, scalable fonts become more practical.

On a computer screen, the bitmap for the character "A" indicates the subset of pixels in a rectangular area that should be illuminated with the foreground color versus the background color. Similarly, traditional dot-matrix printers create an "A" by extending a subset of the wire pins from a pixel matrix in the shape of an "A"; only the protruding pins contact the printer ribbon. Laser printers, with resolutions ranging from 300 DPI (dots per inch) for inexpensive printers to greater than 1200 DPI for high-resolution typesetters, use a similar technique for physically representing a character. That is, a laser printer is a dot-matrix printer that uses toner technology to print a character, as opposed to the older technology in which pins impact a ribbon.

8.2 Device-dependent Display Operations

Because computer screens and dot-matrix printers represent text as images built from a system of pixels/dots, there are several implications for users working with monitors of various sizes and resolutions. First, the size of a laser printer's print area is constant for most users, for example, a letter- or legal-sized page. The ramification of this constancy is that regardless of whether or not your laser printer (and software) uses bitmapped or outline fonts, font size is consistent. That is, if you request a 12-point font size with your word processor, the printed output will be consistent across printers.

On the other hand, the resolution of workstation screens differs significantly: 1152×900, 1024×768, 1280×1024, and so on. Moreover, it's possible for a 16-inch and a 19-inch screen to have the same resolution. The implication is that bitmapped font sizes vary; for example, the character "A" for the 8x13 bitmapped font will be larger on a 19-inch monitor than on a 16-inch monitor, given the same screen resolution. In contrast, a window system that fully supports scalable fonts can take the screen's resolution into consideration, producing on-screen fonts that are consistent from screen to screen to printer. The most well-known display technology based on outline fonts is PostScript® for printers and Display PostScript® for computer screens [Adobe, 1990].

The X Window System is inherently bitmap oriented. It's possible to extend X by translating its bitmap-oriented internal operations into a PostScript-compatible format, so that a Display PostScript-based screen-handling facility would render windows, text within windows, and so on in a device-independent manner. Yet, despite the capability for combining Display PostScript with X, most X software is and will continue to be inherently bitmap oriented.

For example, command windows and text editors use a row- and column-oriented approach to displaying text so that when you request a smaller font size the size of the application window is reduced accordingly. That is, with a reduction in font size the amount of viewable text remains constant, instead of increasing to occupy a constant-size application window. Certain software packages, for example, word processors and desktop publishing software, do maintain a constant window size, based on the size of a printed page, but in some cases they handle device-independent display operations internally. That is, with X's bitmap-oriented design, device independence is often managed on an application-by-application basis.

8.3 Fonts versus Typefaces

Helvetica is a typeface, not a font. In the publishing industry, the term *font* refers to the collection of characters and symbols for a particular typeface, in a particular point size, and so on. A font may include a few characters or many characters and symbols. Thus, properly speaking, the size of a font is the number of symbols it includes, not the dimensions of each symbol. Computer users, and this book (because the practice is so entrenched), typically, use the term *font size* to mean typeface size. The term *font family*, as used in the X community to signify fonts of one typeface—for example, Times Roman or Helvetica—in various sizes, slants, and weight, has no legitimate technical meaning/definition; it is confusing at best.

Font terminology is important because users often misinterpret what they're getting when they purchase a laser printer or a window system with, say, 35 fonts. If, for example, the entire font repertoire for your computer or printer is the typeface Helvetica, in a normal weight and slant, and in the point sizes 8, 10, 12, 14, 18, and 24, you have six fonts, not one. With bitmapped fonts, you must have the bitmap files for every combination of typeface, weight, slant, and point size that you display or print. Thus, a printer that supports 35 bitmapped fonts is quite limited because each combination of typeface, point size, slant, and weight constitutes a different font. Even though X distributions include hundreds of fonts, the number of typefaces and point sizes is rather modest.

8.4 Bitmapped Font Files versus Font Scaling

Most X distributions provide bitmapped fonts in three or more subdirectories within */usr/lib/X11/fonts*: *75dpi*, *100dpi*, and *misc*. There may be other font directories depending on your particular X distribution. For example, X11R5 adds the *Speedo* directory, which includes the Speedo® scalable fonts donated by Bitstream® (a font company) in the Charter® and Courier® typefaces:

```
{your system prompt} ls Speedo
font0419.spd     font0611.spd     font0709.spd     fonts.scale
font0582.spd     font0648.spd     font0710.spd
font0583.spd     font0649.spd     fonts.dir
```

Note the differences in disk usage:

```
{your system prompt} du
5522      ./misc
3204      ./75dpi
3677      ./100dpi
531       ./Speedo
```

These differences do not accurately reflect the fact that the bitmapped font directories include fonts in several typefaces, whereas *Speedo* includes the Charter and Courier typeface only. On the other hand, the bitmapped directories include fonts in limited point sizes, whereas the Speedo fonts are scalable in an arbitrary number of point sizes.

An X server based on X11R4, or earlier X releases, cannot use scalable fonts, unless it has been extended by the vendor to do so. An X11R5 server cannot use scalable fonts *directly*, but it can communicate with a separate application called the font server, *fs*. The font server "serves up" fonts for the X server in a manner that is largely transparent to users.

The disk space devoted to bitmapped fonts becomes a significant problem for system administrators (or the person who must pay for disk drives) in pre-X11R5 environments that support X terminals from multiple vendors. Because bitmapped fonts are device-dependent, a system administrator must maintain a separate set of font directories for *every* supported X server. In general, fonts (when compiled and ready for use) are incompatible across workstation and X terminal platforms. Thus, if you use X from a workstation's primary display, and that workstation also serves X terminals from five vendors, it's likely that you'll have six distinct font directories, each with its own font subdirectories. Moreover, the disk storage overhead for fonts is not the only consideration; for example, fonts often must be downloaded from the file server every time a user starts up an X terminal. For this reason, some X terminals store a limited number of fonts in local read-only memory to minimize the network bandwidth required to start an X session.

In X11R4 environments, the X server loads fonts (actually, the bitmaps for each character in each font) into memory from known directories. You can't use, for example, the Courier 12-point bold font, unless a font file exists with the bitmaps for that font. If multiple applications use the same font, its bitmaps are loaded only once—applications share fonts.

In X11R5 environments, the font server manages the process of locating and delivering fonts. In contrast to an X11R4 server, instead of simply loading fonts from a directory, the X server can also send a message to the font server requesting a particular font. The font server is capable of supplying fonts from bitmaps, as well as scaling bitmaps in different point sizes.

Beyond these standard approaches to providing fonts, some workstation vendors modify their X servers to support outline fonts more directly via Display PostScript extensions, or by other means. For example, the OpenWindows environment incorporates a font-scaling facility with an extensive "font collection." As mentioned, however, because X's internal operations are inherently bitmap-oriented, font scaling is not really a dynamic process. Each font must be scaled first; its bitmapped images are then delivered to the X server, as if they were taken from a bitmapped font file.

8.5 Monospaced and Proportional Fonts

With so-called *proportional fonts*, character widths vary—the width of a lowercase "i" is less than that of a lowercase "m". Desktop publishing software supports proportional fonts because proportional spacing has been common in the publishing field since before the first printing press. The computing industry, in contrast, has progressed from paper-tape readers, to card-punch and teletype machines, to ASCII (character) terminals, and now to graphical window systems. For traditional and practical reasons, it's no surprise that many computer applications are oriented toward characters of constant width.

The typesetting industry uses the term *monospaced font* to describe any font, bitmapped or outline, in which each character has the same width. In terms of human history, proportionally spaced type has existed since the beginning of written language, whereas monospaced type is a relative recent "discovery." Yet, with respect to computer software, we sometimes think of proportional fonts as somehow being more modern than monospaced fonts. The irony is that humans go to great extremes with commercial typesetting software to mimic the type of writing done with a hammer and chisel in ancient times. Proportional fonts may be visually appealing in printed matter, but monospaced fonts are not passé.

X is a graphical window system, hence, constant versus proportional spacing is a nonissue. Every character is represented by a data structure with fields that completely describe its format, including its width. Thus, there is no difference between proportional and monospaced fonts in terms of the time and resources required to display a character. For X clients, however, constant versus proportional spacing can be a significant issue. With a text editor, for example, many operations are simplified when the display routines assume/require constant character spacing.

Suppose you click mouse button 1 to (re)position the text cursor at a particular character. With a proportional font, the text editor must take into consideration the individual widths of every character on the line preceding that character, to calculate the exact positioning of the text cursor as well as that character's relative position from the beginning of the line. In contrast, when each character's width is constant, offsets can be calculated in multiples of the font's character width.

X provides two types of monospaced fonts: (1) traditional monospaced fonts from the publishing industry with typefaces such as Courier, and (2) character-cell, or computer-style, fonts such as "8x13bold". Fonts using monospaced typefaces such as Courier differ from proportional fonts primarily with respect to the character-width restriction—they are still scaled in points. Character-cell fonts, on the other hand, are simple bitmapped fonts defined in terms of their maximum character width and height, for example, 8 pixels wide and 13 pixels high. That is, characters may vary in size, but each character is represented in an invisible box of constant size for that particular font. Character-cell fonts were designed for graphical computer displays because it's still common for software to provide character terminal-style output. In most X environments, character-cell fonts are located in the *misc* subdirectory.

8.6 X's Font Naming Convention

With X, fontnames are lengthy, composed of numerous fields that uniquely describe every conceivable font. Consider the following fontname:

```
-adobe-helvetica-bold-r-normal--12-120-75-75-p-70-iso8859-1
```

Note that unlike UNIX filenames, fontnames are case insensitive. Thus, you do not have to specify, for example, the typeface Helvetica, using the proper (legal) upper- and lowercase character combinations.

Despite the length of a fontname, it is highly organized and logical. For completeness, this section describes each field in the previous fontname. Most users do not have to deal with these fields on a daily basis.

Foundry. Fonts are now "manufactured" electronically by companies such as Adobe® Systems and Bitstream. The term *foundry* is a hold-over from the days when fonts were cast with lead. Bitstream often refers to itself as a *digital typefoundry*.

Family. Whenever you see this confusing term, mentally replace it with "typeface." In an X environment, common typefaces include Charter, Courier, Helvetica, Times Roman, and others. Note that typeface names are trademarked by font manufacturers when they are first developed. Thus, when other font manufacturers develop a typeface similar to an existing one, they often provide their own unique typeface names. For example, Bitstream's equivalent of Times Roman is called Dutch®.

Weight. In essence, the weight is the thickness of the type. The most common weights for display fonts, that is, when displaying text on a computer screen, are bold and medium. Typically, desktop publishing software provides a light stroke weight as well.

Slant. Common slants include roman (r), italic (i), and oblique (o). Oblique text looks much like roman text in which each character has been slanted to the right. Although it's often slanted to the right, italic text typically has a more curly, or fancy, appearance than oblique text.

Set width. Set width is a term from the early days of typesetting that describes the width at which characters are set on average. The number of characters per horizontal page measure is actually a function of multiple typesetting policies such as kerning (squeezing characters together to improve readability), letter spacing (space added between letters during horizontal justification), and so on. In X, set width is really a type of character width; the most common choices are normal and semicondensed.

Pixel size. This field indicates the size of the font in pixel metrics. Bitmapped fonts are provided in two approximations to the specified point size in the directories *75dpi* and *100dpi*. With lower resolution monitors, the fonts in *75dpi* will provide a more accurate approximation to the requested point size (what you'd get on paper with desktop publishing software) than those in *100dpi*. You can, of course, use fonts from *75dpi* with a high-resolution monitor and vice versa.

Point size. The value given in the point-size field is actually the point size multiplied by ten; this metric allows fractional point sizes, although fractions of a point are common only in professional typesetting. A *point* is a standard, arbitrary, linear typesetting measure; there are 72 points per inch. Or, 1.0 points is 0.014 inches or 0.035 centimeters in width. Because X is device dependent, and hence, bitmap and pixel oriented, the point size you get on-screen is only an approximation to what you would get on paper.

Horizontal and vertical DPI. The values in these fields are sometimes referred to as the x and y resolution, respectively. This field indicates the screen resolution for which this font is designed. Their values will be 75 and 75 for fonts in the directory *75dpi*, and 100 and 100 for fonts in the directory *100dpi*.

Spacing. The spacing field will be character-cell (c), monospaced (m), or proportional (p), as described in Section 8.5. Character-cell and monospaced fonts are suitable for X clients such as text editors, whereas proportional fonts are typically used with desktop publishing software.

Average width. This field indicates the average character width in pixel metrics, multiplied by ten. Thus, the value 70 means 7.0 pixels wide on average.

Registry. The character set registry field supports fonts in an arbitrary number of character sets. Currently, most fonts belong to the International Standards Organization (ISO) 8859-1 (Latin-1) character set.

Encoding. There can be an arbitrary number of character set encodings within character set families such as Latin and Greek. Latin-1 is the most common.

8.7 Using Fontnames Directly

To invoke *xwp* from the command line and specify a font directly, you could enter a command such as the following:

```
{your system prompt} xwp ski.article.doc -font \
'-adobe-helvetica-bold-r-normal--12-120-75-75-p-70-iso8859-1' &
```

Of course, most word processors would also allow you to choose fonts dynamically from multiple scrollable lists. That is, you would use the mouse to select a typeface, weight, slant, and point size combination. This capability is important because users want on-screen text formatting that matches their printed output.

Although modern desktop publishing and word-processing software insulates users from low-level font selection via X's fontnames, for many X clients this form of dynamic, high-level font selection is largely unwarranted. Typically, with applications such as file managers, mail tools, and text editors, most users would select the same font day after day. For these situations, X provides three mechanisms that simplify font selection: (1) fontname wildcarding, (2) fontname aliases, and (3) a generic font selection utility, *xfontsel*.

8.7.1 Fontname Wildcarding

If you are familiar with the fonts available on your system, it's easy to use fontname wildcarding to short-cut a lengthy fontname specification. For example, if you know that a particular typeface is available (on your system) from only one foundry, you can wildcard the foundry field:

```
{your system prompt} xterm -fn '*courier-bold-r-normal*12*' &
```

With experience on a particular system, you develop a feeling for other fields that you can omit, yet still get the same font:

```
{your system prompt} xterm -fn "*courier-bold-r*12*" &
```

Note that because of the wildcarding that's occurring, the effect of omitting fields is necessarily system dependent. And, if you install additional fonts, a particular wildcard specification may change.

If multiple fonts match the font specification, typically, you'll get the first one that matches:

```
{your system prompt} xterm -fn "*courier*" &
```

If you intend to specify fonts from the command line, it's a good idea to begin with a vague font specification and add fields as necessary to get the desired font. Why should you type more than you have to? You can determine how many fonts match a particular font specification by providing it as an argument to *xlsfonts*:

```
{your system prompt} xlsfonts -fn "*courier*bold-r*"
-adobe-courier-bold-r-normal--0-0-100-100-m-0-iso8859-1
-adobe-courier-bold-r-normal--0-0-75-75-m-0-iso8859-1
-adobe-courier-bold-r-normal--10-100-75-75-m-60-iso8859-1
-adobe-courier-bold-r-normal--11-80-100-100-m-60-iso8859-1
-adobe-courier-bold-r-normal--12-120-75-75-m-70-iso8859-1
-adobe-courier-bold-r-normal--14-100-100-100-m-90-iso8859-1
-adobe-courier-bold-r-normal--14-140-75-75-m-90-iso8859-1
-adobe-courier-bold-r-normal--17-120-100-100-m-100-iso8859-1
-adobe-courier-bold-r-normal--18-180-75-75-m-110-iso8859-1
-adobe-courier-bold-r-normal--20-140-100-100-m-110-iso8859-1
-adobe-courier-bold-r-normal--24-240-75-75-m-150-iso8859-1
-adobe-courier-bold-r-normal--25-180-100-100-m-150-iso8859-1
-adobe-courier-bold-r-normal--34-240-100-100-m-200-iso8859-1
-adobe-courier-bold-r-normal--8-80-75-75-m-50-iso8859-1
-bitstream-courier-bold-r-normal--0-0-0-0-m-0-iso8859-1
```

Note that fonts with size fields of 0 are scalable fonts.

On the other hand, most users specify fonts as X resources in heterogeneous or class resource files:

```
xclipboard*font:   *courier-bold-r-normal*12*
xterm*font:   7x13bold
```

From the previous examples, note that you should enclose font specifications in quotes from the command line; otherwise, the command interpreter will attempt to expand wildcards as filenames. Quoting is not necessary in resource files.

8.7.2 Fontname Aliasing

Although wildcarding is sometimes necessary, X provides a fontname aliasing capability that is usually more convenient. Each of the standard directories for bitmapped fonts, *75dpi*, *100dpi*, and *misc*, should include the file *fonts.alias*. Each record (line) in this standard text file includes two fields: a fontname alias in the first field and the actual fontname in the second field.

On several occasions we've used values such as "8x13bold" when requesting a specific font. This type of fontname is actually not a fontname at all; it is a fontname alias, or simply *font alias*. The following entries are taken from */usr/lib/X11/fonts/misc/fonts.alias* for a workstation with the Consortium X11R5 distribution:

```
. . .
7x13        -misc-fixed-medium-r-normal--13-120-75-75-c-70-iso8859-1
```

```
7x13bold     -misc-fixed-bold-r-normal--13-120-75-75-c-70-iso8859-1
7x14         -misc-fixed-medium-r-normal--14-130-75-75-c-70-iso8859-1
7x14bold     -misc-fixed-bold-r-normal--14-130-75-75-c-70-iso8859-1
8x13         -misc-fixed-medium-r-normal--13-120-75-75-c-80-iso8859-1
8x13bold     -misc-fixed-bold-r-normal--13-120-75-75-c-80-iso8859-1
8x16         -sony-fixed-medium-r-normal--16-120-100-100-c-80-iso8859-1
9x15         -misc-fixed-medium-r-normal--15-140-75-75-c-90-iso8859-1
9x15bold     -misc-fixed-bold-r-normal--15-140-75-75-c-90-iso8859-1
10x20        -misc-fixed-medium-r-normal--20-200-75-75-c-100-iso8859-1
12x24        -sony-fixed-medium-r-normal--24-170-100-100-c-120-iso8859-1
...
```

Specifying the alias is equivalent to specifying the entire fontname. If you have access to this system-wide directory, you can change the names for the existing aliases as well as add aliases for other fonts. (As mentioned, the fonts in this directory are character-cell fonts, as evidenced by the "c" in the spacing field.)

To determine the complete set of fontnames, examine the file *fonts.dir*. It is a directory, or database, of the fonts in a particular (file) directory:

```
69
6x12.pcf  -misc-fixed-medium-r-semicondensed--12-110-75-75-c-60-iso8859-1
6x13.pcf  -misc-fixed-medium-r-semicondensed--13-120-75-75-c-60-iso8859-1
6x10.pcf  -misc-fixed-medium-r-normal--10-100-75-75-c-60-iso8859-1
7x13.pcf  -misc-fixed-medium-r-normal--13-120-75-75-c-70-iso8859-1
7x14.pcf  -misc-fixed-medium-r-normal--14-130-75-75-c-70-iso8859-1
...
```

The first line specifies the number of entries in the font directory. Subsequent lines associate filenames with fontnames—each font's bitmaps are stored in a separate file.

You really should not modify *fonts.dir*; it is a system-generated file. For information on how to rebuild it after adding fonts to your system, see the man-page for *mkfontdir*.

On the other hand, editing *fonts.alias* is perfectly acceptable. Keep in mind that the X server builds a list of font directories, and reads font aliases *each* time it is started. If you modify *fonts.alias*, you should (1) restart your X server or (2) update the X server's font-related information using the following command:

```
{your system prompt} xset fp rehash
```

See Section 8.10 for more information on *xset* and font paths.

8.7.3 Fontname Selection with *xfontsel*

xfontsel is a utility for point-and-click selection of fonts; it is part of the standard Consortium X distribution. When started in the following manner, it builds a list of all available fonts:

```
{your system prompt} xfontsel &
```

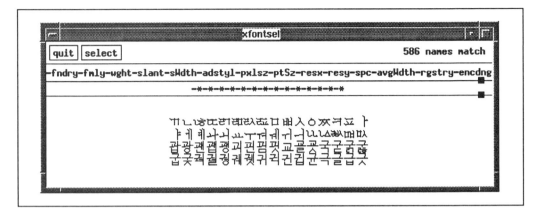

Figure 8.1 *xfontsel* Accessing All Available Fonts

See Figure 8.1. Note that for this particular workstation, there are 586 fonts matching a "completely wildcarded" font specification.

xfontsel can be extremely useful. First, it complements *xlsfonts* when you're experimenting with wildcard font specifications. In particular, *xlsfonts* lists the complete fontnames that match a particular wildcard specification, for example,

```
{your system prompt} xlsfonts -fn "*courier*bold-r*12*"
-adobe-courier-bold-r-normal--12-120-75-75-m-70-iso8859-1
-adobe-courier-bold-r-normal--17-120-100-100-m-100-iso8859-1
```

whereas *xfontsel* with the -pattern command-line option builds a font specification for that pattern, which you can further refine using the menu bar (see Figure 8.2). Typically, *xlsfonts* lists fonts without consideration for the preferred font resolutions for your system;

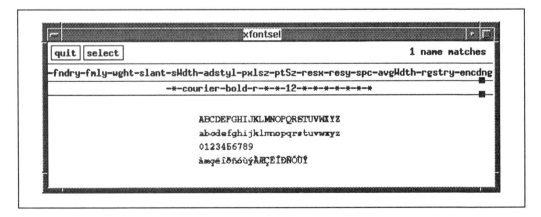

Figure 8.2 *xfontsel* Accessing a Subset of the Available Fonts

that is, it lists fonts from *75dpi* and *100dpi*. *xfontsel*, on the other hand, lists fonts for one or both resolutions, depending on your system configuration. Together these two utilities are indispensable for wildcard experimentation.

A second usage for *xfontsel* is previewing fonts. The top pane in *xfontsel*'s window includes command buttons, as well as a label area that reports the number of matching fonts. The second pane is formatted like a font specification, with hyphen-separated field names, but it is actually a menu bar. Pressing mouse button 1 over a particular field name invokes a pull-down menu; releasing mouse button 1 on a menu item substitutes the menu entry's value in the font specification displayed in the third pane. Lastly, the fourth pane displays a string of text using the selected font. Thus, you can use a trial-and-error technique to preview fonts in various point sizes, weights, and slants.

A third usage is for point-and-click selection of fonts with X clients that don't provide this capability internally. That is, once you've narrowed your font specification so that it targets a unique font, pressing the "select" button makes the font specification the primary selection. You can then paste the primary selection into a command window following `-font`, or into an X resource file.

8.8 *xfd*

xfd (X font display) is another nice utility. For programmers, it's useful because it displays every character and symbol for that font in a grid. Each time you select a particular character, *xfd* displays several programming-related metrics.

Beyond programming, *xfd* is useful for determining the fontname associated with a font alias. To determine the fontname for the alias "8x13bold", simply specify the alias on the command line:

```
{your system prompt} xfd -font 8x13bold &
```

xfd displays the actual fontname in the top of its application window (see Figure 8.3). Lastly, because *xfd* displays every character and symbol for a particular font, it's useful to anyone who must determine the range of characters and symbols included in a particular font. We use *xfd* again in Section 8.11.3 to experiment with scalable fonts.

8.9 Font File Formats

The format of font files in *75dpi*, *100dpi*, and *misc* varies across vendors. These fonts are called *compiled fonts* because they're stored in a format that's compatible with the host hardware and X server. Typically, if you simply copy a compiled font from, say, a Silicon Graphics workstation to a Solbourne workstation, it will be incompatible with the Solbourne's font format.

There are numerous formats for compiled fonts, but the most common type is SNF (server natural format) fonts. SNF fonts have the file extension "snf":

```
{your system prompt} pwd
/usr/lib/X11/fonts/100dpi
```

```
{your system prompt} ls
charB08.snf      helvB10.snf      lubB08.snf      ncenBI14.snf
charB10.snf      helvB12.snf      lubB10.snf      ncenBI18.snf
charB12.snf      helvB14.snf      lubB12.snf      ncenBI24.snf
charB14.snf      helvB18.snf      lubB14.snf      ncenI08.snf
charB18.snf      helvB24.snf      lubB18.snf      ncenI10.snf
...
```

SNF fonts are common in X environments based on X11R4.

You may also encounter freeware fonts distributed in a portable format called BDF (bitmap distribution format). BDF fonts can be compiled into SNF fonts using the utility *bdftosnf* and then added to your font directories; consult your system administrator for guidelines on the best way to do this.

Beginning with X11R5, fonts are distributed in a new format, PCF (portable compiled format), and font files have the extension "pcf":

```
{your system prompt} pwd
/usr/lib/X11/fonts/100dpi
```

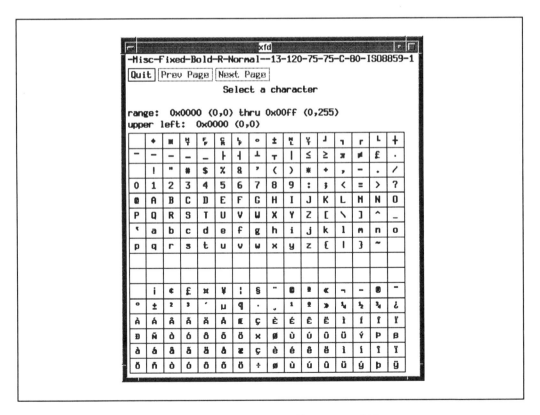

Figure 8.3 *xfd* Displaying a Character-cell Font

```
{your system prompt} ls
charB08.pcf      helvB08.pcf      luRS24.pcf      ncenBI12.pcf
charB10.pcf      helvB10.pcf      lubB08.pcf      ncenBI14.pcf
charB12.pcf      helvB12.pcf      lubB10.pcf      ncenBI18.pcf
charB14.pcf      helvB14.pcf      lubB12.pcf      ncenBI24.pcf
charB18.pcf      helvB18.pcf      lubB14.pcf      ncenI08.pcf
...
```

PCF fonts are designed such that they can be used across any architecture. Performance, however, is optimal for one architecture only. Ideally, if fonts are taken to a different environment, they should be converted to BDF using the utility *fstobdf*, which reads a font directly from the font server and generates a BDF font. After transport to a new X environment, the utility *bdftopcf* can be used to build PCF fonts. Again, system administrators know the particular characteristics of each X environment and typically have experience with font conversions.

There are, of course, several other vendor-specific font formats.

8.10 The Font Search Path

We've mentioned the standard font directories for the Consortium X distribution. The order in which X searches for fonts is based on the font search path. This X server variable is setable with the utility *xset*. You can query the current values for several server characteristics with the q command-line option:

```
{your system prompt} xset q
Keyboard Control:
   auto repeat:  on     key click percent:  0     LED mask:  00000000
   auto repeating keys:   0000000000000000
                          0000000000000000
                          0000000000000000
                          0000000000000000
   bell percent:  50     bell pitch:  400     bell duration:  100
Pointer Control:
   acceleration:  2/1     threshold:  4
Screen Saver:
   prefer blanking:  yes     allow exposures:  yes
   timeout:  600     cycle:  600
Colors:
   default colormap:  0x21     BlackPixel:  1     WhitePixel:  0
Font Path:
   /usr/lib/X11/fonts/misc/,/usr/lib/X11/fonts/Speedo/,
   /usr/lib/X11/fonts/75dpi/,/usr/lib/X11/fonts/100dpi/
Bug Mode: compatibility mode is disabled
```

This output is from a monochrome Sun workstation with X11R5 (from the standard Consortium X distribution). The resolution for the monitor is 1152×900, so the low-resolution font directory (*75dpi*) precedes the high-resolution directory (*100dpi*). If you'd like to modify the search sequence, use *xset* with the fp= command-line option, for example,

```
{your system prompt} xset fp= /usr/lib/X11/fonts/misc/,\
/usr/lib/X11/fonts/Speedo/,/usr/lib/X11/fonts/100dpi/,\
/usr/lib/X11/fonts/75dpi/
```

The space after the "=" is required, because fp= is nothing more than a command-line option; that is, *xset* does not process programming-like statements from the command line.

You can also reset the X server to its default font path:

```
{your system prompt} xset fp default
```

Note that fp= is particularly convenient for eliminating either the low- or high-resolution font directory.

It's important to remember that any time you modify the font path, or files in the font directories, you should rebuild the font path:

```
{your system prompt} xset fp rehash
```

xset is a general-purpose utility for configuring the X server; see its man-page for additional information on configuring your X environment with *xset*, as well as Chapter 11.

8.11 The X Font Server

Prior to X11R5, font access was handled strictly by the X server. That is, an X11R4 server maintains information on all currently loaded fonts. If an X client requests a font that is already memory resident, the X server simply makes it available to the X client. If the font is not memory resident, the X server copies that font (the bitmaps stored in the font file) into memory for the requesting X client.

In the latter case, the X server searches for the font, by fontname, in the appropriate font database/directory, *fonts.dir*:

```
69
6x12.pcf  -misc-fixed-medium-r-semicondensed--12-110-75-75-c-60-iso8859-1
6x13.pcf  -misc-fixed-medium-r-semicondensed--13-120-75-75-c-60-iso8859-1
6x10.pcf  -misc-fixed-medium-r-normal--10-100-75-75-c-60-iso8859-1
7x13.pcf  -misc-fixed-medium-r-normal--13-120-75-75-c-70-iso8859-1
7x14.pcf  -misc-fixed-medium-r-normal--14-130-75-75-c-70-iso8859-1
...
```

If it finds a matching fontname in the second field of each entry, it loads that font based on the filename given in the first field.

As discussed in Section 8.10, the X server sequentially searches the (file) subdirectories given in the current font search path until it finds a *fonts.dir* with a fontname that matches the request, or until the list is exhausted. It's clear that in X11R4 environments in which there are many X terminals, as well as workstations that mount font directories over the network from file servers, font management can be disk and network intensive.

With X11R5, the font server serves two purposes: (1) it allows the X server to offload much of the font management process, and (2) it provides a font scaling facility. Instead of each workstation mounting (accessing) the font directories over the network from the file server, each workstation's X server simply registers for font service with the font server. A single font server can provide fonts for several workstations. Of course, a system administrator can set up multiple font servers per network, and a stand-alone workstation can simply start its own font server.

8.11.1 Font Server Configuration

In most cases, system administrators decide which workstations serve as font file servers (provide the font directories), as well as which workstations host the X font server, *fs*. In a standard X environment, however, it's fairly easy to configure the font server for a stand-alone workstation, and, doing so does not require superuser status, so it's quite common for users to configure a font server locally.

We should emphasize that you do not have to use the font server. By default, the X11R5 server performs font management using the directories specified in the font search path, as described in Section 8.10. To override the default behavior, however, you must register the font server with your X server.

On a stand-alone workstation, if you want the font server to be active all the time, you can execute it from a system start-up file or from a script file in your home directory. If you would like to use the font server occasionally, you can execute it manually. In either case, before you can start the font server, you must set up a configuration file. The man-page for *fs* discusses the configuration options in detail, but the following configuration file, or something similar, should work for most users:

```
#
# File:   fs-config
#
catalogue = /usr/lib/X11/fonts/Speedo
client-limit = 2
clone-self = on
default-point-size = 120
default-resolutions = 75,75,100,100
error-file = FSERRORS
port = 7000
use-syslog = off
```

This file is similar to the example given in the man-page for *fs*. catalogue is the pathname for your scalable fonts. clone-self determines whether or not the font server can start another font server process when it reaches its client limit (the number of X servers it can serve concurrently). We've set the client-limit option to allow service for two X servers, however, with a stand-alone workstation this option is not of interest. The default size and resolution information is used when a font is requested with these fields. port is the TCP/IP (network) port over which the font server and the X server communicate. If you're not familiar with the guidelines for choosing network port numbers, simply use 7000 as we did here.

Next, switch to the directory containing the configuration file and start the font server:

```
{your system prompt} cd
{your system prompt} pwd
/home/jsmith
{your system prompt} fs -config ./fs-config &
```

We've stored our configuration file in the home directory. (Of course, if you specify a complete pathname for the configuration file, you do not have to change to the configuration file's directory.) Note that you *must* start the font server before instructing the X server to use the font server.

You can verify your font server configuration with the utility *fsinfo*:

```
{your system prompt} fsinfo -server jupiter:7000
name of server: jupiter:7000
version number: 2
vendor string:  MIT X Consortium
vendor release number:  5001
maximum request size:   16384 longwords (65536 bytes)
number of catalogues:   1
        all
Number of alternate servers: 0
number of extensions:   0
```

Lastly, to terminate the font server, simply find its process number from the process table and kill it:

```
{your system prompt} ps aux
...
jsmith    895  0.0 10.0 1292 1124 p2 I    09:37   0:04 fs -config fs-config
...
{your system prompt} kill 895
```

In UNIX SVR3 and SVR4 environments use "ps -e" instead of "ps aux" to find the process number.

8.11.2 X Server Configuration

Configuring the X server is easy. In UNIX environments it's common to support network communication via a filesystem-style interface. In the case of communication between the font and X servers, we register the font server with the X server and name the communication channel in one simple operation. Specifically, we prepend a path specification to the existing font search path that encodes: (1) the keyword "tcp", (2) the hostname of the workstation that's hosting the font server, and (3) the port number for network communication:

```
{your system prompt} xset +fp tcp/<hostname>:<port>
```

For example, in our configuration file we specified port number 7000 for network communication between the two servers. Assuming that we've started the font server on a workstation named jupiter, we prepend the following path specification to the X server's default font search path:

```
{your system prompt} xset +fp tcp/jupiter:7000
```

The +fp command-line option prepends its argument to the front of the font search path. If the requested font is part of its "font repertoire," the font server will now automatically provide fonts. If not, the X server will search the remaining font directories in the search path:

```
{your system prompt} xset q
...
Font Path:
  tcp/jupiter:7000,/usr/lib/X11/fonts/misc/,/usr/lib/X11/fonts/Speedo/,\
  /usr/lib/X11/fonts/75dpi/,/usr/lib/X11/fonts/100dpi/
...
```

Although the "tcp/<hostname>:<port>" naming convention is straightforward, it is, perhaps, too low-level for most users, especially those who have no interest in ports, interprocess communication, and so on. In most cases, system administrators will set up environment variables, for example, DEPT_FONT_SERVER_PATH, and/or script files that hide the actual hostnames and port numbers. For most users, access to the font server should be automatic and transparent.

Recall that a stand-alone UNIX workstation constitutes a one-workstation network. Hence, the process of registering the X server with a font server is identical, regardless of whether the font server is running on your workstation or on another workstation on the network. As mentioned, if you run the font server locally in lieu of accessing a font server that's running elsewhere, you must start the font server *before* you register it with the X server.

8.11.3 Using Scalable Fonts

Most users think of the font server in terms of its facility for providing scaled fonts rather than its value in minimizing font-related network bandwidth. In this section we provide examples for using scalable fonts; here, we assume that you've already started the font server and registered it with the X server. For simplicity, we restrict our examples to one typeface, namely, Courier, because it is a monospaced font that's compatible with most X clients. You can, of course, choose other typefaces depending on your X environment.

If you're using an X11R5 implementation other than the one provided by the Consortium X distribution, there may be minor differences in how you configure the font and X servers, as well as the font directory used by the font server and the range of fonts that's available. For example, if you're operating from an X terminal, there may be additional scalable font directories provided by the X terminal vendor and configured by your system administrator. Our examples are restricted to the fonts provided in the *Speedo* directory.

Beyond the fonts provided in scalable font directories, the Consortium X distribution provides, for example, bitmapped fonts in the Courier typeface from Adobe in point sizes up to 24 points. The following aliases are from */usr/lib/X11/fonts/75dpi/fonts.alias*:

```
. . .
acb8  -adobe-courier-bold-r-normal--8-80-75-75-m-50-iso8859-1
acb10 -adobe-courier-bold-r-normal--10-100-75-75-m-60-iso8859-1
acb12 -adobe-courier-bold-r-normal--12-120-75-75-m-70-iso8859-1
acb14 -adobe-courier-bold-r-normal--14-140-75-75-m-90-iso8859-1
acb18 -adobe-courier-bold-r-normal--18-180-75-75-m-110-iso8859-1
acb24 -adobe-courier-bold-r-normal--24-240-75-75-m-150-iso8859-1
. . .
```

In addition, when the font and X servers are communicating, the *Speedo* directory provides fonts in the Charter and Courier typefaces. *fonts.dir* includes the following:

```
8
font0648.spd -bitstream-charter-medium-r-normal--0-0-0-0-p-0-iso8859-1
font0649.spd -bitstream-charter-medium-i-normal--0-0-0-0-p-0-iso8859-1
font0709.spd -bitstream-charter-bold-r-normal--0-0-0-0-p-0-iso8859-1
font0710.spd -bitstream-charter-bold-i-normal--0-0-0-0-p-0-iso8859-1
font0419.spd -bitstream-courier-medium-r-normal--0-0-0-0-m-0-iso8859-1
font0582.spd -bitstream-courier-medium-i-normal--0-0-0-0-m-0-iso8859-1
font0583.spd -bitstream-courier-bold-r-normal--0-0-0-0-m-0-iso8859-1
font0611.spd -bitstream-courier-bold-i-normal--0-0-0-0-m-0-iso8859-1
```

Thus, you can use Courier fonts from either Adobe or Bitstream.

Note, however, that the pixel size, point size, horizontal and vertical DPI, and average width fields are set to 0 for the scalable fonts.

The utility *fslsfonts* lists (font) server-related fonts:

```
{your system prompt} fslsfonts -server jupiter:7000
-bitstream-charter-bold-i-normal--0-0-0-0-p-0-iso8859-1
-bitstream-charter-bold-r-normal--0-0-0-0-p-0-iso8859-1
-bitstream-charter-medium-i-normal--0-0-0-0-p-0-iso8859-1
-bitstream-charter-medium-r-normal--0-0-0-0-p-0-iso8859-1
-bitstream-courier-bold-i-normal--0-0-0-0-m-0-iso8859-1
-bitstream-courier-bold-r-normal--0-0-0-0-m-0-iso8859-1
-bitstream-courier-medium-i-normal--0-0-0-0-m-0-iso8859-1
-bitstream-courier-medium-r-normal--0-0-0-0-m-0-iso8859-1
```

We should reemphasize that we're using the basic font server support provided by X11R5, and we've included only one directory in the so-called font server catalogue:

```
#
# File:  fs-config
#
catalogue = /usr/lib/X11/fonts/Speedo
...
```

Hence, the fonts in *Speedo* are the only ones *explicitly* recognized by the font server. Yet, the other recognized font directories include scalable fonts as well:

```
{your system prompt} xlsfonts -fn "*courier*bold-r*"
-adobe-courier-bold-r-normal--0-0-100-100-m-0-iso8859-1
-adobe-courier-bold-r-normal--0-0-75-75-m-0-iso8859-1
...
-bitstream-courier-bold-r-normal--0-0-0-0-m-0-iso8859-1
-bitstream-courier-bold-r-normal--0-0-0-0-m-0-iso8859-1
...
```

xfd is an ideal utility for testing font access because it displays the complete fontname across the top of its application window. Figure 8.4 shows the font that's accessed with the

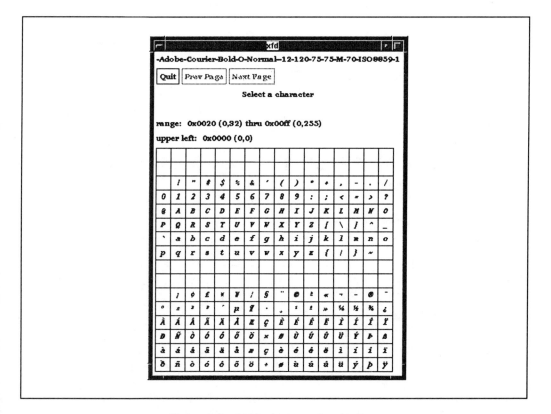

Figure 8.4 *xfd* Displaying a Courier Font

following command:

```
{your system prompt} xfd -fn -bitstream-courier-bold-r-normal--0-0-0-0-
m-0-iso8859-1
```

We've included no size information in our font specification, but in our font server configuration file we specified a default font size:

```
...
default-point-size = 120
...
```

Hence, this configuration information is used to scale the font.

Generally, in requesting a scaled font you should not assume that a monospaced font has
pixel and point sizes that are multiples of each other, and so on. If you do, you may get the
(false) impression that a particular font cannot be generated, simply because the font server
can't generate a font with that particular pixel and point size combination. This erroneous
assumption has led some individuals to assume that the font server is severely limited in its
font scaling capabilities—it is not. The best, and simplest, strategy is to supply only the
point size.

Figure 8.5 shows (part of) *xfd*'s application window for the following command:

```
xfd -fn '-adobe-courier-bold-r-normal--*-420-75-75-m-*-iso8859-1' &
```

In this case, the pixel size is 44.

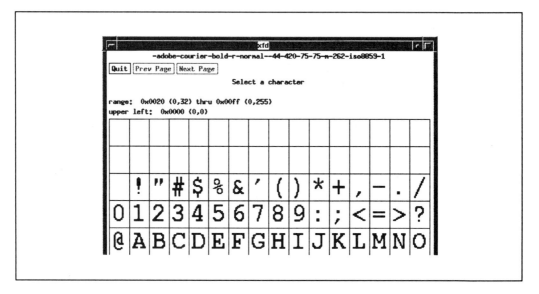

Figure 8.5 *xfd* Displaying a Scaled Font

If you're not convinced that the font server is actually scaling fonts, you may want to try the previous command with a larger point size, for example, 82 (820 in points-times-10 metrics). Also, test the font server's capability for scaling the fonts in the *Speedo* directory:

```
xfd -fn '-bitstream-courier-bold-r-normal--*-420-75-75-m-*-iso8859-1' &
```

It's interesting to compare the Adobe and Bitstream fonts by placing the previous two *xfd* sessions adjacent to each other; that is, the Courier typeface varies from one font manufacturer to another.

We should emphasize that even when you're working with scalable fonts, you don't have to use lengthy fontnames. In particular, you can set up an assortment of fonts in arbitrary point sizes by creating a *fonts.alias* file in the *Speedo* directory. The following *fonts.alias* includes aliases for several common fonts in the Courier typeface:

```
bcb12 -bitstream-courier-bold-r-normal--*-120-75-75-m-*-iso8859-1
bcb18 -bitstream-courier-bold-r-normal--*-180-75-75-m-*-iso8859-1
bcb24 -bitstream-courier-bold-r-normal--*-240-75-75-m-*-iso8859-1
bcb30 -bitstream-courier-bold-r-normal--*-300-75-75-m-*-iso8859-1
bcb36 -bitstream-courier-bold-r-normal--*-360-75-75-m-*-iso8859-1
bcb42 -bitstream-courier-bold-r-normal--*-420-75-75-m-*-iso8859-1
```

You could, of course, add fonts in arbitrary sizes for the Charter typeface. Don't forget to have the X server rebuild the font search path if you add or modify *fonts.alias* (see Section 8.10).

8.12 Guidelines for Choosing Fonts

With a word processor or typesetting software, you typically choose a font that corresponds to the one used for printing the manuscript. In fact, with most typesetting packages, when you choose a font it applies to both the on-screen text and the printed text, because the objective is an on-screen appearance that mirrors the printed output.

On the other hand, if you're using an X text editor, or other text-oriented tools, your objective is probably to minimize eye strain. In this case, you should experiment at length with various fonts, before you develop a habit of using a common font day after day. Even if you have only the fonts supplied with X11R5 from the Consortium distribution, given the font server's scaling capabilities, the font possibilities are enormous. In particular, you (or your system administrator) can experiment with each of the fonts in *75dpi, 100dpi*, and *misc* that have 0 in their size fields, proportional or monospaced. If you have a high-resolution monitor (for example, with a resolution of 1280×1024, or something similar), make sure that *100dpi* is first in your font search path; otherwise, *75dpi* probably should be first.

For some reason, many users automatically choose medium weight fonts. Yet, for most users, especially in fluorescent lighting, a bold font is probably a better choice. Also, with X's support for overlapping windows, there is no reason not to configure at least one or more of your windows to use a large font. Large fonts are especially useful for programmers and writers on a (rapidly approaching) deadline when continued hours behind the monitor are likely.

It has been our personal experience that, for relatively small point sizes, the character-cell fonts in *misc* sometimes produce less eye strain than fonts with, say, the Courier typeface. With larger point sizes, however, the Courier typeface is very pleasing because the Bitstream Speedo fonts produce characters with much smoother edges than a large scaled font from *misc*. Figure 8.6 shows a text editor configured for the following font:

```
ie*font:    -bitstream-courier-bold-r-normal--*-240-75-75-m-*-iso8859-1
```

Note that the figure has been reduced to fit within the page margins of this book. Even though the point size is not accurately reflected in the figure, the quality of the Bitstream Courier typeface is evident.

Of course, you are the only person who can decide which fonts produce the least strain for *your* eyes—and you owe it to your eyes to experiment with typefaces and point sizes.

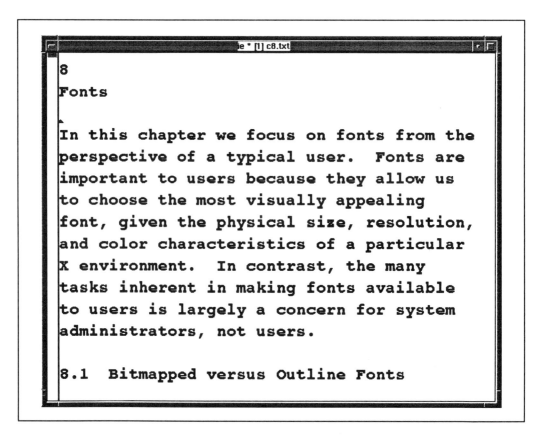

Figure 8.6 A Text Editor Using a Scaled 24-point Courier Font

9

Colors

In this chapter we focus on the rather limited number of color-related issues that are common to all X users. We describe X's color model, as well as how to set color-related resources for X applications whose color configuration is based on X resources. Recall that Appendix A.1 addresses several low-level issues including screen resolution, single- versus multiplane displays, and the relationship between windows and colormaps.

9.1 The Popularity of Color Workstations

The two most popular display colors are still black and white, although this statistic may change soon. For example, Silicon Graphics, a workstation manufacturer known for its high-performance graphics capabilities, focuses exclusively on the color workstation market. Despite the popularity of monochrome displays among programmers, publishing professionals, and others, the demand for color displays is growing rapidly.

In addition to its importance in traditional areas such as CAD/CAM, scientific modeling, medical visualization, a color display is indispensable in emerging areas such as film animation and multicolor publishing. More important, perhaps, many software developers are now recognizing the importance of color in the design of their applications' user interfaces, especially for software that monitors critical plant operations. Even for users who prefer applications with color motifs that are predominately paperwhite, for example, desktop publishing software, the subtle use of color can significantly enhance the user interface.

In all of the arenas in which color is critically important, high-resolution UNIX workstations and X terminals are the systems of choice. Given the steadily declining cost for workstations and X terminals, combined with their increasingly high performance, low- and high-resolution PCs simply cannot compete in terms of the cost-performance ratio (per seat). In terms of the maturity of user interfaces, there's no question that the UNIX/X environment hasn't reached its potential. But, for anyone who requires concurrent execution of multiple high-end applications, the UNIX/X environment provides the most convenient and powerful, network-oriented solution.

There really aren't a lot of color-oriented issues to address, at least not at the generic X level. Primarily, software vendors have the responsibility to make the most appropriate use of color in their user interface, given the characteristics of their applications. On the other hand, in relative terms, color is an expensive commodity. No matter how much computer memory you have, it seems never enough. Thus, in terms of system resources, it is important that applications such as text editors, as well as standard utilities, not overuse color.

9.2 Mixing Colors

Until now, we've chosen colors in our examples using common color names, for example,

```
xterm*background:   SkyBlue
```

In many cases, this type of color specification is ideal. Occasionally, however, it is important (or even intriguing) to experiment with colors, possibly developing and naming your own new colors.

In its simplest form, color specification in X is much like mixing paint from the hardware store, but without the messy clean-up chores. Low-level color selection is performed by mixing/adding together varying portions of red, green, and blue, following the so-called RGB (red-green-blue) color model. Even though there are other ways of specifying colors, it's important to cover the low-level approach so that (1) you recognize it when you see it, for example, in computer-generated configuration files, and (2) if the situation demands it, you have total control over color selection.

In an OpenWindows environment, when you select workspace and window colors from the "Properties" pop-up window (and save your selections), OpenWindows generates a new *.Xdefaults* file containing two color resources:

```
OpenWindows.WorkspaceColor:  #98bfbf
OpenWindows.WindowColor:     #bf9898
...
```

(See Section 12.4.3 for information on adding custom root window colors to the Open-Windows workspace menu. Also, the "Properties" window is implemented in the X client *props*.)

With X11R4 (from which OpenWindows 3.1 is derived), you indicate a low-level color specification with the character "#", followed immediately by three hexadecimal values (with no spacing) that encode the "amount" of color. That is, the format for the color specification is "#<red><green><blue>" where *<red>*, *<green>*, and *<blue>* are one- to four-digit hexadecimal integers. FFFF requests the maximum amount of a particular color and 0000 is the minimum. (In the hexadecimal number system, FFFF is the largest four-digit integer.) For example, the traditional color white is "all colors," that is, the maximum amount of red, green, and blue; in this format, white is #ffffffffffff.

Beginning with X11R5, however, there is a new, preferred RGB color specification: "rgb:<red>/<green>/<blue>". The older format may not be supported in future X releases, and the new format is more explicit, so it's a good idea to switch to the new format (unless your using an X11R4-based X server). Hereafter, we use the "rgb:<red>/<green>/<blue>" format; Section 9.5 provides broader coverage of the new format. Be aware, however, that slashes in the wrong location(s) may cause core dumps in X11R5 releases, so save your work first.

It's unfortunate that for pre-X11R5 X distributions you must have a basic understanding of the hexadecimal number system to use the low-level form of color specification; it is a very convenient mechanism for fine-grained control of color selection. Section 9.3 describes an alternate, rather roundabout, technique that allows you to specify each color component using decimal integers. Section 9.5 describes the RGI Intensity color specification, which supports values that range from 0.0 to 1.0. Also, the freeware X client *xcoloredit* provides a high-level approach to color management.

An important point is that the color components in "rgb:<red>/<green>/<blue>" can be from one to four hex digits, and the number of digits can vary for each color component. In contrast, with the older RGB format, "#<red><green><blue>", the number of digits must be the same for each component within a particular color specification. That is, with the older format there are no delimiters to separate color component, so X divides the digits into groups having an equal number of digits to determine each color component. Thus, the total number of hex digits must be a multiple of 3. Each of the following is a valid (albeit bizarre) color specification:

X11R4:

```
#000
#123
#f6a
#ff00ff
#FF00FF
#aaa444bbb
#000999333
#FFF
```

X11R5:

```
rgb:0/0/0
rgb:1/2/3
rgb:f/6/a
rgb:ff/00/ff
rgb:FF/00/FF
rgb:aaa/444/bbb
rgb:000/999/333
rgb:F/F/F
```

The hex digits A through F can be lower- or uppercase characters, although consistency will probably minimize errors.

Note that there is a difference between `rgb:f/f/f` and `rgb:ffff/ffff/ffff` because the former specification is actually `rgb:f000/f000/f000`. That is, after X divides a color specification into its three components, it pads each component specification on the right size with zeros. Because `F000` is less than `FFFF`, technically, the former color is "less white" than the latter one. That is, even though these two colors have the same *relative* amounts of red, green, and blue, `rgb:ffff/ffff/ffff` is brighter because each RGB component is at its maximum.

Lastly, the real value of this low-level approach to color specification is that once you determine a color that is pretty close to what you are seeking (for whatever purpose), you can increment the red, green, or blue components to fine-tune the color selection to your exact requirements. Once you've done this fine-tuning, you can label your new-found color with a more user-friendly name and add it to the color database.

9.3 The RGB Database

With X, you can use either numeric- or name-oriented color specifications from either the command line or an X resource file. When you use a name-oriented specification such as

```
xterm*cursorColor:   Magenta
```

X must translate it into an "rgb:<red>/<green>/<blue>" specification. X performs this translation via an RGB color database. Each entry in this database contains two fields in the format:

```
<low-level RGB specification in decimal>    <high-level color name>
```

For example, the following entries are taken from the text version of the (Consortium) X11R5 default RGB database, */usr/lib/X11/rgb.txt*:

```
. . .
248 248 255      ghost white
248 248 255      GhostWhite
. . .
255 250 240      FloralWhite
253 245 230      old lace
253 245 230      OldLace
250 240 230      linen
250 235 215      antique white
. . .
245 255 250      MintCream
. . .
240 255 255      azure
240 248 255      alice blue
240 248 255      AliceBlue
230 230 250      lavender
255 240 245      lavender blush
255 240 245      LavenderBlush
```

```
255 228 225        misty rose
255 228 225        MistyRose
255 255 255        white
  0   0   0        black
 47  79  79        dark slate gray
 47  79  79        DarkSlateGray
 47  79  79        dark slate grey
...
100 149 237        CornflowerBlue
 72  61 139        dark slate blue
 72  61 139        DarkSlateBlue
...
 72 209 204        medium turquoise
 72 209 204        MediumTurquoise
 64 224 208        turquoise
  0 255 255        cyan
224 255 255        light cyan
224 255 255        LightCyan
 95 158 160        cadet blue
 95 158 160        CadetBlue
102 205 170        medium aquamarine
102 205 170        MediumAquamarine
127 255 212        aquamarine
  0 100   0        dark green
  0 100   0        DarkGreen
 85 107  47        dark olive green
...
160  82  45        sienna
205 133  63        peru
222 184 135        burlywood
245 245 220        beige
245 222 179        wheat
244 164  96        sandy brown
244 164  96        SandyBrown
...
  0   0   0        gray0
...
227 227 227        grey89
...
240 240 240        gray94
...
255 255 255        gray100
255 255 255        grey100
```

We extracted these entries in the same order as they appear in *rgb.txt*. There is an approximate organization into similar colors, but this ordering is not particularly significant. Also, many colors are represented as multiple entries; thus, the number of distinct colors in the database is considerably less than the number of entries.

The utility *showrgb* displays the entries from the (binary/compiled) RGB database in readable format, similar to listing the text file for the RGB database with *cat(1)*, but typically the ordering will be different. Also, with *showrgb* you don't have to know the full path specification of the text file; the actual location of the RGB database is transparent. *showrgb* lists every entry on standard output (in your command window), so you will probably want to pipe its output into a page display utility such as *more(1)*, or your text editor (if possible):

```
{your system prompt} showrgb | more
```

Note that the highest color component value is `255`, which is equivalent to `FF` (hex), hence, less than `FFFF`. Most users with color displays either (1) have 8-bit color frame buffers, physically limiting them to 256 colors (or less due to memory constraints), or (2) cannot (or do not care to) distinguish the difference between specifying `FF` versus `FFFF` for a color component. Thus, "everything is relative," literally, with respect to color specifications. Note that the previous database entries for gray0 down to gray100 range from black to white (white is the same as gray100).

It's important to emphasize that *rgb.txt* is *not* the actual database. In particular, if you add entries to this file, X won't be aware of the new colors until you add them to the real database, implemented in *rgb.dir* and *rgb.pag*. Actually, you shouldn't modify *rgb.txt*. If you want to supplement this database, make a copy of it under an alternate filename, for example, *alt-rgb.txt*, and modify the latter file. Of course, the location of these files is vendor specific: */usr/lib/X11* on many systems, *$OPENWINHOME/lib* in OpenWindows environments, and so on.

Although its location is not widely advertised, there is another utility, *rgb*, with which you can update the X server's RGB database. It takes new database entries from standard input, for example,

```
{your system prompt} rgb < alt-rgb.txt
```

These entries are added to the current RGB database, possibly overwriting existing entries. Note that in some environments, *rgb* may not work properly without some system modifications, because some vendors include the version from the Consortium X distribution without modifying it to take into consideration the location of the RGB-related files on their systems.

In Section 9.2 we suggested that users often like to experiment with low-level color specifications, to create "personally crafted" colors, but aren't comfortable working with hexadecimal integers. If you have *rgb* (and if it works properly), you can avoid the hexadecimal values by running *rgb* from a command window. (As mentioned, *rgb* interprets its input as decimal integers.) You can add new database entries on the fly in the following format:

```
<low-level RGB value in decimal>    <high-level color name>
```

You can redefine a color as many times as you'd like until you're satisfied with it. Simply start *rgb* without redirecting input from a file so that it will read (consume) whatever you type at the command line as new entries for *rgb.txt*:

```
{your system prompt} rgb
152 191 191 MyWorkspaceColor
191 152 152 MyWindowColor
<type <Ctrl>-D to terminate input>
```

These entries are added to the current RGB database immediately; thus, you can add an entry and then test it, repeating this cycle until you're satisfied with the color. When you're finished entering new colors, simply type **<Ctrl>-D** to terminate database entry. Once you're satisfied with a color definition, record it in a text file such as *alt-rgb.txt* and use this new text file to rebuild the RDB database. Your system administrator should be able to provide assistance, if necessary. Also, your X environment may have a vendor-supplied utility, or the freeware utility *xcoloredit*, for editing the color database.

9.4 Testing Colors

When you define a new color, what's the best way to test it? Some vendors provide a utility for displaying various colors, for example, Solbourne Computer's X distribution includes the freeware utility *xcolor*, which displays colors from the RGB database. Similarly, Silicon Graphics X distribution includes the application *colorview* that displays a color chosen from a selection box (see Figure 9.1).

If you don't have a utility for displaying colors, one of the best ways to see a new color (in a big way) is with *xsetroot*:

```
{your system prompt} xsetroot -solid MyWorkspaceColor
```

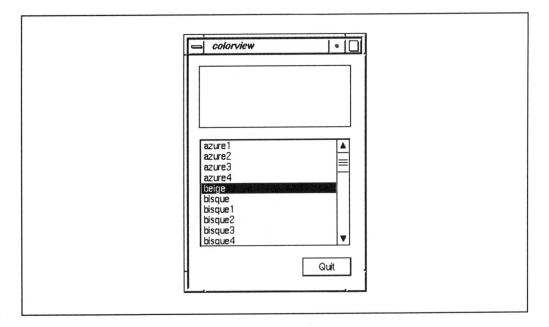

Figure 9.1 Silicon Graphics *colorview*

This command sets the entire background color for the root window to the specified color.

If you prefer to see the effect of the color change for a particular GUI object, simply create a class file in your home directory for any X client having that GUI object. In this file, set the appropriate X color resource using your potential new color(s):

```
*SimpleMenu*Background:   MyNewColor
```

Save the class file and then start the application to test your new color in this particular context.

9.5 Device-independent Color Specifications

RGB color specifications are device dependent. If you use the color rgb:bf/98/98 (a pleasant, earthy brown) for your window title bar color on two different X workstations/terminals, you'll get two similar, yet different, colors. Beginning with X11R5, X supports several device-independent color spaces, or strategies, through the X Color Management System (Xcms). These color strategies, or models, support color specification in a variety of formats. In fact, the support for multiple color spaces beginning with X11R5 is the reason for changing the RGB format to include the keyword rgb. That is, the RGB color space is one of several that the Xcms recognizes.

With large color-oriented applications such as publishing software, color specification is managed internally, that is, via dynamic customization menus or color palettes. And, with traditional applications such as text editors, color specification is achieved directly via X resources using traditional color names such as SkyBlue, possibly with the assistance of a utility such as *editres*. With the former type of application, users typically aren't confronted with the issue of whether to choose a device-dependent or device-independent color model. Hence, the color specification format is typically an issue only in situations where you specify X resources directly, and must (or prefer to) use low-level color specifications.

For users making low-level color specifications, X currently supports the following color spaces:

Color Space	Color Specification Format
RGB	rgb:<red>/<green>/<blue>
RGB Intensity	rgbi:<red-i>/<green-i>/<blue-i>
CIE XYZ	CIEXYZ:<f>/<f>/<f>
CIE u'v'Y	CIEuvY:<f>/<f>/<f>
CIE xyY	CIExyY:<f>/<f>/<f>
CIE L*a*b*	CIELab:<f>/<f>/<f>
CIE L*u*v*	CIELuv:<f>/<f>/<f>
TekHVC	TekHVC:<f>/<f>/<f>

where *<red>*, *<green>*, and *<blue>* are one- to four-digit hexadecimal integers; *<red-i>*, *<green-i>*, and *<blue-i>* are floating-point numbers in the range 0.0 to 1.0; and *<f>* is a floating-point value that varies across color spaces.

RGI Intensity is simply the RGB device-dependent color space, but with a color specification that supports values in the range of 0.0 to 1.0, which you may find more convenient than hex values. The following color specifications (for the color red) are equivalent:

```
rgb:ffff/0/0
rgbi:1.0/0.0/0.0
```

With X11R5, Xcms processes color specifications from an alternate color database, not from *rgb.dir* and *rgb.pag*. The Xcms database is maintained and processed in text format, so there is no need to modify a text file and then regenerate the binary version, as for the X11R4 RGB database. The sample Xcms database for X11R5, *Xcms.txt*, includes the following:

```
XCMS_COLORDB_START 0.1
red                     CIEXYZ:0.371298/0.201443/0.059418
green                   CIEXYZ:0.321204/0.660070/0.159833
blue                    CIEXYZ:0.279962/0.160195/1.210705
aquamarine              CIEXYZ:0.34672401/0.54832153/0.44658871
cadet blue              CIEXYZ:0.22601070/0.28905571/0.47233452
cornflower blue         CIEXYZ:0.05658276/0.04476296/0.17063955
navy blue               CIEXYZ:0.06713718/0.03366278/0.31293880
navy                    CIEXYZ:0.06713718/0.03366278/0.31293880
brown                   CIEXYZ:0.08443233/0.06011398/0.01840693
gray0                   TekHVC:0.0/0.0/0.0
gray10                  TekHVC:0.0/10.0/0.0
gray20                  TekHVC:0.0/20.0/0.0
gray30                  TekHVC:0.0/30.0/0.0
gray40                  TekHVC:0.0/40.0/0.0
gray50                  TekHVC:0.0/50.0/0.0
gray60                  TekHVC:0.0/60.0/0.0
gray70                  TekHVC:0.0/70.0/0.0
gray80                  TekHVC:0.0/80.0/0.0
gray90                  TekHVC:0.0/90.0/0.0
gray100                 TekHVC:0.0/100.0/0.0
XCMS_COLORDB_END
```

In contrast with the RGB database, with the Xcms database, the named color is given first.

Working with Xcms is much easier than using the older approach based on the RGB database. You can specify colors using any of the supported color strategies, including RGB. Also, you can define synonyms for existing colors. For example, we could add the following entry anywhere following the entry for aquamarine but before the keyword XCMS_COLORDB_END:

```
ocean                   aquamarine
```

A discussion of how to use each of the device-independent color spaces would be quite lengthy and is beyond the scope of this book. Typically, however, anyone working in an area that requires this type of color specification is already familiar with one or more of these color spaces.

9.6 Color-related X Resources Settings

For completeness, in this section we should mention the color-related X resources that we've used as examples throughout the book. Virtually all X clients support *background* and *foreground*; hence, nonspecific resource settings (in heterogeneous resource files) such as

```
*background:   AntiqueWhite
*foreground:   DarkSlateGray
```

should affect many X clients.

Of course, in heterogeneous resource files, you can preface these resource settings with client names to introduce client-by-client color distinctions; in class resource files, this specificity is not needed.

Also, many X clients follows *xterm*'s lead and provide the resource *cursorColor*. It's amazing how many users squint their eyes and strain their necks searching for a text cursor that's displayed, by default, in the application's foreground color, when setting the text cursor to a color such as Magenta would make it significantly more visible.

Lastly, if you prefer applications that have menus and dialog boxes that differ in color, you can usually achieve the desired effect by setting widget class resources, as outlined in Chapter 5. For example, with Athena-based X clients, use the *SimpleMenu* class to set all menu colors:

```
*SimpleMenu*Background:   SaddleBrown
*SimpleMenu*Foreground:   OldLace
```

With Motif-based X clients, you may have to set menus and other GUI objects at the widget instance level, because the Motif widget set uses the *XmRowColumn* widget class for a variety of GUI objects. *editres* is useful determining widget instance names as well as setting resources dynamically.

10

Graphics

X, of course, is a graphical window system. Even though much of what we do as users involves text, for example, writing a memo, the text images that we see in a window are displayed by graphics routines. As users, however, when we think of graphics applications we think of CAD/CAM, line-drawing, medical-imaging, and paint packages, to name only a few.

Typically, hardware vendors enhance their X distributions with simple graphics utilities, for example, OpenWindows' *iconedit* and *snapshot*. In this chapter, however, we focus on the basic graphics utilities provided with Consortium X because they are included with most vendor-specific X releases as well.

10.1 Graphics Handling within X

The X toolkit provides widget-level functionality. That is, applications employ Xt routines for creating, managing, and deleting user-interface objects. Xlib, on the other hand, is the low-level X library that provides routines for creating, managing, and deleting X system resources such as bitmaps (pixmaps) and windows, as well as an extensive set of routines for drawing curves, lines, rectangles, text, and other graphics images.

Commercial software developers often employ Xt with, say, the Motif widget set, to design the user interface for a graphics application. In some cases, developers use Xlib, or another library of graphics primitives, to implement the graphics tasks requested by the user, for example, drawing a line. Workstation vendors, however, sometimes prefer proprietary graphics libraries, designed specifically for their graphics hardware—including non-X graphics. That is, even though you may be operating in an X environment, it's possible that the application and the X server have been designed to exploit a more powerful graphics library that by-passes X's normal set of graphics requests. Applications that require this level of graphics performance typically are not displayed remotely, so the absence of X's network-based graphics support is not a problem.

10.2 X Bitmaps and Bitmap Files

In Appendix A.2 we discussed X drawables, specifically, pixmaps and windows. A pixmap is an off-screen memory area that accepts graphics requests, much like a window. Applications often draw graphics images in pixmaps for subsequent use. At any time, an application can copy a pixmap's image to a window. Thus, a pixmap can serve as a "slate," or work area, for building images that an application must display repeatedly. As with windows, X applications typically create pixmaps with the same depth (the same number of planes) as the display screen. For each pixel on a color screen, the workstation must store multiple bits (hence, multiple layers or planes) in order to represent that pixel's color (indirectly via a colormap). (See Appendix A.1.)

A *bitmap* is a single-plane pixmap; thus, a bitmap can directly represent a graphics image displayed on a monochrome screen. In addition, however, bitmaps are ideally suited for representing icon images, for tiling a window with a background pattern, for simulating gray-scale colors on a monochrome screen, and so on.

Bitmaps are also used with color workstations. Consider an icon. Window managers typically display an icon image using two colors, one for the foreground (the image) and one for the background. This *pattern*, however, is easily represented in two dimensions. That is, a two-dimensional array of 1s and 0s completely describes the icon's image. In the bitmap, a 1 represents a pixel that should be drawn in the foreground color and a 0 represents a background pixel. Because of its two-dimensional simplicity, a bitmap is easily *represented* in a file.

When the X server is running, bitmaps are maintained in off-screen memory allocated to the server. When you start X, a number of bitmaps are created from two-dimensional representations stored as 1s and 0s in ASCII files, commonly referred to as *bitmap files*. A bitmap file is a representation of a bitmap; it is not a bitmap. For convenience, however, we often say "bitmap" when we mean "the bitmap created in memory by the X server from the (pattern) representation stored in a bitmap file."

For example, the following bitmap file represents the 3×3 bitmap shown in Figure 10.1:

```
#define plus_width 3
#define plus_height 3
static char plus_bits[] = {
   0x02, 0x07, 0x02};
```

It's easy to see that the bitmap file is a regular text file. C programmers will recognize its contents as C source code. The first two lines of every X bitmap file specify the dimensions, in this case, 3×3. Some bitmap files also contain statements that define a hot spot:

```
#define plus_x_hot 1
#define plus_y_hot 1
```

A hot spot is used in bitmaps that define cursors; it is the area of the bitmap that defines the "point of the pointer."

The remaining lines define an array of 1s and 0s in hexadecimal format compatible with the C programming language. Every X bitmap file follows this format, although the number of lines required for the array varies. Here, 02 hex is 010 binary; 07 hex is 111 binary; 02 hex is 010 binary. Hence, the pattern "010" represents the first row in the bitmap, "111" represents the second row, and "010" represents the third row.

Fortunately, as users we rarely have to decipher bitmap files. The main point is that X provides tools for creating custom bitmaps (actually, bitmap files), which you can then use to customize your X environment. Because X bitmap files are in ASCII/C format, you can transport them across workstations of different architectures. Note that the names used in the C source code are derived from the bitmap filename. Thus, if you inadvertently misname or overwrite a bitmap file, you can use a text editor to examine it and possibly identify its original filename.

The Consortium X distribution includes a variety of bitmaps in the directory */usr/include/X11/bitmaps*. The location of system-wide bitmaps varies across vendors; for exam-

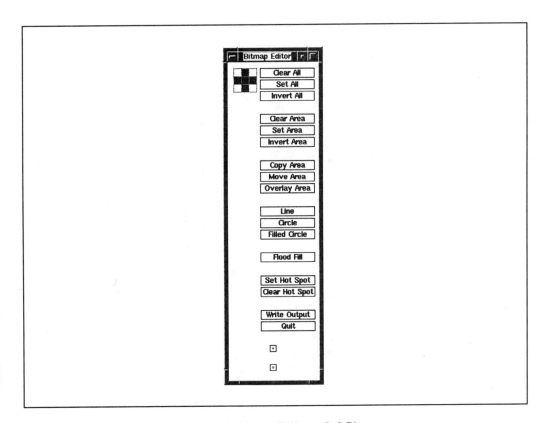

Figure 10.1 *bitmap* Editing a 3x3 Bitmap

ple, OpenWindows provides bitmap files in two directories: *$OPENWINHOME/share/in-clude/X11/bitmaps* and *$OPENWINHOME/share/include/Xol/bitmaps*. If you ever need a custom bitmap, there may be an existing bitmap that is similar, which you can then edit to create the desired bitmap. (Don't modify the existing system-wide bitmaps; copy them first.)

10.3 Creating Bitmap Files with *bitmap*

bitmap is the standard X utility for creating and modifying bitmap files (see Figure 10.2). There are other bitmap utilities, for example, OpenWindows' *iconedit*, but *bitmap* should be included with every X distribution.

The X11R4 version of *bitmap* (Figure 10.2) is a very simple, easy-to-use utility. It displays a column of command buttons down the right side of the window and the bitmap grid appears to their left. The grid is a super-enlarged bitmap where each pixel is represented by a square pixel area. Below the command buttons, *bitmap* displays the actual bitmap in normal and reverse video as it would appear during normal use, for example, when used for an icon image.

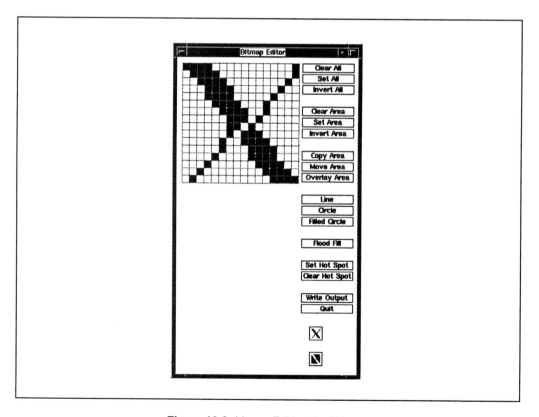

Figure 10.2 *bitmap* Editing the X Logo

To create a bitmap file, simply specify the bitmap filename and the bitmap's dimensions on the command line:

```
{your system prompt} bitmap my.bitmap 32x32 &
```

To edit an existing bitmap file, you do not have to specify the dimensions.

With *bitmap*, you simply click mouse button 1 in the grid to turn on pixels, or mouse buttons 2 or 3 to erase pixels. There are command buttons for clearing and setting the entire grid and specific grid areas. You specify an area by pressing mouse button 1 and dragging the area from the top-left to bottom-right corners.

You can also copy, move, and overlay an area of the grid. First, you drag mouse button 1 to select the source area and then click mouse button 1 at the top-left corner of the target area.

bitmap provides two short-cut commands for drawing lines and circles. To draw a line, simply click mouse button 1 at each of its end points. To draw a circle, simply click mouse button 1 first at its center and then at any point along its circumference (simply designate the radius).

Because *bitmap* is often used for creating cursors for the mouse pointer, it has commands for clearing and setting a hot spot. As mentioned, the hot spot is the pixel in the grid that the X server interprets as the central point of the cursor during pointing operations. For example, for an arrow-shaped cursor, you would set the hot spot at the pixel (grid element) representing the arrow point. In Figure 10.3 *bitmap* is displaying the left-pointer cursor, which many applications request when the mouse pointer is inside command buttons and menus. You can see the hot-spot at the arrow's tip.

With X11R5, *bitmap* has changed considerably (see Figure 10.4). The column of command buttons is now located to the left of the bitmap grid; there are two pull-down menus, "File" and "Edit"; the current bitmap filename appears along the top of the window; there are command buttons for directional manipulation of the image; the normal and reverse video images have been relegated to a secondary window, available by pressing **<Meta>-I**; and fundamental operations such as clear and set are now distinct from the type of object, thus supporting additional operation-object combinations.

With this version of *bitmap*, you first choose the type of object, for example, a rectangle, and then drag out its shape with mouse button 1. Using the directional commands, you can also move the current object within the grid; when part of an object is moved passed the edge of the grid, it reappears on the opposite edge.

The marked block concept is very useful. With "Mark" you can designate a subset of the grid for various tasks such as cut and paste, directional movement, and so on.

It's important to note that you must be careful not to use a window manager "Close" or "Delete" operations to terminate *bitmap* (or the top-level image window for the X11R5 *bitmap*), because *bitmap* is missing the functionality for graceful window termination that's provided with other utilities such as *xload*; that is, it is not ICCCM compliant in some environments. If *bitmap* has unsaved edits, (in some environments) closing the window will immediately kill the application without saving your work.

10.4 Other Bitmap-related Utilities

bmtoa and *atobm* are UNIX filters that complement *bitmap*. *bmtoa* is used more often than *atobm*; it converts bitmap files to an approximate visual ASCII representation of the bitmap. Suppose you're searching for a particular bitmap file, but you can't recognize it by its filename. In this case, as you examine various bitmap files, you require only a quick approximation to the bitmap represented by each file. *bmtoa* is ideal for snooping through bitmap files because you can display the bitmap approximation directly in a command window. For example, in Section 10.2 we described *plus.xbm*, a bitmap file representing a plus sign. To view the plus bitmap in a command window, simply redirect *plus.xbm* as standard input to *bmtoa*:

```
{your system prompt} bmtoa < plus.xbm
-#-
###
-#-
```

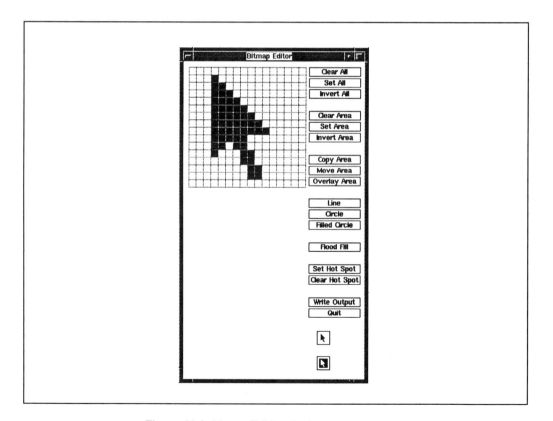

Figure 10.3 *bitmap* Editing the Left-pointer Cursor

In the output, foreground pixels are represented by "#" and background pixels by "-".

If necessary, you can store this representation in a file by redirecting the standard output from *bmtoa* to a text file:

```
{your system prompt} bmtoa < plus.xbm > plus.ascii
```

To produce a bitmap file from this type of ASCII representation, use *atobm*:

```
{your system prompt} atobm < plus.ascii > plus.bitmap
```

Note that the name portion of the C statements in the bitmap file will be absent:

```
{your system prompt} atobm < plus.ascii
#define _width 3
#define _height 3

static char _bits[] = {
  0x02, 0x07, 0x02 };
```

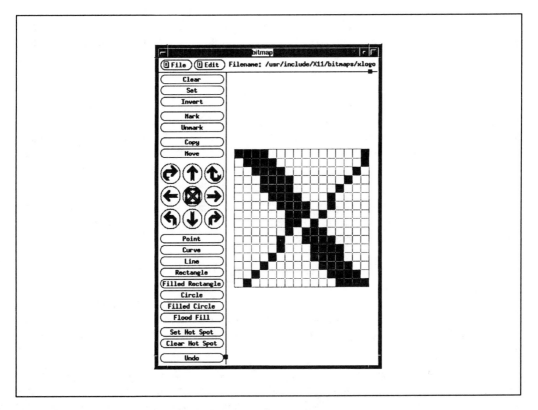

Figure 10.4 *bitmap* for X11R5

If you create a bitmap file in this manner, you can use *bitmap* to name (rename) the bitmap filename; it will automatically set the name components in the bitmap file.

10.5 Taking Screen Shots with *xwd*

xwd (X window dump) captures a window's image. In most cases, the output from *xwd* is stored in a file for subsequent input to other utilities such as *xpr* (X printer). Most of the screen shots in this book were taken with *xwd*, filtered through *xpr* to produce PostScript output, and then converted to Encapsulated Postscript for subsequent typesetting.

Typically, you designate the window for the screen shot by selecting it with mouse button 1. Optionally, you can supply a window ID with the -id command-line option, or the window name using the -name command-line option. See the man-page for *xwd* for a complete list of options.

The following usage is typical with *xwd*:

```
{your system prompt} xwd -frame > figure1.xwd
```

The -frame command-line option requests that *xwd* include the window manager frame as part of the image; otherwise, the captured image would be similar to one taken when there is no window manager running. In the previous example, the captured image is redirected to a file. A common alternative is to pipe the output into another filter/utility such as *xpr*:

```
{your system prompt} xwd -frame | xpr ...
```

When you capture an image for a window, that image does not include the contents of windows that overlay the captured window, for example, menus and dialog boxes (unless they are children of the captured window, which is very rare). By definition, *xwd* captures the image of *a* top-level window. Menus and dialog boxes aren't included in the captured image, even though they may be part of the application, because they are not part of the application's top-level window—they are distinct top-level windows.

Thus, with earlier versions of *xwd* it is quite difficult to make a screen shot of an application while one of its menus is active. Beginning with X11R5, however, *xwd* includes the -screen command-line option:

```
{your system prompt} xwd -frame -screen > figure1.xwd
```

If you specify this option, *xwd* directs the capture operation to the root window, but restricts it to that region of the root window occupied by the selected window. Because all windows are children of the root window, this option makes it convenient to capture images of overlapping top-level windows.

If you want to make a screen shot of an application window when a dialog box is active, a command similar to the previous one should be adequate. In many cases, however, when you activate a menu the application only displays the menu while a mouse button is pressed, or it performs something called a *pointer grab* which restricts pointer usage to the menu while it's active. In either case, the mouse is "busy," preventing you from executing an *xwd* command.

Some vendors provide alternative screen-shot utilities, such as OpenWindows' *snapshot*, that provide a timer facility (see Figure 10.5). Thus, you can start the capture operation with an arbitrary delay, allowing you enough time to invoke the menu before the actual screen shot takes place.

Suppose you'd like to make a screen shot with *xwd* of a UI object such as a menu that "restricts the pointer" while the menu is active. In this case, the standard use of *xwd* is inappropriate because (1) you cannot move the pointer to a command window to execute *xwd*, and (2) you cannot use the pointer to select the target window.

One solution is to select the target window using its window ID and delay *xwd*'s execution with *sleep(1)*. For example, to capture an image of *xrolodex* with an active menu, first determine its window ID with *xwininfo*:

```
{your system prompt} xwininfo

xwininfo: Please select the window about which you
          would like information by clicking the
          mouse in that window.

xwininfo: Window id: 0x200005f "xrolodex"

  Absolute upper-left X:   648
  Absolute upper-left Y:   185
...
    -geometry 432x290-63+159
```

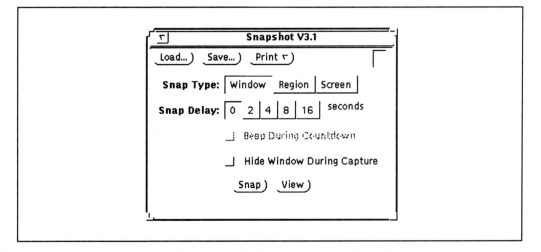

Figure 10.5 OpenWindows *snapshot*

Next, precede the *xwd* command with an arbitrary delay, in this case, five seconds:

```
{your system prompt} sleep 5 ; xwd -frame -screen > xrolodex.xwd \
-id 0x200005f
```

This delay provides enough time to use the mouse to invoke the menu. (Placing a semicolon between commands executes them sequentially.)

Enhanced utilities such as *snapshot* simplify this process, providing a higher level user interface that does not require users to be fluent in command-line computing.

Lastly, we should mention *xwud* (X window undump). If you've made a screen shot with *xwd* you can view it on-screen with *xwud*:

```
{your system prompt} xwud -in xrolodex.xwd &
```

xwud allows you to preview, and hence, verify, the image before proceeding with operations that transform it into PostScript for printing, Encapsulated PostScript for typesetting, and so on.

10.6 Converting Window Dumps to Printable Output with *xpr*

Once you've captured an image with *xwd*, it's common to convert it to one printable form or another with *xpr*. *xpr* has several command-line options; see its man-page for complete details. For example, the following (minimal) command converts the window dump to a PostScript file:

```
{your system prompt} xpr -device ps xrolodex.xwd
```

Beginning with X11R5, PostScript is the default output device; with X11R4, however, if you don't specify PostScript, *xpr* will produce a printer file for an archaic output device.

Parenthetically, the input and output command-line options for *xwd*, *xwud*, *xpr*, and others are inconsistent; for example, *xwud*'s option is -in followed by a filename, whereas *xpr* expects the filename only. Thus, unless you use these utilities regularly, you may need to refer to their respective man-pages each time you use them. *xman* makes it convenient to do so.

Using *xpr* is usually not as simple as the previous command suggests. *xpr* is a very powerful utility and typically there are many decisions to make in preparing a screen shot for printing. For this reason, it's unlikely that *xpr*'s default printer preparation decisions will be appropriate, except for preliminary output. For example, *xpr* adjusts the scale and orientation of an image based on the image size, which may be inappropriate in preparing screen shots for typeset documentation.

In many cases, using *xpr* to prepare typeset documents requires considerable typesetting experience. (Typesetting is an inherently difficult, and often underappreciated, task.) A complete discussion of *xpr*'s options is beyond the scope of this book. We can, however, describe a common use of *xpr*, namely, producing a PostScript file suitable for inclusion into another document, either directly or after conversion to an Encapsulated PostScript file.

To produce this type of intermediate file, one approach is to use the `-portrait` option and the `-scale` option with the argument 1:

```
{your system prompt} xpr xrolodex.xwd -device ps -scale 1 \
-portrait > xrolodex.ps
```

In particular, by explicitly choosing the portrait orientation, each screen shot will have a consistent orientation, which your desktop publishing software should be able to accommodate.

When your objective is to produce a PostScript file that you can print directly, the default scale factor, or something similar, is probably adequate. A scale factor of 1 would mean that one pixel on screen would translate to one dot in the laser printer output; hence, the printed image would be too small in most situations. On the other hand, if your objective is to produce a PostScript file that you will scale to the proper size during a subsequent typesetting process, a scale factor of 1 is probably appropriate. Otherwise, if you scale the image before delivering it to the typesetting software, you've lost the original image. That is, when *xpr* scales an image generated by *xwd*, it translates each pixel into several pseudopixels, or dots, based on the scale factor. This scaling may have a negative impact on a high-resolution image.

10.7 *xmag*

xmag is an X utility for magnifying a portion of the screen, although it has other uses as well. Note that *xmag*'s point of reference is not a specific window. (Window-oriented screen capture would prevent screen magnifications that encompass multiple windows. Also, *xwd* is available for window-oriented dumps.)

Figure 10.6 shows *xmag* capturing a portion of *xman*'s main window with a magnification factor of 3 (the default magnification factor is 5):

```
{your system prompt} xmag -mag 3 &
```

We've taken this screen shot from a monochrome workstation to illustrate that bitmaps are used for many purposes. For example, from this screen shot we can see that the root window pattern (visible outside the window decoration) is a simple bitmap in which every other pixel is active. This form of shading with a pixel density of 50 percent produces a uniform gray appearance (unmagnified). In contrast, the window decoration uses a lower pixel density for a lighter, simulated gray-scale appearance (in this case, for a nonactive application window).

xmag has a command-line option for directing the magnification to a particular area of the screen:

```
{your system prompt} xmag -source 100x300+10+20 &
```

In this case, the top-left corner of the magnification begins ten pixels from the left border and 20 pixels from the top border of the screen (root window), and the captured screen area extends 100 pixels horizontally and 300 pixels vertically.

In most cases, however, users drag/sweep the source area using mouse button 2. Without a source specification, if you press mouse button 1, *xmag* magnifies a 64x64 area with the top-left corner originating at the point of the mouse click. To drag out the area for the screen magnification, simply press mouse button 2 at the top-left corner and drag out a rectangular area; releasing mouse button 2 defines the bottom-right corner.

A sometimes-overlooked use for *xmag* is taking unmagnified screen shots when you want to capture a portion of the screen, as opposed to capturing a window (*xwd*). Prior to X11R5, *xwd* didn't provide screen-oriented image capture. Figure 10.7 captures a portion of the screen containing *xman*'s main window:

```
{your system prompt} xmag -mag 1 &
```

Normally, however, you use *xwd* and *xpr* to make screen shots of windows that you can transform into PostScript and Encapsulated PostScript® files for inclusion in documentation.

10.8 Using Bitmaps to Tile the Root Window

In Section 9.4 we mentioned that *xsetroot* is useful for testing colors, as well as for customizing your root window for each X terminal and workstation environment. Recall that the -solid command-line option sets the root window to an arbitrary color:

```
{your system prompt} xsetroot -solid "Plum"
```

Figure 10.6 *xmag* with a Magnification Factor of 3

Similarly, with the -bitmap option you can specify a pattern for tiling the root window:

```
{your system prompt} xsetroot -bitmap /usr/include/X11/bitmaps/root_weave
```

The argument to -bitmap is a bitmap file from which X builds the actual bitmap. By default, the Consortium X environment uses the root-weave bitmap. In fact, executing *xsetroot* with no options is equivalent to the previous command. The root-weave bitmap is a well-tested bitmap that works well in a variety of lighting conditions. Many users who abandon it for something a little more exciting eventually rediscover it. */usr/include/X11/bitmaps* includes other bitmap files that are suitable for tiling the root window including *cross_weave*. Experimenting with bitmaps such as *mensetmanus* may be a useful diversion, but for most users the more uniform background provided by a smaller tile leads to less eye strain.

If you use a monochrome screen and you'd like to experiment with alternatives to the root-weave pattern, use *bitmap* to create a custom bitmap. You can test it using *xsetroot* manually, but eventually you may want to add it to your start-up script for X:

```
{your system prompt} xsetroot -bitmap graytile.bit
```

```
(See the script segment in Section 6.7.)
```

The bitmap in Figure 10.8 provides a uniform gray background, and may be useful as a starting point. Note that some bitmap sizes are more appropriate for tiling operations than others; in general, a 4×4 or a 16×16 bitmap is usually quite efficient.

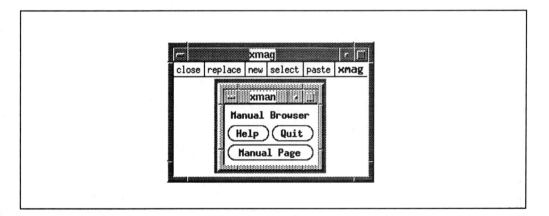

Figure 10.7 *xmag* with a Magnification Factor of 1

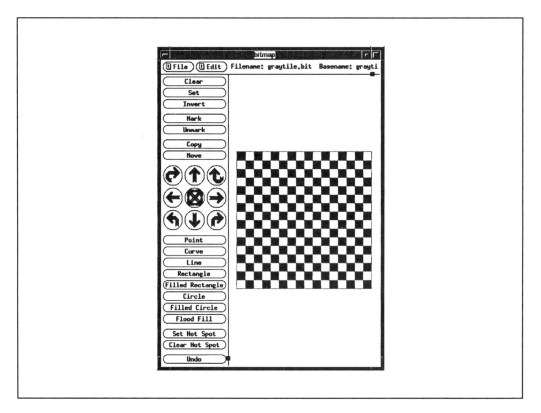

Figure 10.8 A Bitmap Pattern Suitable for Simple Grayscale Operations

11

X Server-related Customizations

In other chapters we provide examples for customizing your X environment, but always in the context of a particular topic; we describe ways to set resources at the class level in order to customize UI objects such as menus; we discuss how to define logical names for colors in order to augment the color database; and other customizations. In addition to building on the information presented elsewhere, this chapter addresses additional opportunities for keyboard-, mouse-, and other X server-related customization.

11.1 Configuring the X Server with *xset*

X terminals often provide pop-up windows for configuring a number of terminal characteristics, including X server characteristics controlled by *xset*. If you're working from an X terminal, using the configuration window is typically more convenient than using a command-line utility such as *xset*. With workstations, however, *xset* often is the only tool available for configuring the X server. In some cases, vendors provide additional configuration tools for non-X server customizations. For example, the OpenWindows "Properties" window sets several characteristics such as scrollbar placement, dialog behavior, and menu behavior for OpenWindows clients. The point is that there may be several configuration tools for your X environment.

If you execute *xset* with the q (query) command-line option (as we did in Section 8.10 to determine the font path), *xset* prints the current settings in the command window:

```
{your system prompt} xset q
Keyboard Control:
  auto repeat:  on      key click percent:  0      LED mask:  00000000
  auto repeating keys:  0000000000000000
                        0000000000000000
```

```
                          0000000000000000
                          0000000000000000
   bell percent:   50     bell pitch:   400     bell duration:   100
Pointer Control:
   acceleration:   2/1     threshold:   4
Screen Saver:
   prefer blanking:   yes     allow exposures:   yes
   timeout:   600     cycle:   600
Colors:
   default colormap:   0x21     BlackPixel:   1     WhitePixel:   0
Font Path:
   /usr/lib/X11/fonts/misc/,/usr/lib/X11/fonts/Speedo/,
   /usr/lib/X11/fonts/75dpi/,/usr/lib/X11/fonts/100dpi/
Bug Mode: compatibility mode is disabled
```

Warning: We should point out that X servers vary considerably in terms of whether or not you can modify certain characteristics. If, for example, you attempt to modify the bell volume and nothing happens, you haven't necessarily made an error. It could be that this modification simply isn't possible with your particular X server-workstation combination. Also, if you set a characteristic to a particular value, for example, key-click volume to 100 percent, the q may reflect this setting even though the X server does not honor it. In other words, *xset* typically is not customized to each X server-workstation combination.

11.1.1 The Terminal Bell

The b command-line option sets bell characteristics, for example:

```
{your system prompt} xset b off
{your system prompt} xset -b
{your system prompt} xset b on
{your system prompt} xset b
{your system prompt} xset b 100
{your system prompt} xset b 50 400 500
```

Users most often use this option to turn off the terminal bell with "noisy" X clients that provide no client-specific option for suppressing incessant bell ringing.

Inconsistencies abound in the UNIX/X community in the use of a "-" as the first character in a command-line option. In terms of UNIX, X, and command interpreters, there is nothing special about the character "-". Applications traditionally have used a hyphen as the first character of a command-line option to make it easier to process options and their accompanying values, if any. Many UNIX utilities, however, are designed to accept command-line options either with or without a hyphen, especially utilities such as *tar(1)* that have single-character options, many of which are optional and often packed together in a string-like form:

```
{your system prompt} tar -cvf /dev/diskette *
{your system prompt} tar cvf /dev/diskette *
```

Here, *tar(1)* creates an archive file on the device diskette that consists of any file matching "*". The command-line options are "c", "v", and "f" (for create, verbose, and file, respectively).

With *xset*, however, -b and b are not equivalent because the hyphen (minus sign) is used to turn off a specific option. Hence, "b off" and "-b" are equivalent and "b on" and "b" are equivalent. Unfortunately, and quite inconsistently, +b is not an option, but +fp is a valid option. These inconsistencies often make sense to long-time UNIX users, but are an ongoing thorn in the side for many end-users.

In addition to enabling and disabling the bell, you can also set its volume, pitch, and duration:

```
xset b <volume-in-percent> <pitch-in-hertz> <duration-in-milliseconds>
```

If you specify a single numeric value, *xset* modifies the bell volume; to modify the bell duration, you must specify all three values.

11.1.2 Bug-compatibility Mode

The bc and -bc command-line options enable and disable bug-compatibility mode. Developers should never enable bug-compatibility mode while they're developing applications because this option requests that the X server emulate run-time errors in older X servers. Today, users should very rarely use this option. If you're using X software that recommends enabling bug-compatibility mode, you probably should upgrade to a later release that doesn't require compatibility with pre-X11R4 X servers. If a modern version of the software is unavailable, consider a competing product.

11.1.3 Keyboard Click

The c and -c command-line options enable and disable keyboard click with certain X servers. In addition to specifying on and off values with c, you can specify the key-click volume as a percent:

```
xset c 75
```

11.1.4 Pointer Characteristics

One of the most useful options is m, which sets the acceleration and movement threshold for the pointing device, typically, a mouse:

```
xset m <acceleration-ratio> <threshold-in-pixels>
```

If you specify a single numeric value, it is interpreted as the pointer acceleration with 1/1, or 1, being the baseline:

```
{your system prompt} xset m
{your system prompt} xset m 1/2
{your system prompt} xset m 2/1
```

```
{your system prompt} xset m 2
{your system prompt} xset m 5
```

The larger the fraction (or integer), the greater the pointer cursor movement relative to the pointing device movement. That is, the larger the integer, the faster the mouse; "m 1/2" typically yields a slow mouse; "m 5" makes the mouse scamper very quickly; and "m 10" requests a jet-propelled mouse. To set the mouse acceleration back to the default value, simply enter "xset m".

The threshold value controls the sensitivity of the mouse, that is, the number of pixels you must move the mouse before the mouse cursor actually moves. If you're consuming large amounts of (caffeinated) coffee, you may want to decrease the threshold.

On the other hand, if you continually find your mouse at the edge of your mousepad (or the edge of the desk with a mechanical mouse), try increasing the acceleration. If, for example, the current value is 2/1, try 3/1 (or 3), and so on. If you regularly perform very delicate drawing operations with a paint program, you will probably want to experiment with both the acceleration and the threshold.

11.1.5 The Screen-saver

The s command-line option controls the X server's screen-saver facility. In many environments the default action is to blank the screen after several minutes; in a few environments the screen-saver may be "permanently disabled;" and, in some environments you may be able to activate the screen-saver but not control its method of saving the screen from "phosphoric burnout."

You can turn the screen-saver on or off, set its save operation to "blank" or "noblank", set its time-out and cycle thresholds, and so on:

```
{your system prompt} xset s on
{your system prompt} xset s off
{your system prompt} xset s blank
{your system prompt} xset s noblank
{your system prompt} xset s expose
{your system prompt} xset s noexpose
{your system prompt} xset s 300 10
```

You can, of course, enter multiple *xset* commands and screen-saver options.

The option "s blank" requests that the screen-saver cover the screen with a nonactive background after an arbitrary period of X server inactivity (no one at the keyboard or mouse). For a CRT, "blank" implies that the screen would become black, that is, the radiation that illuminates the phosphorescent material at each pixel area would be turned off, hence, saving the screen from premature burnout. With a different display, for example, an LCD, deilluminating the screen would have a slightly different effect, depending on the display technology.

The "s blank" option is a problem sometimes because you can't distinguish between an inactive display and a monitor that's turned off. Thus, suppose you'd like to set the screen-saver so that it displays the familiar X logo when the display is inactive for more than 2 minutes, and you'd like to vary the X logo (its cycle) every 10 seconds. To select the no-blank mode, enter the following command:

```
{your system prompt} xset s noblank
```

Next, to set the time-out (inactivity) period and the X logo cycle, enter the following command:

```
{your system prompt} xset s 120 10
```

Both values must be expressed in seconds, so we must specify 120 seconds instead of 2 minutes. (Hint: While you're experimenting with the screen-saver, set the inactivity period to a small value, say, 20 seconds, so that you don't have to wait a long time to observe modifications.)

It's unlikely that you will use "s noexpose". This option specifies that the X server activate the screen-saver *only* if it can record, and hence regenerate, the contents of every application window without requesting that X clients redisplay their windows by sending them expose events. This option could be useful in an environment where an X client requires a long time to build a complex image, which it cannot redisplay without recalculating the image.

We've mentioned *xset*'s most interesting options. There are others that you will probably never use, for example, disabling keyboard auto-repeat, as well as options such as `fp` (font path) that we've discussed elsewhere (Chapter 8). For additional information, use *xman* to examine the man-page for *xset*.

11.2 X's Logical Keycodes: Keysyms

One very nice feature of X is key symbols, commonly called *keysyms*. Keysyms provide a mechanism for binding logical keyboard operations to physical keys. Keysyms allows X clients to respond to higher level key mappings, which users can reassign, instead of the low-level keycodes generated directly by the keyboard, which vary across workstations and X terminals. Although many X terminal manufacturers supply their terminals with PC-style keyboards, there is no keycode standard for PC-style keyboards, so the keycodes vary considerably, even among keyboards with a similar appearance.

Keyboards generate integer values that identify each key, for example, the "A" key might generate the integer 84 while <**Enter**> might generate 96. The integers are arbitrary; the only requirement is that each key generate a different integer, so that every key is distinguishable. An X server does not simply pass these integers along to the application. Instead, it maps a higher level, logical key symbol to each key (keycode) generated by the keyboard; examples of keysyms include `a`, `A`, `Delete`, and `Find`. This type of service is central to the X server; it manages the display on behalf of X clients, and the keyboard is part of the display.

X provides a standard set of keysyms that X server vendors are encouraged to support (see Appendix E). X server vendors vary, however, in the completeness of their support for X's keysyms. For example, some X servers do not map (assign) keysyms to many of the cursor keys such as **<Home>** and **<End>**; others map less-than-obvious keysyms to certain keys, often based on older, pre-X software environments. For example, the Consortium X server implementation for Sun SPARCstations® maps the keysym F27 to **<Home>**. In many Sun workstation environments, **<F11>** and **<F12>** do not generate the F11 and F12 keysyms as most users would expect; instead, they generate SunF36 and SunF37! This situation is quite ludicrous.

Yes, this keysym mapping may make sense to a few users, but for the most part it is very confusing when a key such as **<Home>** sends something other than the "Home" keysym. Moreover, when X servers do not fully support the display (which includes the keyboard), it introduces problems for vendors of other X clients, as well as for users. When the X server doesn't provide a keysym (or one that makes sense) for the **<Home>** key, some software vendors provide keyboard-specific solutions, or even assume, for example, that the "F27" keysym should be interpreted as the "Home" keysym, simply because of their relationship on a specific keyboard—a very undesirable solution.

Keyboard-dependent software presents problems for users because they often use X clients from a workstation, as well as in a heterogeneous X terminal environment. Software vendors simply cannot provide different keyboard configurations for every conceivable X terminal and keyboard, because of inconsistent use of keysyms. In other words, when X servers are inconsistent in their logical-to-key assignments (each assigning a different keysym to the physical key **<Home>**), using keysyms becomes as problematic as using physical keycodes. As users, we can only hope that X server vendors become more responsible.

Fortunately, X provides a utility, *xmodmap*, for modifying keyboard and pointer mappings. Before you can modify keysym-to-keycode mappings, however, you must have a way of discovering the keycodes generated by the keyboard. If the X client *xev* is provided with your X environment (it's in the *demo* directory for the Consortium X distribution), you can examine the keycodes and keysyms supported by your hardware and X server, respectively. *xev* creates a top-level application window that includes a smaller, nested application window; it then reports (in the command window where you execute *xev*) every X event that occurs in these windows, including keyboard-related events.

When *xev* first starts there is a flurry of events, so the output is quite large (see Figure 11.1). Once you've placed the pointer cursor inside *xev*'s window and stopped moving the mouse, you can simply press various keys to see the event information generated by the X server and reported by *xev*, including the keycode and keysym for each key. Typically, there is a key-press and a key-release event each time you press and release a key. Pressing the "A" key for a Sun SPARCstation running Consortium X11R5 generates the following output:

```
{your system prompt} xev &
...
[omitted output]
...
KeyPress event, serial 13, synthetic NO, window 0x2800001,
    root 0x23, subw 0x0, time 2688150310, (70,139), root:(460,269),
    state 0x0, keycode 84 (keysym 0x61, a), same_screen YES,
```

```
       XLookupString gives 1 characters:  "a"

KeyRelease event, serial 15, synthetic NO, window 0x2800001,
    root 0x23, subw 0x0, time 2688150430, (70,139), root:(460,269),
    state 0x0, keycode 84 (keysym 0x61, a), same_screen YES,
    XLookupString gives 1 characters:  "a"
. . .
```

The third line of output for each event lists the keycode and the keysym; in this case, the actual keysym is a, but for clarity it is often shown as a string in double quotes, "a". It is a lowercase "a" because <Shift> and/or <Caps Lock> were not active.

For X server keyboard customizations, the output from *xev* is somewhat overwhelming. Hence, programmers and system administrators often develop a higher level X client that reports only the information relevant to key mappings. For example, we regularly use a simple X client named *xkeymap* that reports this information and, optionally, logs it to a disk file (see Figure 11.2). For users, the logging feature is quite useful in communicating key mappings to technical support staff at a remote location who can assist them with keysym modifications.

11.3 Modifier Keys

Modifier keys include <Shift>, <Ctrl>, <Caps Lock>, and others. Actually, a modifier key represents a symbolic, or logical key state, not a physical key. The keysym facility for mapping physical keys to logical keyboard operations is used to define modifier keys as well.

It's important to recognize that modifiers are distinct from keysyms. Keysyms are used to define modifiers, but they are not equivalent; for example, the keysym Control_L (or Control_R) usually generates the modifier state control.

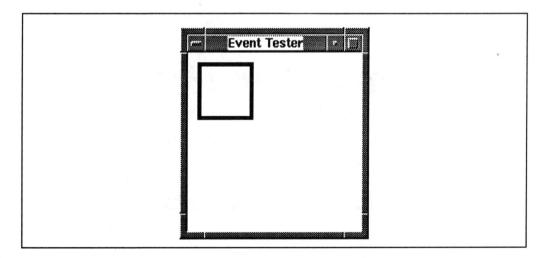

Figure 11.1 *xev*'s Event-processing Windows

xmodmap is an X utility designed primarily for manipulating modifier key assignments, although it is also used to modify keysym-to-keycode bindings. If you execute *xmodmap* with no arguments, it prints the current modifier-to-keysym mappings:

```
{your system prompt} xmodmap
xmodmap:  up to 3 keys per modifier, (keycodes in parentheses):

shift        Shift_L (0x6a),   Shift_R (0x75)
lock         Caps_Lock (0x7e)
control      Control_L (0x53)
mod1         Meta_L (0x7f),   Meta_R (0x81)
mod2         Num_Lock (0x69)
mod3         F13 (0x8),   F18 (0x50),   F20 (0x68)
mod4
mod5
```

(Here, we're using the Consortium X server for a Sun workstation; the output probably will be different in your X environment. The keycodes in parentheses are hexadecimal integers—"Ox" means hex.)

Here, both `Shift_L` and `Shift_R` generate the modifier state `shift`. With respect to an X client, this mapping implies that when you press either **<Shift>** key *in isolation*, its keysym is delivered to the application by the X server via a key-press event—the modifier state is not set. But, when you press a **<Shift>** key *in conjunction with*, say, the "A" key, the A keysym is delivered via a key-press event and the modifier state is set to `shift`. Likewise, in isolation **<Ctrl>** generates a key-press event for `Control_L`, but combined with the "A" key, it generates the a (lowercase) keysym with the modifier state set to `control`. In other words, modifier keys modify the state of a keyboard event.

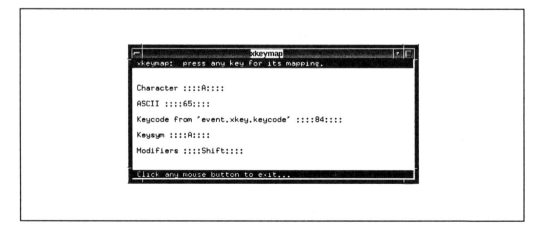

Figure 11.2 *xkeymap*'s Key-related Information

11.4 The Meta Key

Consider the meta key. For the previous *xmodmap* output, the `Meta_L` and `Meta_R` keysyms generate the modifier state `mod1`. Most X applications, when they receive a key-press event with the modifier state set to `mod1`, assume that you've pressed the meta key, so you would not want to modify the association between your meta key and `mod1`.

The meta key, however, represents a logical key operation. Because the UNIX operating system has been ported to many different hardware platforms (and keyboards), many UNIX applications have traditionally supported a logical command key. The term *meta* reflects this higher level usage. (The meta key concept is not unique to X.) In contrast, PC keyboards are consistent in their support for <Alt>, so <Alt> always functions as a general-purpose command key with PC software.

Thus, even though you would not want to modify the meta-to-`mod1` association, you are free to modify what constitutes the meta key in one of two ways: (1) by having some other key generate the `Meta_L` (or `Meta_R`) keysym, if `Meta_L` is mapped to `mod1`, or (2) by mapping another keysym to the modifier state *mod1*. As stated in the output from *xmodmap*, each modifier state supports up to three keysyms for this particular X server.

With Sun workstations, for example, the diamond keys are the meta keys. Most X terminals, on the other hand, have PC-style keyboards; hence, <Alt> typically functions as the meta key. For example, consider the modifier mappings for a particular HDS X terminal (its X server):

```
{your system prompt} xmodmap
xmodmap:  up to 2 keys per modifier, (keycodes in parentheses):

shift       Shift_R (0xab),   Shift_L (0xae)
lock        Caps_Lock (0xaf)
control     Control_L (0xb0),   Control_R (0xb3)
mod1        Alt_L (0xac),   Alt_R (0xb2)
mod2
mod3
mod4
mod5        Help (0x7c)
```

Parenthetically, note that the keycodes differ from those for the previous Consortium X server implementation for a Sun workstation. Thus, in general, X software should not depend on keycodes.

This X terminal has a left and right <Alt>, so the keysyms for both are mapped to the modifier state `mod1`. Some workstations, for example, those from Silicon Graphics, have PC-style keyboards as well; thus, the use of <Alt> for meta-key operations is not restricted to X terminals. Although it's convenient to view <Alt> as "the meta key" in certain X environments, the actual situation is that arbitrary keys generate the modifier state `mod1`, which most X clients interpret as the meta key.

11.5 Modifying Key and Mouse Bindings with *xmodmap*

In this section we provide several customizations, some of which may be useful in customizing your X environment. All of these customizations, however, are useful in understanding the utility of *xmodmap*, as well as the keycode, keysym, and modifier concepts.

11.5.1 Adding <Alt> as a Modifier Key

Again consider the modifier mappings for the Consortium X server running on a Sun workstation:

```
{your system prompt} xmodmap
xmodmap:  up to 3 keys per modifier, (keycodes in parentheses):

shift         Shift_L (0x6a),  Shift_R (0x75)
lock          Caps_Lock (0x7e)
control       Control_L (0x53)
mod1          Meta_L (0x7f),  Meta_R (0x81)
mod2          Num_Lock (0x69)
mod3          F13 (0x8),  F18 (0x50),  F20 (0x68)
mod4
mod5
```

Users coming from a PC environment are accustomed to using **<Alt>** for commands, for example, **<Alt>-F** for the file menu, but on a Sun workstation they typically have to use **<Meta>-F**. To add consistency across the PC and X environments, we can simply add **<Alt>** as a modifier key.

xmodmap has several command-line options; see its man-page for a complete description. At present, we are interested in the `-e` option, which processes one of several types of expressions (in string form) that modify the current modifier mappings:

```
xmodmap -e <expression>
```

To add a modifier, use the `add` keyword as follows:

```
{your system prompt} xmodmap -e "add mod1 = Alt_L"
```

We can verify our modification with *xmodmap*:

```
{your system prompt} xmodmap

shift         Shift_L (0x6a),  Shift_R (0x75)
lock          Caps_Lock (0x7e)
control       Control_L (0x53)
mod1          Meta_L (0x7f),  Meta_R (0x81),  Alt_L (0x1a)
mod2          Num_Lock (0x69)
mod3          F13 (0x8),  F18 (0x50),  F20 (0x68)
mod4
```

```
mod5
```

This modification is particularly appropriate in a Motif environment because the menus for *mwm* and other Motif applications often specify "Alt" as part of the keyboard accelerator, even though the meta key is actually the proper key. This inconsistency can be confusing for users new to X, so adding <**Alt**> as a modifier key is a good idea. Given that <**Alt**> is already assigned the `Alt_L` keysym, mapping <**Alt**> to the `Meta_L` keysym would be an inferior solution.

11.5.2 Swapping <Ctrl> and <Caps Lock>

Another popular customization for both PCs and workstations is swapping the <**Ctrl**> and <**Caps Lock**> keys. Many users are still accustomed to a keyboard with <**Ctrl**> adjacent to the "A" key and <**Caps Lock**> on the bottom row, left of the space bar, even though many PC keyboard manufacturers have been inverting this arrangement for several years.

For this customization, the modifications are more involved than simply adding a new modifer mapping. Specifically, you must remove existing modifier mappings, reassign two keysyms, and then add the new modifier mappings. The following actions accomplish the key swap for a particular HDS X terminal:

```
# Reverse Control and Caps Lock keys:
#
xmodmap -e "remove lock = Caps_Lock"
xmodmap -e "remove control = Control_L"
xmodmap -e "keycode 176 = Control_L"
xmodmap -e "keycode 175 = Caps_Lock"
xmodmap -e "add control = Control_L"
xmodmap -e "add lock = Caps_Lock"
```

(These commands are taken from an *.xsession* script that applies similar operations for different X terminals, depending on the manufacturer, which is coded in the X terminal's network name.)

Typically, there are multiple ways to accomplish this type of key swap. Here, we first remove two of the default modifer mappings:

```
xmodmap -e "remove lock = Caps_Lock"
xmodmap -e "remove control = Control_L"
```

Next, we modify the existing keycode-to-keysym mappings:

```
xmodmap -e "keycode 176 = Control_L"
xmodmap -e "keycode 175 = Caps_Lock"
```

To rebind the keysyms we must know the keycodes for this particular's X terminal's <**Ctrl**> and <**Caps Lock**> keys; in Section 11.2 we used *xev* to obtain this information:

```
. . .
KeyPress event, serial 15, synthetic NO, window 0x1c00001,
    root 0x29, subw 0x1c00002, time 4614800, (34,32), root:(112,110),
    state 0x0, keycode 176 (keysym 0xffe3, Control_L), same_screen YES,
    XLookupString gives 0 characters:   ""
. . .
KeyPress event, serial 15, synthetic NO, window 0x1c00001,
    root 0x29, subw 0x1c00002, time 4623830, (34,32), root:(112,110),
    state 0x0, keycode 175 (keysym 0xffe5, Caps_Lock), same_screen YES,
    XLookupString gives 0 characters:   ""
```

Here, we're showing the key-press events *after* performing the reassignments, verifying the intended modifications. Of course, to perform this type of key reassignment, you must determine the keycodes generated for your keyboard.

Once the keysym reassignments are in place, we simply put back the original modifier mappings:

```
xmodmap -e "add control = Control_L"
xmodmap -e "add lock = Caps_Lock"
```

At this point, you should relabel **<Ctrl>** and **<Caps Lock>**, so that an innocent user doesn't go crazy when first using your X terminal or workstation. (You can make key labels from a high-quality mailing label.)

Why couldn't we simply reassign the keysyms (step 2) without first removing and then replacing the modifier mappings? Even though modifier mappings are specified in terms of keysyms, the X server records the mappings as keycodes. Thus, if you perform step 2 alone, pressing **<Caps Lock>** in isolation would in fact send `Control_L` in the key-press event. But, in conjunction with another key, the modifier state would still be set to `lock`.

11.5.3 <Backspace> versus <Delete>

In most X environments, the `BackSpace` keysym is mapped to **<Backspace>** and `Delete` is mapped to **<Delete>**. Some X clients, however, only honor the `Delete` keysym for deleting the previous character. For users coming from a PC environment where **<Backspace>** traditionally performs this task, the lack of support for **<Backspace>** is a real burden. Of course, when **<Backspace>** doesn't work with one X client, for example, *xterm*, there's also an inconsistency with other X clients such as *xedit* (or most other clients built from the widget sets) that do support **<Backspace>** in the traditional manner.

To reassign **<Backspace>** (or any key that assigned the `BackSpace` keysym) so that it generates the `Delete` keysym, simply enter the following command:

```
{your system prompt} xmodmap -e "keysym BackSpace = Delete"
```

Of course, you could include this statement in your start-up script.

As we mentioned in Section 11.5.2, the X server records key bindings in terms of the lower level keycodes, not keysyms. That is, the previous command requests that the X server assign the `Delete` keysym to whatever key is currently assigned the `BackSpace` keysym; it does *not* equate the `BackSpace` and `Delete` keysyms. In particular, in some environments the `BackSpace` keysym could be assigned to multiple keys. Thus, even though the `keysym` keyword supports key (re)assignments at a higher level than `keycode` (you don't have to determine the actual keycodes for a particular keyboard), it is potentially ambiguous and should be used with care.

This customization is a good example of a keysym-level modification, as opposed to the keycode-level modifications that we used to swap **<Ctrl>** and **<Caps Lock>**. Even so, we normally would not recommend this approach to customizing **<Backspace>** and **<Delete>** because it takes place at the server level, potentially affecting every X client, even those that provide higher level mechanisms for customizing character-deletion operations. Also, this customization introduces a discrepancy between the physical key **<Backspace>** and the logical key operation represented by the `Delete` keysym. Compare this type of customization to the translation-based reassignment of **<Delete>** in Section 7.5.1.

11.5.4 Adding Common Keysyms to Unused Keys

Many keyboards have a few keys that virtually no application uses. You may want to reassign these keys to specific keysyms that a few applications support, or to very common keysyms that you'd simply like to have available with multiple keys. We must preface this customization with the warning that these modifications could affect applications in ways that you haven't considered in advance. If you add this type of customization to your start-up script, keep it in mind for several days. If there are unintended side effects to other applications, simply remove it from the script, or make some type of adjustment that resolves any conflicts.

Many X clients interpret **<F1>** as a help key. For this reason, window managers generally do not usurp **<F1>** for their own use. If, however, your window manager has been configured to use **<F1>** for window manager operations, consider assigning the `Help` keysym to an unused key. Many X applications interpret the `Help` keysym as a help key, even though **<Help>** may not exist on your keyboard.

Keyboards often have keys such as **<Pause>**, **<Print Screen>**, and others that are essentially unused, especially in a UNIX environment. To reassign **<Print Screen>** so that it generates the `Help` keysym, add something similar to the following to your start-up script:

```
xmodmap -e "keycode <keycode> = Help"
```

You must replace `<keycode>` with the keycode generated by **<Print Screen>** for your keyboard.

Quite a few X clients support the `Find` keysym. For example, an X text editor might associate a find-next or find-selection operation with this keysym. Hence, if you never use **<Pause>**, you could reassign it so that it generates the `Find` keysym:

```
xmodmap -e "keycode <keycode> = Find"
```

You must replace ⟨keycode⟩ with the keycode generated by your keyboard for the designated key.

11.5.5 Restoring <F11> and <F12> on Sun Workstations

For many Sun workstations, **<F11>** and **<F12>** generate the keysyms SunF36 and SunF37, respectively. If you need to modify these bindings, please verify with *xev* (or some other utility) that they actually exist before attempting to change them. You can make a keysym-level reassignment as follows from a start-up script:

```
xmodmap -e "keysym SunF36 = F11"
xmodmap -e "keysym SunF37 = F12"
```

Or, you can first determine the keycodes for your keyboard in order to make a keycode-level reassignment:

```
xmodmap -e "keycode 16 = F11"
xmodmap -e "keycode 18 = F12"
```

11.5.6 Overruling a Problematic Keysym Mapping

You may discover that an X server maps a common keysym to a particular key that is problematic or illogical in your X environment. For example, with many Sun workstations **<Stop>** and **<Again>** generate the keysyms F11 and F12, respectively. To disable a key mapping, simply assign a rarely-used keysym to that key.

To determine the entire list of allowable keysyms, you must consult the keysym definition file that's shipped with your X implementation (if it's available). Often, this file exists as */usr/include/X11/keysymdef.h*. (Ignore the "XK_" prefixes.) Also, in some cases, your system may have a keysym database, *XKeysymDB*, possibly in a system directory such as */usr/lib/X11*, that includes all or part of the recognized keysyms.

If, for example, a keysym such as "Execute" is unused, or won't conflict with other keysym mappings in your X environment, you can replace problematic keysym mappings as follows:

```
xmodmap -e "keycode 8 = Execute"
xmodmap -e "keycode 10 = Execute"
```

Again, you must use the keycodes generated by your keyboard for the problem key(s).

If you don't have access to the entire set of legal keysyms, you may be able to choose a keysym from the currently assigned keysyms. To view the current keysym mappings, use *xmodmap* with the -pk command-line option:

```
{your system prompt} xmodmap -pk
There are 2 KeySyms per KeyCode; KeyCodes range from 8 to 132.

     KeyCode      Keysym (Keysym) ...
```

```
Value          Value    (Name)   ...

  8            0xffca  (F13)
  9
 10            0xffca  (F13)
 11
 12            0xffbe  (F1)
 13            0xffbf  (F2)
...
...
129            0xffe8  (Meta_R)
130
131
132            0xffab  (KP_Add)  0xffab  (KP_Add)
```

11.5.7 Reversing Pointer Button Bindings

When you press a mouse button, the X server sends an event to the appropriate X client indicating which button was pressed: 1, 2, or 3. In particular, to the X server and X clients there are no left, middle, and right mouse buttons. Normally, however, mouse buttons are assigned from left to right so that mouse button 1 is the leftmost button:

```
{your system prompt} xmodmap -pp
There are 3 pointer buttons defined.

   Physical          Button
   Button            Code
     1                 1
     2                 2
     3                 3
```

For convenience, we often say "click the left mouse button" when we really mean "click mouse button 1."

If you prefer to operate the mouse with your left hand, you may want to modify the direction of the mouse button bindings so that mouse button 1 is located under the left index finger. To reverse the button assignments, put the following in your start-up script:

```
xmodmap -e "pointer = 3 2 1"
```

This command assigns logical mouse button 1 to physical mouse button 3:

```
{your system prompt} xmodmap -pp
xmodmap -pp
There are 3 pointer buttons defined.

   Physical          Button
   Button            Code
     1                 3
     2                 2
```

```
          3                        1
```

(Don't forget to click right when the documentation says to click left!)

The man-page for *xmodmap* provides additional customization examples, as well as complete description of *xmodmap*'s command-line options.

12

Window Managers

This chapter describes various customizations for three popular window managers: *mwm*, *olwm*, and *twm*.

12.1 The Window Manager's Role

As we've mentioned, the window manager is responsible for decorating and managing the top-level windows for X clients. The level and type of decoration varies considerably among window managers. With many window managers, you can set a resource that controls the level of window decoration. For example, minimal decoration could include nothing more than a window border, whereas maximal decoration typically includes a title bar, an application menu, an icon button, and resize handles.

Window decoration is more than decorative. That is, it often provides convenient short-cuts for common functions, for example, resizing a window. The disadvantage of customizing your window manager for minimal window decoration is that you must select window manager operations from a background menu, for example, the "Resize" entry, and then click on the target window. Most users prefer the more direct approach allowing you simply to stretch the window's dimensions with the mouse.

We should mention a special type of application window that receives no window manager decoration, regardless of the level of decoration you've requested for application windows. For the record, the technical term for this type of decoration-free window is an *override-redirect window*; we prefer to call them, for lack of a better term, *lightweight windows*. Applications sometimes employ lightweight windows for transient dialog boxes (even though style guides discourage their use), because they can significantly reduce network overhead.

In general, the term *transient window*, or *transient dialog*, describes a window that requires an immediate response, after which it disappears. Applications employ transient windows for warning dialogs, work-in-progress dialogs, and so on. Transient windows often have less-than-maximal window decoration, for example, no iconify or maximize buttons. Your window manager may provide an X resource for transient windows; *mwm*, for example, supports the resource *transientDecoration*.

Even though we've characterized the window manager as a provider of window decoration, users often still view window decoration as something that belongs to the application—it does not. In some cases, when dialog boxes are slow to appear, it's because the window manager provides extensive decoration, involving the dynamic creation of many small subwindows. In this sense, activating a so-called pop-up dialog involves much more than the name implies.

Most window managers *reparent* an application's top-level windows. To decorate an application window, the window manager must surround it with numerous windows that implement the title bar, resize handles, and other decoration. Yet, to the user, this assemblage must behave as a unit—the high-level perception of the application window. The most logical way to handle the window decoration process is to create a new top-level window (child of the root window), and then create the window decoration (windows) and configure the application window as children of this new window.

In this manner, an application window starts out as a child of the root window (having no grandparent), but the window manager dynamically reparents it, making it a grandchild of the root window. This laborious process occurs every time an application creates a top-level window, and it is a significant contributor to network bandwidth and memory overhead. With a stand-alone workstation for which the network is simply a local communication pathway, network-intensive operations are fairly insignificant. On the other hand, when an X client's display is at a remote location or there is a significant shortage of memory for X server resources (pixmaps and windows), overall system performance may be quite sluggish. In this case, you may want to consider a relatively economical window manager such as *twm*.

12.2 Starting and Terminating the Window Manager

In Section 2.4 we described a hypothetical start-up script for either *xdm* or *xinit*:

```
<command to start a window manager>   &
<command to start an on-screen clock>   &
<command to start a command window>   &
<command to start a command window>
```

Here, the window manager is started as a background process and the last command window is started in the foreground. When you exit the foreground command window, the script completes and the X session terminates.

Some users like to switch window managers from time to time. With this arrangement, you can terminate the window manager and start another window manager at any time. If your X environment is properly configured, there is nothing wrong with this approach. In particular, the X session is uninterrupted, although the window decoration disappears until you start the alternate window manager. The only danger with this approach is that it's possible in some environments to lose the keyboard focus when you terminate the window manager, preventing you from entering a command to start another window manager, and from exiting X from the command window.

Because the command window terminates the X session, the window manager menu's exit entry should be "Exit *<window manager>*", where *<window manager>* is the name of your window manager, not "Exit X".

In general, you shouldn't trust window managers to the extent of having unsaved work for any application when you terminate one window manager to start another. With one particular window manager, for example, if there are errors in its configuration file, attempting to restart it kills the entire X environment, including all X clients, culminating in a core dump in your home directory. Save often, especially when experimenting with window managers.

If you prefer to terminate X by terminating the window manager, the window manager should be started last in the start-up script:

```
<command to start an on-screen clock>   &
<command to start a command window>   &
<command to start a command window>   &
<command to start a window manager>
```

In this case, the window manager menu's exit entry should be something similar to "Exit X" or "Exit X/mwm", in order to reflect the more significant task, namely, terminating the X environment. Although you don't have the luxury of switching among window managers with this approach, it is the most intuitive one for many users.

12.3 The Motif Window Manager

mwm, the Motif window manager [OSF, 1992a], is, perhaps, the most powerful, most enjoyable, and most configurable window manager (see Figure 12.1). One of its best features is that it makes any application very accessible, even when the desktop is quite crowded. If any portion of an application window's border area is visible, you can simply click on the resize border to raise that window to the top of the stack. In the default configuration, the resize borders are quite wide, thus, raising a window is almost effortless. In contrast, with some window managers, you must click on the title area, or on a resize corner, to bring an application window forward.

Currently, there are several window manager implementations based on the Motif style guide [OSF, 1992b]. In general, their behavior and operations differ in certain ways from *mwm*. Moreover, because *mwm* is distributed in source code form to many workstation and third-party software vendors, you can expect subtle differences in *mwm* in different X environments.

Each *mwm* vendor is responsible for correcting a variety of errors. For example, *mwm* releases as recent as 1.1.4 failed to follow the Motif Programmer's Reference [OSF, 1992a] and the ICCCM with respect to the "Close" operation in the application menu. The Motif widget set provides a mechanism for overriding these errors, but this approach assumes that all X clients are Motif-based applications.

The preferred solution is to fix the original error(s) so that *mwm*'s "Close" operation conforms to the ICCCM and the programmer's reference, and is consistent with other window managers such as *olwm*, *swm*, and *twm*. HP and IBM have corrected these errors for their *mwm* distribution in their X environments, but several other vendors have not.

12.3.1 X Resources versus the Configuration File

Many of *mwm*'s characteristics are configured with X resources. The man-page for *mwm* describes each X resource, and the number of resources is quite large. The instance and class names are *mwm* and *Mwm*, respectively (or *vuewm* and *Vuewm* with VUE). Thus, you can choose from a variety of X resource repositories for system-wide and user-local configuration. Chapters 6 and 7 describe the resource-processing strategies for X clients. As with other X clients, one of the most convenient locations for personal customizations is the class file (in this case, *Mwm*) in each user's home directory. Of course, you can modify the location with the environment variable XUSERFILESEARCHPATH.

Also, note that in some situations XUSERFILESEARCHPATH may be set so that class files in the home directory are not recognized. To remedy this situation, set XUSERFILE-SEARCHPATH to include <home-directory>/%N; that is, append this colon-separated value to the current setting. For example, if your home directory is "/home/mary", you would append :/home/mary/%N to the current value of XUSERFILESEARCHPATH.

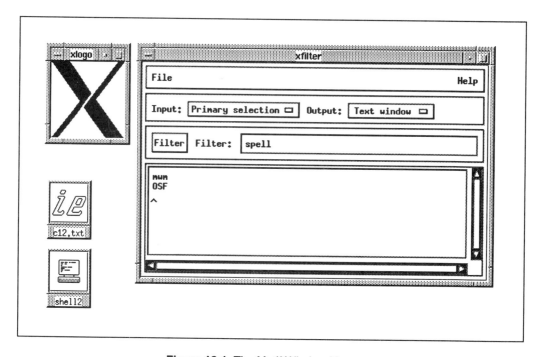

Figure 12.1 The Motif Window Manager

12.3.2 *mwm*'s Configuration File

For some configuration options, an X resource specification would be quite awkward, for example, defining *mwm*'s root menu. For this reason, *mwm* reads a variety of customizations from the file specified by the *configFile* resource. Most users do *not* set this resource, so that *mwm* chooses the filename based on a built-in strategy.

If *configFile* is not set, or the specified file doesn't exist, *mwm* checks for certain default configuration files. To support multiple language environments, *mwm* includes the value of the environment variable LANG in the search path. The following locations are searched until there is a match or the list is exhausted:

1. *$HOME/$LANG/.mwmrc*
2. *$HOME/.mwmrc*
3. */usr/lib/X11/$LANG/system.mwmrc*
4. */usr/lib/X11/system.mwmrc*

Most users copy *system.mwmrc* to *.mwmrc* in their home directories and customize *mwm* from *.mwmrc*. (With VUE, copy */usr/vue/config/sys.vuewmrc* to *$HOME/.vue/vuewmrc*.)

Unless your system administrator has made changes to *system.mwmrc*, it will be unsatisfactory because the root menu, for whatever reason, does not include an entry for terminating the window manager. *system.mwmrc* defines the following root menu:

```
. . .
Menu RootMenu
{
    "Root Menu"         f.title
    "New Window"        f.exec "xterm &"
    "Shuffle Up"        f.circle_up
    "Shuffle Down"      f.circle_down
    "Refresh"           f.refresh
    no-label            f.separator
    "Restart..."        f.restart
}
. . .
```

Thus, when you press mouse button 1 over the root window, you should get the menu in Figure 12.2.

Virtually everyone should modify the root menu definition in *.mwmrc* to include "Quit mwm" or "Quit X / mwm", depending on your start-up script (see Section 12.2):

```
. . .
Menu RootMenu
{
    "Root Menu"         f.title
    "New Window"        f.exec "xterm &"
    no-label            f.separator
    "Shuffle Up"        f.circle_up
    "Shuffle Down"      f.circle_down
```

```
      "Refresh"              f.refresh
      no-label               f.separator
      "Restart..."           f.restart
      "Quit X / mwm"         f.quit_mwm
}
...
```

For this menu, the first component of each entry is the label and the second component is the *mwm* function that's associated with that entry: f.<function>. When there is no label, as with a separator item, an empty string or an arbitrary symbol such as no-label serves as a placeholder. The man-page for *mwm* includes a complete description for each window manager function.

A common customization is using the function f.menu to define pull-right, or cascading, menus. For example, the previous menu contains a mix of window-manipulation functions, restart and terminate functions, and one f.exec item that starts an *xterm* window. Most users prefer to organize common functionality into submenus, so that a class of operations remains hidden, except when needed. This approach minimizes the size of the root menu.

To illustrate f.menu, consider a subordinate menu for common commands, such as starting an *xterm* window, a calculator application, and so on. First, we add menu entries for invoking two submenus:

```
Menu RootMenu
{
      "Root Menu"            f.title
      "Shuffle Up"           f.circle_up
      "Shuffle Down"         f.circle_down
      "Refresh"              f.refresh
      "Applications"         f.menu ApplicationMenu
      "Root Background"      f.menu BackgroundMenu
      no-label               f.separator
```

Figure 12.2 *mwm*'s Root Menu

```
    "Restart..."        f.restart
    "Quit X / mwm"      f.quit_mwm
}
```

The menu name following f.menu connects the parent and child menus. We've put the submenus after root menu entries that might be executed on a frequent basis.

Next, we define the application menu:

```
Menu ApplicationMenu
{
    "Applications"      f.title
    "Command Window"    f.exec "xterm &"
    "Text Editor"       f.exec "ie &"
    "Calculator"        f.exec "xcalc -rpn &"
    "Analog Clock"      f.exec "xclock -g 150x150+5+5 &"
    "Digital Clock"     f.exec "xclock -digital -g 200x35+5+5 &"
    "Manual Pages"      f.exec "xman &"
    "Screen lock"       f.exec "xlock.logo &"
}
```

Here, you would substitute your favorite X clients, possibly further broken down by submenus for clock applications, command windows, and so on. This menu is shown in Figure 12.3.

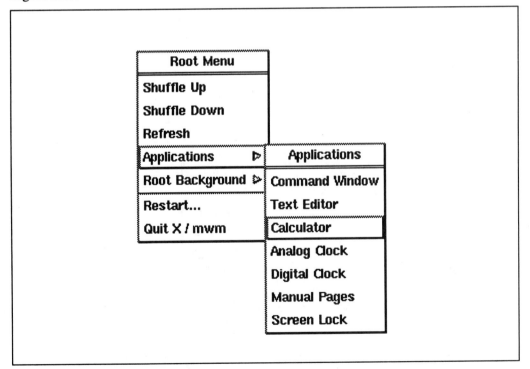

Figure 12.3 An Application Menu for *mwm*'s Root Menu

Because we sometimes work in a variety of lighting conditions (for example, at home on weekends where the light varies greatly throughout the day), we also define a menu for controlling the root window background (see Figure 12.4). In poor lighting conditions, especially with monochrome gas-plasma and LCD screens, the mouse pointer cursor can be difficult to see. From this menu we can instantly tile the root window using one of several patterns that we've created with *bitmap* and stored in the same local directory as our custom application icons, as well as bitmaps from */usr/include/X11/bitmap*:

```
Menu BackgroundMenu
{
    "Background"        f.title
    "Gray Mono"         f.exec "xsetroot -bitmap \
                        /home/jsmith/icon/graytile.bit &"
    "Gray 2Dot"         f.exec "xsetroot -bitmap \
                        /home/jsmith/icon/2pixtile.bit &"
    "Gray 3Dot"         f.exec "xsetroot -bitmap \
                        /home/jsmith/icon/3pixtile.bit &"
    "Gray 4Dot"         f.exec "xsetroot -bitmap \
                        /home/jsmith/icon/4pixtile.bit &"
    "Root Weave"        f.exec "xsetroot -def &"
    "Cross Weave"       f.exec "xsetroot -bitmap \
                          /usr/include/X11/bitmaps/cross_weave &"
```

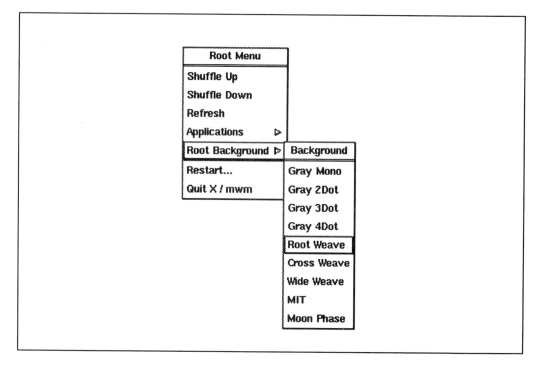

Figure 12.4 A Desktop Background Menu for *mwm*'s Root Menu

```
      "Wide Weave"          f.exec "xsetroot -bitmap \
                              /usr/include/X11/bitmaps/wide_weave &"
      "MIT"                 f.exec "xsetroot -bitmap \
                              /usr/include/X11/bitmaps/mensetmanus &"
      "Moon Phase"          f.exec "xphoon &"
}
```

The bitmap associated with the "Gray Mono" entry is described in Section 10.8. For variety we've also included the popular moon-phase program, *xphoon*, available from various X distribution sites in the *contrib* directory. Of course, for color environments, we typically use a solid background.

Note that the default menu, as defined in *system.mwmrc*, does not include a complete path specification for the *xterm* entry:

```
Menu RootMenu
{
      "Root Menu"       f.title
      "New Window"      f.exec "xterm &"
      . . .
}
```

In some environments, however, you may have to include the complete path specification, or take steps to ensure that the shell environment started by f.exec includes the proper search path. By default, *mwm* executes a command associated with f.exec within a Bourne shell [*sh(1)*]. You can set environment variables, however, that request *csh(1)* instead; see the man-page for *mwm*. Note that the X client executes within a *noninteractive* shell. Thus, if your X clients aren't executing, check your *.profile* [for *sh(1)*] or *.cshrc* [for *csh(1)*] to make sure that the search path for executables is being set properly for noninteractive shells.

In addition to the root menu, *mwm* supplies a menu for each application window:

```
Menu DefaultWindowMenu MwmWindowMenu
{
      "Restore"     _R   Meta<Key>F5  f.normalize
      "Move"        _M   Meta<Key>F7  f.move
      "Size"        _S   Meta<Key>F8  f.resize-
      "Minimize"    _n   Meta<Key>F9  f.minimize
      "Maximize"    _x   Meta<Key>F6  f.maximize
      "Lower"       _L   Meta<Key>F3  f.lower
      no-label                        f.separator
      "Close"       _C   Meta<Key>F4  f.kill
}
```

The second and third columns specify mnemonics and accelerators, respectively. You, of course, can modify the mnemonics, accelerators, or functions.

Mnemonics have the format "_<character>"; when a window menu is posted, pressing the specified character selects that menu entry. Accelerators differ in that the specified key sequence selects that menu entry, even when the menu is not posted. To accomplish this feat, window managers must usurp these keystrokes, never delivering them to the application.

The presence of accelerators often causes conflicts for applications that provide their own function key-based accelerators. If this happens, you must redefine the accelerators for either the window manager or the application. A potentially better solution is to remove the window manager's accelerators entirely. Accelerator keys are usually quite valuable in applications, and relatively unimportant in window manager application menus. Most users prefer, for example, to resize a window directly with the mouse instead of initiating the resize operation from the menu. Also, the window menus are more attractive without the accelerators. (HP's VUE includes optional window menus without accelerators.)

We should mention that some *mwm* environments include "Alt" as the modifier in the accelerator key sequence, whereas others specify "Meta". If your X environment supports **<Meta>** instead of **<Alt>**, you may want to modify the menu entries to specify the correct modifier key.

Rather than removing the accelerators from the default menu, it preferable to define a new menu (or see `NoAcceleratorWindowMenu` in **VUE**'s configuration file, *vuewmrc*):

```
Menu NoAccMenu
{
    "Restore"      _R        f.normalize
    "Move"         _M        f.move
    "Size"         _S        f.resize
    "Minimize"     _n        f.minimize
    "Maximize"     _x        f.maximize
    "Lower"        _L        f.lower
    no-label                 f.separator
    "Close"        _C        f.kill
}
```

Thus, both menus are now available and you can choose between them simply by modifying the value of the *windowMenu* resource:

```
Mwm*windowMenu:                        NoAccMenu
```

Also, with both menus available, you have the option of client-specific configuration for the type of application window menu (see Section 12.3.4).

Next, consider the "Close" entry in the window menu. With certain *mwm*s, and *mwm*-variants, the "Close" behavior is noncompliant. Although the man-page and the Motif Programmer's Reference [OSF, 1992a] state that `f.kill` follows the ICCCM guidelines for terminating X clients [Rosenthal, 1992], in many *mwm* environments it simply does not. For these "broken" *mwm*s, beware of *mwm*'s "Close" button, especially for terminating applications that have unsaved changes.

Another customization option is modifying the key and button bindings, both of which post the window menu among other tasks. Consider the default key bindings:

```
Keys DefaultKeyBindings
{
    Shift<Key>Escape             icon|window           f.post_wmenu
    Meta<Key>space               icon|window           f.post_wmenu
    Meta<Key>Tab                 root|icon|window      f.next_key
    Meta Shift<Key>Tab           root|icon|window      f.prev_key
    Meta<Key>Escape              root|icon|window      f.next_key
    Meta Shift<Key>Escape        root|icon|window      f.prev_key
    Meta Ctrl Shift<Key>exclam   root|icon|window      f.set_behavior
    Meta<Key>Down                root|icon|window      f.circle_down
    Meta<Key>Up                  root|icon|window      f.circle_up
    Meta<Key>F6                  window                f.next_key transient
}
```

(These key bindings differ from one third-party *mwm* vendor to the next.) Note that there are two key sequences—within the application window—for posting the window menu. That is, the second field describes the context in which the bindings apply. If any of these bindings interfere with the key bindings for one or more application, and you don't want to modify the application's bindings, one solution is to remove the "window" context for that key binding. To minimize interference, we use a very abbreviated set of key bindings:

```
Keys AlternateKeyBindings
{
    Meta<Key>Down             root|icon|window         f.circle_down
    Meta<Key>Up               root|icon|window         f.circle_up
}
```

The resource *keyBindings* requests these bindings:

```
Mwm*keyBindings:                         AlternateKeyBindings
```

Next, consider the default button bindings:

```
Buttons DefaultButtonBindings
{
    <Btn1Down>   icon|frame   f.raise
    <Btn3Down>   icon|frame   f.post_wmenu
    <Btn3Down>   root         f.menu   RootMenu
!   <Btn1Up>     icon         f.normalize
}
```

These bindings are rather limited. We use the following alternate bindings:

```
Buttons AlternateButtonBindings
{
```

```
        <Btn1Down>       frame|icon        f.raise
        <Btn2Down>       frame|icon        f.lower
        <Btn3Down>       frame|icon        f.post_wmenu
        <Btn3Down>       root              f.menu   RootMenu
        Meta<Btn1Down>   window            f.raise
        Meta<Btn2Down>   window            f.lower
        Meta<Btn3Down>   window            f.move
}
```

To request these bindings, set the *buttonBindings* resource:

```
Mwm*buttonBindings:      AlternateButtonBindings
```

12.3.3 Common X Resources

Typically, users modify *mwm*'s resources at the local level, as described in Section 12.3.1.
The man-page for *mwm* describes many X resources, three of which are demonstrated in the
previous section:

```
Mwm*windowMenu:      NoAccMenu
Mwm*buttonBindings:  AlternateButtonBindings
Mwm*keyBindings:     AlternateKeyBindings
```

Most users have a distinct preference when it comes to keyboard focus policy. With *mwm*,
explicit (often called click-to-type) keyboard focus is the default. Thus, you must explicitly
click mouse button 1 in an application window before it will receive keyboard events. The
advantage of this policy is that if the mouse cursor drifts out of the application window by
accident while you're typing, that window doesn't lose the keyboard focus.

On the other hand, having to click the mouse button before you can type into an application
window is a real disadvantage for "fast users," so it's common to request pointer-based
(often called focus-follows-mouse) keyboard focus:

```
Mwm*keyboardFocusPolicy:  pointer
```

With *mwm*, the entire window border serves as a system of resize handles. The default width
of this border is 10 pixels. Some user prefer a thinner border for aesthetic reasons, but with
anything smaller than 5 pixels it becomes difficult to resize a window quickly. The
following setting provides a border width of 8 pixels:

```
Mwm*resizeBorderWidth:  8
```

In Section 12.1 we mentioned that window managers typically support different levels of
decoration for transient windows. To request less than complete decoration, either specify
each type of decoration explicitly or use a minus sign to suppress a particular type of
decoration:

```
Mwm*transientDecoration:  none
```

```
Mwm*transientDecoration:   all
Mwm*transientDecoration:   border maximize minimize resizeh menu
Mwm*transientDecoration:   border resizeh
Mwm*transientDecoration:   -maximize -minimize -menu
Mwm*transientDecoration:   -maximize
```

In the previous (mutually exclusive) examples, the second and third settings are equivalent, and the fourth and fifth settings are equivalent. Note that menu determines whether or not the menu button is present; it does not inhibit activation of the window menu based on key and mouse bindings. Also, depending on the type of requests made by the X client during start-up operations, you may not be able to request a minimize button for certain transient windows.

There are several icon-related resources. First, users often have a preference for the area of the screen where their icons congregate. For the *iconPlacement* resource, the keywords top, bottom, left, and right in the following interpretation:

```
Mwm*iconPlacement:   <primary-layout> <secondary-layout>
```

For many of the screen shots in this book we've used the following layout:

```
Mwm*iconPlacement:   right top
```

These values indicates the general area of the screen where icons are placed, as well as the orientation. The default values are "left bottom", indicating that icons are arranged from left to right at the bottom of the screen. In contrast, "bottom left" requests that *mwm* arrange icons from bottom to top on the left side of the screen.

If you regularly execute many X clients simultaneously, you probably also iconify many of them to maximize the available screen area. Even so, having a large number of icons can occupy a significant portion of the screen. The solution is to request an icon box, as shown in Figure 12.5:

```
Mwm*useIconBox:   True
```

The best way to control the placement of the icon box is with the *iconBoxGeometry* resource:

```
Mwm*iconBoxGeometry:   -0+0
```

These offsets are analogous to an *iconPlacement* value of "right top". The default location in offsets is +0-0, analogous to an *iconPlacement* value of "left bottom".

12.3.4 Client-specific Resources

One nice feature of *mwm* is its client-specific resources. For this type of resource specification, you should interpose a client name (or class) before the resource:

```
Mwm*<client>*<resource>:   <value>
```

This facility is easily illustrated with client-specific icon specifications. The *useClientIcon* resource controls whether or not *mwm* substitutes your preferred icon for an X client's default icon. If *useClientIcon* is False, *mwm* uses an alternate icon on a client-by-client basis, based on client-specific settings for the *iconImage* resource.

For example, to specify alternate icons for *xcalc* and *xterm*, you could include something similar to the following:

```
Mwm*useClientIcon:      False
Mwm*xcalc*iconImage:    /home/jsmith/icon/xcalc.icon
Mwm*xterm*iconImage:    /home/jsmith/icon/xterm.icon
```

The first resource setting requests that *mwm* honor alternate icons—but only if you specify them. Here, for example, we've specified alternate icons for only two X clients; thus, for other clients such as *xman*, *mwm* will continue to use the client's default icon.

You can use client-specific resource settings to customize, for example, window menus, on a client-by-client basis:

```
Mwm*xterm*windowMenu:   NoAccMenu
```

12.3.5 *mwm* Component Names

For several key components, *mwm* uses the following instance names: client, feedback, icon, and menu. The names are useful in restricting resource settings to a class of components such as dialog boxes. For example, to set the background color for *mwm*'s dialog (feedback) boxes, you would interpose feedback in the normal resource specification:

```
Mwm*feedback*background:   Plum
```

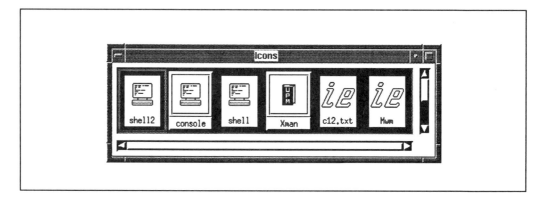

Figure 12.5 *mwm*'s Icon Box

Similarly, you can set distinct background colors for inactive client window frames as well as all menus:

```
Mwm*client*background:   Cornsilk
Mwm*menu*background:     RosyBrown
```

With *mwm*, the number of customizations is virtually infinite; see the *mwm* man-page for more information.

12.4 The OPEN LOOK Window Manager

olwm, the OPEN LOOK Window Manager, is used primarily in Sun environments as part of OpenWindows [Sun Microsystems, 1992]. Overall, there are significant differences between the OpenWindows and Consortium X environments: X-related files occupy different filesystem locations; certain X utilities from the Consortium X distribution aren't available; OpenWindows applications are built with an alternative toolkit, namely, XView [Heller, 1991b]; an alternative copy and paste strategy; and others. Also, most of the X clients shipped with OpenWindows, including all XView-based applications, conform to the OPEN LOOK user interface.

Despite these differences between OpenWindows and other X environments, *olwm* is one of the most compliant window managers with respect to theICCCM. For example, *olwm* properly handles delete-window operations from the application menu. In terms of window manager functionality, *olwm* is vendor-neutral. For example, if your workstation includes *olwm* and the requisite shared libraries, you can run *olwm* with the Consortium X distribution, as well as with applications based on the Athena and Motif widget sets and other custom X toolkits. Of course, in this heterogeneous environment *olwm* will have an OPEN LOOK user interface, while other X clients exhibit the Athena and Motif look and feel. The point, however, is that these X clients all work together because they are X clients.

12.4.1 The OPEN LOOK User Interface

Figure 12.6 presents a portion of an OpenWindows desktop that includes two applications from the OpenWindows deskset, *snapshot* and *textedit*. Both of the X clients conform to the OPEN LOOK user interface. Likewise, *olwm*'s dialog boxes and menus exhibit the same look and feel; see Figure 12.7. We often use OpenWindows applications in our discussions of the OPEN LOOK user interface because OpenWindows is the most common OPEN LOOK-based X environment.

OPEN LOOK-based applications have a 3-D appearance on a color screen, but the OPEN LOOK 3-D effect is more subtle than Motif's. When reduced to monochrome (for this book), the OPEN LOOK 3-D effect essentially disappears. In contrast, Motif provides distinct 3-D designs for monochrome and color screen, both of which are quite successful in rendering a 3-D appearance.

Although trade publications often focus on look-and-feel issues, especially the differences between OPEN LOOK and Motif, we like to think that most users are quite flexible. Are users overwhelmed, or even noticeably inconvenienced, by the inconsistencies between these two user interface styles? Virtually all hardware vendors continue to ship all or a subset of the

Athena-based X clients from the X Consortium, introducing a third user-interface style. It has been our experience that the ongoing inconsistencies in command-line arguments among X clients, inconsistencies and outright failures in ICCCM compliance by many X clients, and a nagging command-line predisposition present more problems for new users than look-and-feel inconsistencies.

In any case, there are many similarities. For example, both Motif and OPEN LOOK *suggest* that applications use mouse button 3 for pop-up menus. Motif applications often have a primary menu bar with pull-down menus, activated by mouse button 1. OPEN LOOK applications such as *textedit* (see Figure 12.6) typically have a row of menu buttons for activating pull-down menus. Although the menu buttons are not visually connected, as with Motif's menu bar, they, in effect, constitute a menu bar.

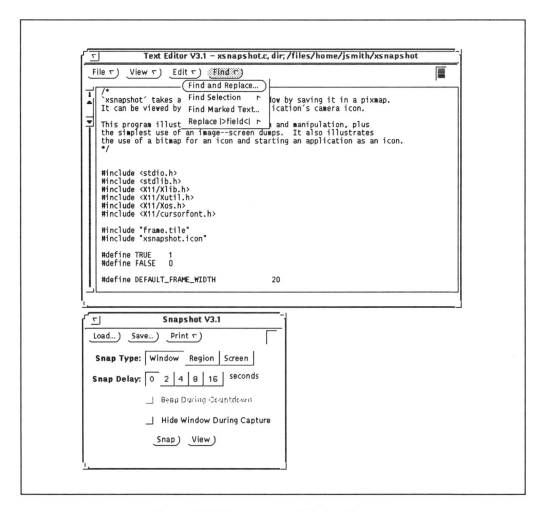

Figure 12.6 The OPEN LOOK Window Manager

Much has been made of the fact that with OpenWindows applications mouse button 3 (often called the "menu" button) activates pull-down menus, which is deemed inconsistent with Athena and Motif applications. These criticisms, however, overlook the fact that the use of mouse button 3 for both pop-up and pull-down menus is a logical, user-interface design decision—many users like this consistency. Similarly some critics have protested the OPEN LOOK behavior whereby mouse button 1 (often called the "select" button) selects the default menu option, instead of simply activating the menu. These complaints continue despite the fact that OpenWindows provides an X resource, *SelectDisplaysMenu*, for requesting the more common Athena- and Motif-like pull-down menu behavior with mouse button 1.

12.4.2 Customizing *olwm*

olwm's approach to customization differs from other X clients. There is no configuration file that's equivalent to *mwm*'s *.mwmrc*. You can customize the root menu (often called the workspace menu), but you cannot customize application menus with respect to mnemonics, accelerators, menu functionality, and so on from a configuration file.

Except for the root menu definition, *olwm* is configured via X resources. The man-page for *olwm* documents an extensive set of X resources, as well as various command-line options.

12.4.3 *olwm*'s Root Menu

As with *mwm*, an alternate root menu is defined in a file. The following locations are searched until there is a match, or the list is exhausted:

1. *$OLWMMENU*
2. *$HOME/.openwin-menu.<locale>*
3. *$HOME/.openwin-menu*

If there is no definition for the root menu, *olwm* uses a small built-in menu. Also, *<locale>* is the language locale defined by your system, if any. We should reiterate that even though the second and third filenames contain "openwin" in their names, *olwm* can be used with other X distributions, for example, the Consortium X server. In fact, the built-in menu's command-window entry invokes *xterm*, not OpenWindows' *cmdtool*.

One nice feature is that recent versions of *olwm* automatically/dynamically update the root menu. That is, *olwm* monitors changes to the menu definition file, redefining the root menu each time you update this file. The feature is very convenient when you're configuring the root menu, but the computing overhead is significant. Once you've configured your root menu, you can turn off menu-file monitoring with the X resource *AutoReReadMenuFile*.

To define a custom root menu, open a menu file—most users simply place their menu definition in *$HOME/.openwin-menu*. The format differs greatly from that used by *mwm*. With *mwm*, the `f.<function>` mechanism associates menu entries with menu actions, which is applicable to the root menu as well as window menus. In contrast, *olwm* defines a number of keywords such as `TITLE`, `REFRESH`, `MENU`, and others; see the man-page for a complete description of menu keywords. The number of operations available through *olwm*'s menu keywords is significantly less than with *mwm*'s window manager functions.

The following menu definition creates a very simple root menu, shown in Figure 12.7:

```
"Root Menu"          TITLE
"Refresh"            REFRESH
"Properties..."      PROPERTIES
"Command Window"     xterm
"  "                 NOP
"Restart"            RESTART
"Exit X..."          EXIT
"Root Menu"          END
```

There is no menu separator function, but you can use a null entry, signified by the NOP keyword, to create space between item groups.

Warning: The label field for NOP menu entries should contain at least one blank; otherwise, the menu definition is incorrect. *olwm*, in effect, ignores incorrect menu definitions.

Consider the menu entry for invoking a command window:

```
...
"Command Window"     xterm
...
```

If the keyword field contains anything other than a keyword, it is interpreted as an external command. Unlike with *mwm*'s f.exec function, commands should not be enclosed in double quotes, and a trailing ampersand should not be included because commands are automatically started as background processes.

The following menu definition illustrates submenus, as well as variety of external commands, some of which have command-line options:

```
"Root Menu"     TITLE
"Refresh"       REFRESH
Applications    MENU
```

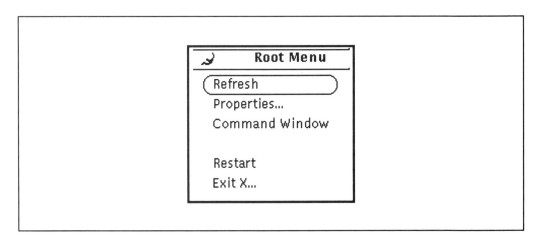

Figure 12.7 *olwm*'s Root Menu

```
        "Command Window"      DEFAULT xterm
        "Text Editor"         ie
        "Calculator"          xcalc -rpn
        "Analog Clock"        xclock -g 150x150+5+5
        "Digital Clock"       xclock -digital -g 200x35+5+5
        "Manual Pages"        xman
        "Screen Lock"         xlock
Applications     END PIN
"Root Background"    MENU
        "Root Weave"          DEFAULT xsetroot -def
        "Cadet Blue"          xsetroot -solid CadetBlue
        "Gray"                xsetroot -solid Gray
        "Lavender"            xsetroot -solid Lavender
        "Peach Puff"          xsetroot -solid PeachPuff
        "Powder Blue"         xsetroot -solid PowderBlue
        "Rosy Brown"          xsetroot -solid RosyBrown
        "Salmon"              xsetroot -solid Salmon
        "Sky Blue"            xsetroot -solid SkyBlue
        "Tomato"              xsetroot -solid Tomato
"Root Background"    END PIN
"Properties..."  PROPERTIES
" "                  NOP
"Restart"        RESTART
"Exit X..."      EXIT
"Root Menu"      END
```

OPEN LOOK supports pinnable, that is, sticky, pop-up windows. Clicking or releasing on a menu's pin icon, "pins the menu." To make a submenu pinnable, simply add the keyword PIN following the END keyword for that menu:

```
"Root Background"    MENU
   ...
"Root Background"    END PIN
```

Figure 12.8 demonstrates this menu system with the root menu and each submenu pinned to the root window.

For both submenus, we've included the DEFAULT keyword before the first menu entry. There can be one DEFAULT keyword per menu; it can be associated with any menu entry, not necessarily the first entry. If a submenu definition includes DEFAULT, this entry is chosen when you select the parent menu entry for that submenu instead of explicitly activating the submenu. For this reason, it's a good idea to choose logical, nondestructive operations for default menu entries.

We should point out that the OpenWindows "Properties" window allows you to set the root window (workspace) color from a palette, or with sliders that vary the brightness, hue, and saturation. The "Apply" button saves this color in *$HOME/.Xdefaults* using the "#<red><green><blue>" format (see Chapter 9):

```
OpenWindows.WorkspaceColor:  #98bfbf
```

Thus, each time you restart OpenWindows, *olwm* uses this custom workspace color. If, from root-window boredom, you change the color by selecting one of the entries in the "Root Background" menu, you can restore the original root color by selecting "Apply" in the "Properties" window. Alternatively, you could create one or more personal colors and color names from the "Properties" window by (1) choosing a color, (2) saving this color to *$HOME/.Xdefaults*, and (3) entering the color from *$HOME/.Xdefaults* as a "Root Background" menu entry:

```
"Root Background"    MENU
    . . .
    "Earthy Green"   xsetroot -solid \#98bfbf
    . . .
"Root Background"    END PIN
```

Note the use of "\" to force the proper interpretation of "#" in the "#<red><green><blue>" format.

Our example demonstrates the more common menu keywords, but there are several others. See *olwm*'s man-page for a complete listing of menu keywords and operations.

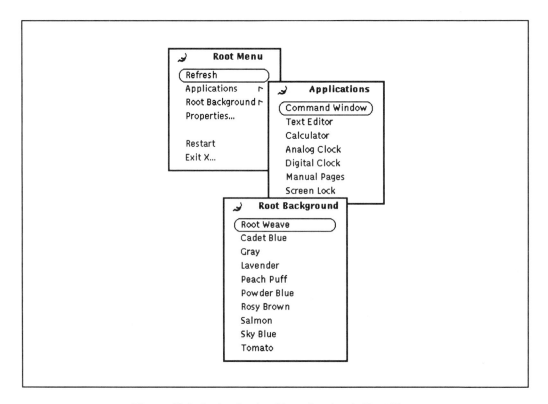

Figure 12.8 An Application Menu for *olwm*'s Root Menu

12.4.4 Common X Resources

Although *olwm* is less configurable in many ways than *mwm*, the set of X resources is quite extensive. You can specify a default icon, a language locale, the window manager's beep propensity, and so on; *olwm* provides several configurations that are not available with *mwm*. In this section, we mention several of *olwm*'s X resources.

olwm's naming convention for X resources is somewhat nonstandard. Generally, the application name should be "olwm". Because *olwm* is the standard window manager in Sun's OpenWindows environment, for consistency with OpenWindows X clients you can set selected X resources with the name "OpenWindows". (With this approach, common resources apply to *olwm* and other OpenWindows applications.) The OpenWindows "Properties" window uses the latter name when it writes resource specifications to *.Xdefaults*. Generally, however, the preferred strategy is to use "olwm*<resource specification>" for setting *olwm* X resources outside an OpenWindows environment. Also, note that the first character in resource names is not lowercase.

Like *mwm*, *olwm* uses the click-to-type keyboard focus model unless you specify otherwise. The documentation sometimes refers to this policy as the *click-to-focus input focus mode*. You choose this model with the resource *SetInput* and the resource value `select`:

```
olwm.SetInput:   select
```

If you prefer the focus-follows-mouse approach, use the resource value `followmouse`:

```
olwm.SetInput:   followmouse
```

olwm offers less configurability than *mwm* with respect to transient window decoration. For transient windows, window decoration is either present or absent. You cannot remove selected title bar components, as with *mwm*, because *olwm* provides most of its functionality through window menus. To disable the (default) window decoration, set the *TransientsTitled* resource to `False`.

```
olwm.TransientsTitled:   false
```

Alternatively, you can specify minimal window decoration for a list of X clients with *MinimalDecor*:

```
olwm.MinimalDecor:   xclock
```

Another transient window-related resource is *KeepTransientsAbove*. Enabling this resource prevents pop-up windows from being hidden by accident behind primary application windows:

```
olwm.KeepTransientsAbove:   true
```

You can set the screen area where icons congregate with *IconLocation*:

```
olwm.IconLocation:   top-rl
```

The component preceding the hyphen is `top`, `bottom`, `left`, or `right`, with the obvious meanings. The component following the hyphen is `lr`, `rl`, `tb`, or `bt`, for left-to-right, right-to-left, top-to-bottom, or bottom-to-top arrangements, respectively.

Like *mwm*, *olwm* simultaneously supports two selection styles for menus: drag-and-release and click. The resource *ClickMoveThreshold* determines the distance (in pixels) that the mouse pointer must move to activate the drag-and-release approach to selecting menu entries. You may want to increase this value beyond the default value, 5 pixels, if you always use click-style menu operations:

```
olwm.ClickMoveThreshold:   10
```

ClickMoveThreshold should not be confused with *DragRightDistance*, which determines the number of pixels that you must move the mouse pointer to the right within a menu entry before a submenu (a pull-right, or cascade, menu) is activated. This resource applies to the drag-and-release mode of menu entry selection. Modifying the default value of 100 to, say, 50, results in quick-responding menus:

```
olwm.DragRightDistance: 50
```

Another nice resource is *EdgeMoveThreshold*, which determines a window's "reluctance to travel" beyond the edge of the screen. Increasing this value beyond the default value of 10 makes it easier to position a window quickly and exactly at the screen's edge.

```
olwm.EdgeMoveThreshold:   20
```

Lastly, we mentioned *SelectDisplaysMenu* in Section 12.4.1. If you set this resource to `True`, clicking mouse button 1 activates pull-down menus. *olwm*'s root menu is, of course, a pop-up menu, and this resource is not really useful with pop-up menus. It does apply, however, to the pull-down menu associated with the menu button in *olwm*'s "Properties" window. Otherwise, it is useful primarily as an OpenWindows resource for X clients such as *filemgr*, *textedit*, and others.

See the *olwm* man-page for a complete discussion of X resources.

12.5 The Tab Window Manager

At one time, *uwm* (universal window manager) was the standard window manager shipped with the Consortium X distribution. *uwm* is a simple window manager; it provides no title bar, no resize handles, no iconify button—no window decoration. Operations such as moving and resizing windows are initiated from the root menu. The Consortium X distribution now includes *twm* as a replacement for *uwm*; the latter window manager is still available as part of the supplemental distribution of user-contributed X software.

twm is, perhaps, the most successful (based on its continued popularity) of the early X window managers. It's common to view *twm* and subsequent window managers as intermediate steps toward some ultimate window manager, but not everyone wants the advances provided by *mwm*, *olwm*, and others. *twm* provides several features that are not available with *uwm*, and, following this progression, *mwm* provides several features that are not available with *twm*. Regardless of whether or not you view the progression to larger, more feature-filled window managers as "advancements," both *uwm* and *twm* represent significant early contributions to a now large base of X software.

twm was originally written by Tom LaStrange (Tom's window manager). It is now called the *tab window manager*, based on a configuration option that allows the title bar to be reduced to a tab. This feature gives a *twm* window a unique appearance, similar to a file folder, but it is generally unuseful. For most users, manipulating windows from the title area is a highly desirable feature. Reducing the size of the title bar makes window manipulation more difficult, especially with a crowded desktop.

12.5.1 *twm*'s Simplicity

twm is simpler than *mwm* and *olwm* in several ways. First, its appearance is two-dimensional (see Figure 12.9). Without question, *mwm*'s three-dimensional effect is very attractive. Hence, if you prefer 3-D window managers, it's unlikely that you'll consider *twm* as an alternative. If, on the other hand, your eyes prefer less complex user interfaces, consider *twm*.

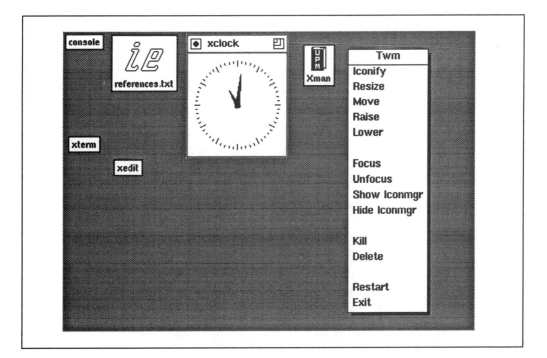

Figure 12.9 The Tab Window Manager

twm does not automatically organize icons in one particular area of the screen. When you first iconify an X client under *twm*, the icon is positioned at the point on the root window where you clicked the icon button; hence, the icon appears near the top-left corner of the application window. Unless you manually move them to another area, icons often become hidden by other application windows. If you do move them to a particular screen area, you may have to reposition them if you restart *twm*.

Another consideration is that *twm* provides no default, standard-sized icons. For applications such as *xedit* and *xterm* that provide no client icon, *twm* creates an minimal-sized icon containing the application name. If you prefer icons with graphical images, you can create and then define icons on a per-application basis, as described in Section 12.5.4. Regardless of the size of the actual icon image, *twm* will enlarge the icon to accommodate the icon label (recommended and supplied by the application). In Figure 12.10, even though the icon image is constant, the icons differ in size for two distinct sessions of the X editor *ie*; *twm* expands the icon to include the filename supplied by the X client.

Another difference with respect to more recent window managers is that *twm* provides no window menu in its default configuration. Hence, operations that cannot be performed from the title bar, must be done in two stages: (1) select the operation from the root menu and (2) click on the target window. (All window manager operations are performed in this fashion with *uwm*.) For example, to terminate an X client via the window manager, you must choose the "Delete" root menu entry and then click on the "victim" window.

twm is a relatively lightweight window manager, developed in a bygone era when programmers were genuinely concerned with the efficiency of an application and the overall drain on system resources. Users often complain about the increasing-taxing memory requirement of current X applications. Despite these complaints, however, users rarely demand or support applications and developers who strive to develop efficient software. If your workstation is straining under the load of huge, inefficient applications, consider *twm*.

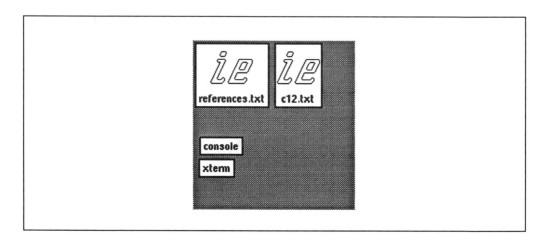

Figure 12.10 *twm*'s Default Icons

12.5.2 Keyboard Focus Policy

twm's default focus style is focus-follows-mouse. When you move the mouse cursor from one application window to the next, *twm* highlights the border of the window that currently has the keyboard focus, as well as the interior of the title bar. In Figure 12.11, *xclipboard* has the keyboard focus.

If you want the key events to be delivered to a specific window, regardless of the location of the pointer (the explicit focus policy), simply select the "Focus" entry from *twm*'s root menu (Figure 12.9). In this mode, *twm* highlights the title area of the focus window, but not it's border. To return to pointer-based keyboard focus, choose the "Unfocus" entry.

12.5.3 Title Bar and Root Menu Functionality

twm's title bar contains an iconify button (on the left side) and a resize button (on the right side). There are no resize handles along a window's border for dynamic resizing in any direction. You must resize a window by pressing the resize button (or choosing the "Resize" menu entry) and stretching the title bar upward or to the right. With this approach, you may have to move the window first in order to create space in the direction of the resize operation.

The title bar also manipulates a window's stacking order. In the default configuration, clicking mouse button 1 raises the window to the top of the stack; clicking mouse button 2 lowers the window. As with resize operations, stack operations are also available via the root menu.

The "Show Iconmgr" and "Hide Iconmgr" entries control the presence or absence of *twm*'s icon manager, which is quite different from that of *mwm* (see Figure 12.12). Entries having a small X logo to the left of the application name represent applications in icon form. You can iconify or deiconify an application by clicking on the appropriate entry. Unlike with *mwm*'s icon manager, however, the icon manager does not encompass the icon. That is, an iconified application has a normal icon, in addition to its entry in the icon manager.

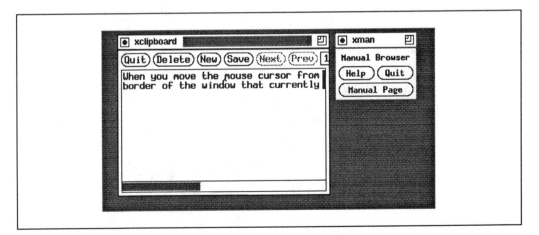

Figure 12.11 *twm*'s Keyboard Focus Highlighting

The default root menu contains two entries for terminating an application: "Delete" and "Kill". When you select "Delete", the window manager sends a request to the application to terminate that window. Every ICCCM-compliant X application is responsible for terminating windows gracefully, in an application-specific manner. When you select "Kill", the window manager forcefully kills (exterminates) the application. In general, you should not kill application windows. If you do, typically, you'll receive messages in a command window or on the root window, notifying you of the application's "painful and unexpected demise."

twm's "Restart" and "Exit" menu options are consistent with those of *mwm* and *olwm*, as described earlier in this chapter. If *twm* is the last command in your start-up script, "Exit" terminates the window manager; shortly thereafter, the X server and all X clients terminate.

12.5.4 Configuring *twm*

Unlike other X clients, *twm* does not support configuration via X resources. Instead, *twm* processes three types of specifications from its configuration file: variables, bindings, and menus.

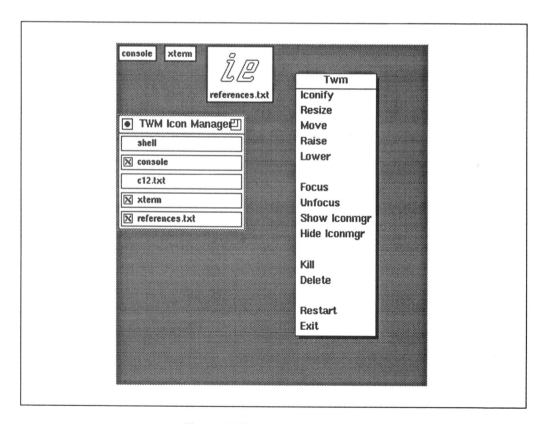

Figure 12.12 *twm*'s Icon Manager

Typically, customizations are provided in the file _.twmrc_ in the user's home directory.
(Actually, you can have multiple configuration files, one for each screen attached to your
workstation, named _.twmrc.<screen-number>_. If this file is not found, _twm_ consults a
system-wide configuration file, typically, _/usr/lib/X11/twm/system.twmrc_.)

If there is no configuration file, _twm_ assumes its default behavior, _but provides no root menu_.
If there is no configuration file, you may not be able to terminate _twm_. If your start-up script
depends on _twm_ exiting in order to terminate your X session, you may have to kill the _twm_
process from a command window, assuming that you have one running. With _twm_, the best
approach is to copy _system.twmrc_ into your home directory as _.twmrc_ and then add your
personal customizations.

twm has many configuration variables, each of which is thoroughly described in the
man-page. Variables should be defined at the top of the configuration file. Boolean
(true-false) variables are set simply by their presence or absence, as reflected by _twm_'s
naming convention, for example, _DecorateTransients_, _NoMenuShadows_, _NoRaiseOn-
Deiconify_, and others. Note that even though the man-page indicates that a variable is _not_
set by default, for example, _DecorateTransients_, it may be set in your system-wide file,
system.twmrc. It's a good idea to group all of your Boolean variables near the top of _.twmrc_:

```
. . .
DecorateTransients
NoMenuShadows
NoRaiseOnDeiconify
. . .
```

twm has numerous string variables, for which values are enclosed in double quotes, for
example,

```
IconDirectory   "~/icon"
```

Here, icons are searched for in the directory _icon_ with the user's home directory. (In UNIX
environments, "~" expands to the value of $HOME.)

Variables often have lists as values. A list is specified with curly brackets and elements in
the list are separated by whitespace, for example,

```
NoTitle {"client-1" "client-2" "client-3" ... }
```

or

```
NoTitle
{
    "client-1"
    "client-2"
    "client-3"
    . . .
}
```

After variable definitions, the configuration file should contain key and button bindings according to the following format:

```
<key or button> = <modifier list> : <context> : <window manager function>
```

Keys are designated by their keysyms, specified in quotes, for example, "F1"; see Section 11.2 for a discussion of keysyms. Buttons are designated by the keywords Button1, Button2, and so on.

Modifiers, see Section 11.3, are designated with the keywords s, l, c, m, m1, ..., m5, for , shift, lock, control, meta, mod1, ..., mod5, respectively. If an operation requires multiple modifiers they are separated by a vertical bar.

The context field describes the context in which a key or button event is significant, with modifiers, if any. Context keywords include all, icon, iconmgr, menu, root, title, and window. Multiple contexts are separated with a vertical bar.

system.twmrc includes the following button bindings among others:

```
Button1 = : root : f.menu "defops"
...
Button2 = m : window|icon : f.iconify
```

Interpretation: Pressing button 1 over the root menu invokes the menu named "defops" (default operations). Pressing button 2 with the meta key (see Section 11.4) over a window or an icon invokes the iconify operation. (f.iconify is a toggle; that is, when applied to an icon, it undoes the iconify operation.)

The third type of specification in a configuration file is a menu. Note that menus may be defined after they are referenced in, say, a binding definition:

```
Button1 = : root : f.menu "defops"
...
menu "defops"
{
...
}
```

(*mwm* and *twm* have similar menu definition styles because *mwm* is a successor to *twm*.)

system.twmrc includes the following root menu definition:

```
menu "defops"
{
"Twm"         f.title
"Iconify"     f.iconify
"Resize"      f.resize
"Move"        f.move
"Raise"       f.raise
"Lower"       f.lower
```

```
""                  f.nop
"Focus"             f.focus
"Unfocus"           f.unfocus
"Show Iconmgr"      f.showiconmgr
"Hide Iconmgr"      f.hideiconmgr
""                  f.nop
"Kill"              f.destroy
"Delete"            f.delete
""                  f.nop
"Restart"           f.restart
"Exit"              f.quit
}
```

The previous button binding associates this menu with the root window. The f.nop (no operation) functions create space, as with *mwm*'s f.separator. Figures 12.9 and 12.12 illustrate this menu.

You may have noticed that entities such as menu names and colors are enclosed in double quotes:

```
menu "defops"
{
...
}
```

These quotes are necessary with *twm*. In general, if a name is not a keyword, it should be in double quotes. If you omit these quotes, your configuration option may be ignored.

12.5.5 A Sample *twm* Configuration File

Warning: *twm* does not provide any default root menu functionality in the event that your configuration file has errors. Thus, if you restart *twm* from the menu after modifying *.twmrc* and there are errors, the root menu may disappear, providing no opportunity to exit *twm*. In this situation, to terminate *twm* you must kill the *twm* process from a command window. We recommend that you add a key bindings for terminating *twm*, as we do in our sample configuration file.

As mentioned, the man-page for *twm* includes a complete discussion for the many *twm* variables and functions. Rather than duplicate that information here, in this section we illustrate a practical *twm* configuration. Our configuration file is rather modest; the objective is to illustrate various types of variables while keeping the configuration file small. You can easily add many more customizations.

Previously in this chapter we've illustrated root menus for *mwm* and *olwm* that have submenus. For consistency, it is convenient to illustrate a similar menu system for *twm*. Also, unlike *mwm* and *olwm*, *twm* does not provide a window menu in its default configuration. Even though *twm* has no provision for a window-menu button, it's still possible to activate a window menu from the title bar, as with *mwm* and *olwm*. Our configuration file includes a simple window menu that is easily expanded.

Our *.twmrc* file begins as follows:

```
#
# .twmrc -- sample twm(1) configuration file
#

#
# Decorate the pop-ups so that it's easier to manipulate them:
#
DecorateTransients
...
```

Our file begins with Boolean variable definitions. Hereafter, we omit the comment statements for conciseness. Our Boolean variable definitions include

```
...
DecorateTransients
ForceIcons
NoGrabServer
RandomPlacement
...
```

As mentioned, `DecorateTransients` adds window manager decoration for pop-up windows. Next, in the event that we specify an icon for an application that already defines a client icon, `ForceIcons` requests that our icon override the client's default icon. Next, `NoGrabServer` requests that *twm* not seize the X server (in essence, temporarily suspend processing of other events) during certain window-movement and pop-up menu activities. `RandomPlacement` requests that *twm* automatically place new application windows on the desktop at random locations; the default is to engage the user in an interactive placement strategy.

We define one numeric variable:

```
...
MoveDelta 3
...
```

`MoveDelta` is used to distinguished a simple mouse click from an attempt to drag an object. For example, clicking on an icon should open the application window, whereas dragging an icon should move it to a new location.

Next, come several string variables from *system.twmrc*:

```
...
TitleFont "-adobe-helvetica-bold-r-normal--*-120-*-*-*-*-*-*"
ResizeFont "-adobe-helvetica-bold-r-normal--*-120-*-*-*-*-*-*"
MenuFont "-adobe-helvetica-bold-r-normal--*-120-*-*-*-*-*-*"
IconFont "-adobe-helvetica-bold-r-normal--*-100-*-*-*-*-*-*"
IconManagerFont "-adobe-helvetica-bold-r-normal--*-100-*-*-*"
...
```

We add our personal icon directory:

```
...
IconDirectory    "~/icon"
...
```

This directory includes several icons of our own design that we next associate with particular X clients:

```
...
Icons
{
    "xterm"       "xterm.icon"
    "xedit"       "xedit.icon"
    "xclipboard"  "clip.icon"
    "xcalc"       "xcalc.icon"
}
...
```

Our icon list is our first example of a variable with a list for its value. You may prefer to use class names, as opposed to instance names, in this context. Figure 12.13 illustrates several icons.

The next list variable overrides the maroon colors in *system.twmrc*:

```
...
Color
{
    BorderColor "Chocolate"
    {
        "XTerm"      "Navy"
```

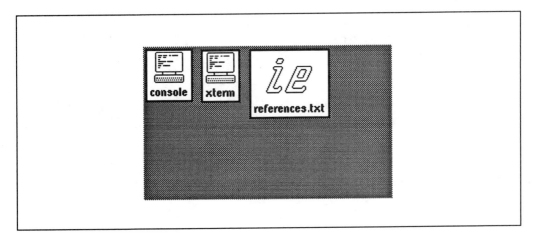

Figure 12.13 *twm* Icons

```
        "XCalc"      "Purple"
        "XClock"     "AquaMarine"
        "Xedit"      "Plum"
    }
    DefaultBackground "Bisque"
    DefaultForeground "Navy"
    TitleBackground "Bisque"
    TitleForeground "Navy"
    MenuBackground "Bisque"
    MenuForeground "Navy"
    MenuTitleBackground "Salmon"
    MenuTitleForeground "Bisque"
    IconBackground "Bisque"
    IconForeground "Navy"
    IconBorderColor "Navy"
    IconManagerBackground "Bisque"
    IconManagerForeground "Navy"
}
...
```

A common error is to define a list variable such as `BorderColor` at the highest level (scope) in your configuration file, when it must be defined within the definition for `Color`. The man-page descriptions for each variable indicate when they must be defined within a special context. Again, *twm* does not explain this type of error, so don't forget to consult the man-page.

In this example, we've requested a chocolate border color for all X clients, unless otherwise specified. The default color is black. Within the list, we've specified an alternate border color for X clients from four classes.

Next, we include three user-defined functions from *system.twmrc*:

```
...
Function "move-or-lower" { f.move f.deltastop f.lower }
Function "move-or-raise" { f.move f.deltastop f.raise }
Function "move-or-iconify" { f.move f.deltastop f.iconify }
...
```

The keyword `Function` signals a function definition. The function name should be in double quotes and the operation should be in list format. To invoke a user-defined function, specify `f.function` followed by the function name:

```
    ... f.function "move-or-raise"
```

Consider the function `move-or-raise`:

```
Function "move-or-raise" { f.move f.deltastop f.raise }
```

Each function in the list is executed sequentially. `f.move` will move a window if and only if there is actual pointer movement; otherwise, a window is moved 0 pixels. The function `f.deltastop` terminates the execution of any remaining functions in a user-defined function's list, if the pointer moves more than `MoveDelata` pixels. Thus, `move-or-raise` terminates after a move operation; `f.raise` is never executed because of `f.deltastop`. If, however, there is no pointer movement, all three functions are executed. In this case, `f.move` and `f.deltastop` do nothing (from the user's perspective) and `f.raise` raises the window.

With this function, one button binding provides the functionality for moving and raising an application window from the title bar:

```
Button1 = : title : f.function "move-or-raise"
```

Here's our complete set of button bindings:

```
. . .
Button3 = : root : f.menu "RootMenu"

Button1 = : title : f.function "move-or-raise"
Button2 = : title : f.lower
Button3 = : title : f.menu "WindowMenu"

Button1 = m : window : f.raise
Button2 = m : window : f.lower
Button3 = m : window : f.move

Button1 = : icon : f.function "move-or-iconify"
Button2 = : icon : f.lower
Button3 = : icon : f.menu "WindowMenu"
. . .
```

As with *mwm* and *olwm*, mouse button 3 activates the root menu. In the title bar, our buttons have the same functionality as defined for *mwm* in Section 12.3.2:

```
. . .
Buttons AlternateButtonBindings
{
        <Btn1Down>        frame|icon        f.raise
        <Btn2Down>        frame|icon        f.lower
        <Btn3Down>        frame|icon        f.post_wmenu
        <Btn3Down>        root              f.menu   RootMenu
        Meta<Btn1Down>    window            f.raise
        Meta<Btn2Down>    window            f.lower
        Meta<Btn3Down>    window            f.move
}
. . .
```

Likewise, we've defined similar functionality for the icon and window contexts. Note that mouse button 3 invokes a window menu in the icon and title contexts.

The issue is not whether or not our arbitrary button bindings are the best. The point is that you can configure your window manager environment to match your preferences and to have consistent behavior across different window managers.

Next, we provide a single key binding that serves as a "panic button":

```
. . .
"F10" = c|m : root : f.quit
. . .
```

You can use any uncommon key sequence, but you definitely should have this type of key definition. In our case, <**Ctrl**>-<**Meta**>-<**F10**> terminates *twm*. You should not depend on your menu for terminating *twm*, because if there is an error in .*twmrc* the menu may not appear. This feature is especially important if you start *twm* in the foreground as the last process in your start-up script.

All that remains is our menu definitions. First, the root menu is

```
. . .
menu "RootMenu"
{
    "Root Menu"            f.title
    "Raise"                f.raise
    "Lower"                f.lower
    "Refresh"              f.refresh
    "Applications"         f.menu "ApplicationMenu"
    "Root Background"      f.menu "BackgroundMenu"
    ""                     f.nop
    "Restart twm"          f.restart
    "Quit X / twm"         f.quit
}
. . .
```

Menu definitions are very similar for *mwm* and *twm* (see Figure 12.14). The function f.nop is similar to *mwm*'s f.separator, except that it does not provide a separator graphic; instead, vertical space is provided by a menu entry with a null name field.

f.menu associates two submenus with the root menu:

```
. . .
menu "ApplicationMenu"
{
    "Applications"         f.title
    "Command Window"       f.exec "xterm &"
    "Text Editor"          f.exec "ie &"
    "Calculator"           f.exec "xcalc -rpn &"
    "Analog Clock"         f.exec "xclock -g 150x150+5+5 &"
```

```
     "Digital Clock"      f.exec "xclock -digital -g 200x35+5+5 &"
     "Manual Pages"       f.exec "xman &"
     "Screen Lock"        f.exec "xlock.logo &"
}

menu "BackgroundMenu"
{
     "Background" f.title
     "Gray Mono"  f.exec "xsetroot -bitmap /home/jsmith/icon/graytile.bit &"
     "Gray 2Dot"  f.exec "xsetroot -bitmap /home/jsmith/icon/2pixtile.bit &"
     "Gray 3Dot"  f.exec "xsetroot -bitmap /home/jsmith/icon/3pixtile.bit &"
     "Gray 4Dot"  f.exec "xsetroot -bitmap /home/jsmith/icon/4pixtile.bit &"
     "Root Weave"    f.exec "xsetroot -def &"
     "Cross Weave"   f.exec "xsetroot -bitmap \
                     /usr/include/X11/bitmaps/cross_weave &"
     "Wide Weave"    f.exec "xsetroot -bitmap \
                     /usr/include/X11/bitmaps/wide_weave &"
     "Cadet Blue"    f.exec "xsetroot -solid CadetBlue &"
     "Gray"          f.exec "xsetroot -solid Gray &"
     "Lavender"      f.exec "xsetroot -solid Lavender &"
     "Peach Puff"    f.exec "xsetroot -solid PeachPuff &"
     "Powder Blue"   f.exec "xsetroot -solid PowderBlue &"
     "Rosy Brown"    f.exec "xsetroot -solid RosyBrown &"
     "Salmon"        f.exec "xsetroot -solid Salmon &"
     "Sky Blue"      f.exec "xsetroot -solid SkyBlue &"
     "Tomato"        f.exec "xsetroot -solid Tomato &"
}
...
```

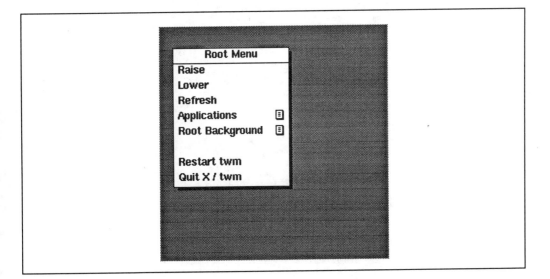

Figure 12.14 The Enhanced *twm* Root Menu

For consistency across window managers, which is only important if you use multiple window managers regularly, we've designed these menus to be very similar to those defined for *mwm* and *olwm*. Figure 12.15 shows the submenu for common X clients.

Lastly, we provide a window menu:

```
. . .
menu "WindowMenu"
{
"Window Menu"     f.title
"Restore"         f.fullzoom
"Move"            f.move
"Resize"          f.resize
"Iconify"         f.iconify
"Maximize"        f.fullzoom
"Lower"           f.lower
" "               f.nop
"Close"           f.delete
}
. . .
```

Figure 12.16 illustrates the window menu. Note that f.fullzoom is a toggle function; it will "unzoom" a zoomed window. Thus, the functionality of "Restore" and "Maximize" are consistent with *mwm*—if you use them in the proper order. Having the "Resize" menu option is particularly convenient because it's often more convenient than using the resize button in the title bar. With the "Resize" option, you simply move the pointer toward one

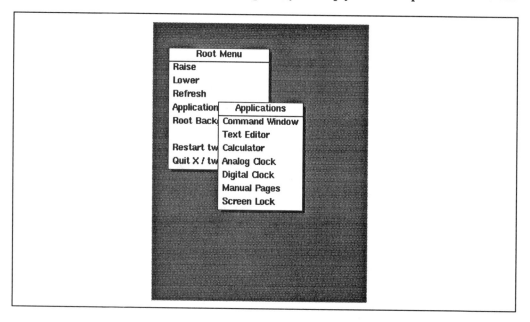

Figure 12.15 The *twm* Application Menu

side of the window. When the pointer crosses the window's edge, that side of the window is dynamically resized with the pointer movement. You can, of course, tailor your window menu to include a variety of operations; see the *twm* man-page for a complete list of window manager functions.

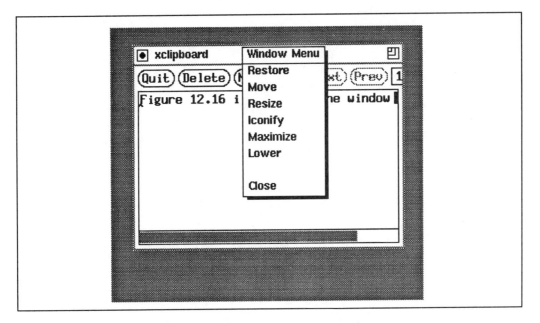

Figure 12.16 The *twm* Window Menu

13

X from X Terminals

Section 1.12 provides a brief overview of X terminals, primarily in comparison to UNIX workstations and PC X servers. In this chapter we consider X terminals in greater detail, but primarily from the perspective of an X terminal user. X terminal administration is straightforward for experienced system administrators, but an exhaustive treatment is, by definition, beyond the scope of an X user's guide. On the other hand, users need to be somewhat aware of the many configuration possibilities for X terminals. For this reason, we include a measured amount of coverage of system administration details. For additional information see Mui and Pearce [1993], and, of course, your X terminal user's manual.

At this point, there are many X terminal manufacturers. Each X terminal manufacturers' set-up menus, windows, and dialog boxes differ in relatively unimportant ways. For that reason, we do not show examples that illustrate modifying text fields in various set-up windows. These manufacturer-specific illustrations are readily available, however, in X terminal user's manuals.

13.1 X Display Stations

Throughout this book we've emphasized that an X server manages a display. The X server is software and the display is hardware; a display typically includes a monitor (screen), a keyboard, and a mouse. Display functionality can be provided by a variety of hardware devices.

With a UNIX workstation running X, the X server operates as a standard UNIX process, albeit one that takes over the entire display. You could, for example, log in to the workstation remotely from another workstation, or from a character terminal, and run other UNIX applications from the remote command window. You could perform any task that did not conflict with the X server's display operations, for example, printing files and backing up a file system to magnetic tape.

In this X environment, the X clients, the X server, and the display are local to each other. Communication between X clients and the X server is implemented within the workstation's local, or software-based, networking facilities. Instead of communication taking place over a physical Ethernet®-based network, the network is implemented via memory or filesystem structures. X is network-transparent in the sense that X clients request services from an X server managing a named display, for example, "saturn:0.0". The workstation's networking facilities, not X, provide the communication services, which, in this case, occurs on one machine.

If a physical network exists and machines at each network node can communicate with each other, X clients running on one node can use the display at another node (if they have permission). It is not necessary for there to be an X server running on the computer that executes the X clients, because they are using a remote display. Thus, with permission, an X client running on saturn can "borrow" jupiter's display. Both jupiter and saturn could be UNIX workstations.

Although we often think of X in conjunction with desktop UNIX workstations, X clients could exist on an entirely different type of computer, either a mainframe or a minicomputer. In this type of computing environment, any type of X display station could provide display services for the central computer: UNIX workstations running X, PCs equipped with network cards and PC X servers, and X terminals.

This network-transparent capability makes X a tremendously powerful enabling technology for heterogeneous computing environments. In human terms, an X client's attitude is: "Just give me the name of a display, any display (with an X server), and (with permission) I'll display my windows there."

13.2 X Terminals

In many cases, the ideal X display station is an X terminal. An X terminal is a dedicated X display station. That is, it is designed specifically to provide display services for X clients running on a remote computer. The remote computer could be a UNIX workstation, a minicomputer, a mainframe, even a supercomputer. In some network environments, X terminals can connect to multiple computers on the local network. Users choose the remote connection dynamically when an X terminal starts up via a window that lists each available remote computer, the so-called *chooser box*.

Traditional ASCII terminals include fairly minimal microprocessor support, for example, an integrated circuit for keyboard operations. In comparison, X terminals are much more sophisticated. In most cases, when you purchase an X terminal, you're getting more technology on your desktop than when you purchase a traditional PC. Although it's true that PCs include a hard disk and can run software locally, with X terminals you get a much higher-powered graphics display environment, typically including a RISC-based CPU and other dedicated processors. Even though you can add X display station capabilities to a PC for approximately $500, its performance will be greatly inferior to an entry-level X terminal.

In many cases, a 14-inch, color X terminal represents a minimal X user environment. It is suitable for running two or three concurrent X applications, and its cost is comparable with a PC with an equivalent amount of memory. Many workstation users are accustomed to 16-inch, or larger, monitors. In these configurations, X terminals often can be purchased for 25 percent, or less, of the cost of a workstation with similar graphics capabilities. In considering workstations versus X terminals for each user's desktop, it's easy to overlook the ongoing software maintenance fees that accompany each workstation, even diskless workstations.

13.3 Sharing Computing Resources

In essence, X terminals provide a high-powered graphics interface to one or more remote computers, allowing you to dynamically mix and match computing environments. In a heterogeneous computing environment, for example, you could maintain user accounts on several different remote computers. Each file server could be designed to provide the best assortment of X clients available for that hardware platform or computing project. Each of these remote application environments would be accessible from a single X terminal on your desktop.

Recently, there has been a dramatic movement from centralized computing to client-server computing with UNIX workstations, with the exception of application areas that require mainframes or supercomputers. X terminals, by definition, are ideally suited for use with central compute and file servers such as supercomputers. X terminals, however, are ideal in a client-server environment as well because they facilitate the sharing of computing resources within a department. It is now common for small departments within a larger organization to take responsibility for their own computing needs.

For users with one workstation platform on their desktop, adding an X terminal provides parallel access to other workstations in the department. Remote log-ins from your local workstation provide one mechanism for accessing other workstations on a local network (see Section 2.8). With a dedicated X terminal, however, these remotely executing X clients don't have to compete for the desktop with local X clients.

13.4 X Terminal Hardware Configurations

Some older X terminals were available only in nonupgradable configurations. That is, if you purchased an X terminal with a 14-inch monitor, there was no realistic way to upgrade to a 19-inch monitor. The trend, however, is toward modular X terminal designs, which some manufacturers have supported from the very beginning. With a modular design, if you need to upgrade to a larger monitor, you simply purchase the required components.

In general, any decisions regarding monitors are similar to those faced with workstations. Like workstation manufacturers, most X terminal manufacturers supply monitors from well-known manufacturers of computer monitors such as Hitachi® and Sony®. For this reason, an X terminal's monitor should be the same quality as those supplied with UNIX workstations, assuming that you've purchased from a reputable X terminal manufacturer.

In terms of screen resolution, most 19-inch X terminals are 1280×1024 pixels. Midsized monitors, either 16- or 17-inch, are more likely to have a resolution such as 1024×1024 pixels or 1152×900 pixels. For some midsized monitors and most 14-inch monitors, 1024×768 pixels is a common resolution.

X terminal manufacturers sometimes provide multiple keyboard configurations. PC-style keyboards are often supplied as standard equipment with smaller, UNIX workstation-like keyboards available as options. Be aware that some X terminal manufacturers supply PC-style keyboards, but their X servers do not support the cursor and secondary keypads. You should reconsider before buying an X terminal for which the keypads do not generate the appropriate keysyms.

As with workstations, the type of mouse supplied with X terminals varies. Mechanical mice are probably more common, but optical mice aren't necessarily better or worse than mechanical mice. Even though optical mice tend to cost more, some of the more expensive workstations are equipped with mechanical mice.

13.5 X Servers for X Terminals

An X server is *the* control program for an X terminal, managing the screen, keyboard, and mouse. An X terminal's X server honors requests by X clients running on a remote computer, for example, drawing a line in a window, and it reports screen-, keyboard-, pointer-related events to these remote X clients (as requested). Typically, this communication takes place over a local area network via coaxial cabling.

Each X terminal executes an X server designed specifically for its hardware configuration. Standard memory (RAM, random-access memory) is volatile; that is, when you turn off an X terminal, information stored in RAM is lost. For this reason, during start-up operations an X terminal loads its X server into RAM from a known storage location. Typically, the X server is loaded from either (1) a file residing on a remote computer or (2) from nonvolatile memory (ROM, read-only memory). (One exception is that some older X terminals retained and executed the X server directly from a private ROM. To upgrade the X server, you had to replace these ROM chips.)

In terms of the cost of X terminals, the most inexpensive configuration is to load the X server from a file on a remote computer. The X server could, for example, be stored on and loaded from computer A, even though the X terminal might be configured to display X clients running on some other computer, say, B. In this case, the X terminal requires no dedicated memory chips for permanent storage of the X server. Another advantage is that X server upgrades are very simple; you essentially have to replace the old X server stored on a remote computer with the new X server.

The disadvantage of this approach is that a certain amount of time is required during start-up operations to download the X server. When the remote computer is on the same local network, this time may not be significant (30 seconds or so), but if you communicate with an X terminal over a dial-up phone line, the time required to download the X server could be prohibitive. In some cases, however, this download operation can become significant with a heavily loaded local network, especially for users who start their X terminals often.

To minimize network overhead, most X terminals are available in configurations that store the X server locally in a type of nonvolatile memory that can be updated (PROM, programmable read-only memory). In this case, each time you receive an X server upgrade, you (or a system administrator) copy it from the distribution medium (cartridge tape) to a file, from where you then copy it to the X terminal's PROM.

13.6 The Physical Network Connection

Assuming that you have the required components, physically connecting an X terminal is quite straightforward. Typically, you simply plug the X terminal into the network using the appropriate type of connector. Typically, there are three possible broadcast connection types. (1) A twisted-pair Ethernet connection uses telephone-style connectors, specifically, IEEE 10BaseT. This type of connection requires a Ethernet hub. (2) A thin-net, or thin-wire Ethernet, connection uses coaxial cabling with BNC connectors (a twist-click, no-tool-required type of connector). This type of connection is also known as IEEE 10Base2. (3) A thick-wire Ethernet connection uses heavier cabling and connectors, similar to a keyboard or printer cable. This AUI (Attachment Unit Interface) connector, specifically, IEEE 10Base5, attaches directly or indirectly to a transceiver, which is then connected to an Ethernet network.

Traditional Ethernet connections allow an X terminal to connect to any remote computer on the local network for which there is a proper logical connection. (Minimally, a logical connection requires an entry for the X terminal in the host database, typically, */etc/hosts*.) Thus, during log-in you can choose among different X environments, depending on your current computing needs. If your X terminal is configured to use a chooser box, you simply select the appropriate host dynamically; if not, you may have to choose the remote computer via a set-up window.

X terminals also support serial connections to a remote computer via an RS-232 C connector. In this case, you can only connect to the remote computer to which you have a serial link.

Some X terminal manufacturers require that you choose from a subset of the connection types when you purchase an X terminal, whereas other manufacturers, for example, Human Designed Systems (HDS), automatically support all of these connection types. Unless you know that your local network implementation will not change in the future, support for all connection types is very desirable.

Note that, typically, after making the physical connection you will have to choose the appropriate connection type from a set-up menu.

13.7 The X Protocol versus Network Protocols

In Section 1.5 and elsewhere in Chapter 1 we describe the X protocol as a messaging system, or protocol, whereby X clients communicate with an X server. X clients request display services from the X server, such as drawing a line in a window, and they request information, such as the screen coordinates of the mouse cursor. The X server replies to specific requests for information from X clients and it reports event information that occurs in application windows, as requested by each X client. The X protocol uses simple byte-oriented message packets, typically, 16- to 32-byte messages.

This messaging system is independent of the lower level networking protocol that physically transports information between X clients and an X server. A complete discussion of networking protocols is beyond the scope of this book; see Kochan and Wood [1989] for a thorough coverage of UNIX networking. The remainder of this section provides a brief description of the most common networking services.

Network services are provided in layers. The lowest level data services, the so-called physical layer, send and receive header and data packets that include a small amount of overhead data, including information that assists in detecting low-level, data transmission errors. Higher level services, at the network layer, implement addressing schemes that support systems of local networks and subnetworks within wide-area networks. Although similar in principal, these electronic addressing schemes are more sophisticated than the traditional address systems used by postal services. At a higher level, the transport layer, additional network services provide mechanisms for managing network loads, handling transmission errors, and so on.

Communication between UNIX workstations, minicomputers, and X terminals is typically implemented via an Ethernet network (the physical layer). Ethernet is a bus-oriented system. That is, all interfaces, for example, workstations and X terminals, connect to a common communication channel, specifically, a coaxial cable. Ethernet is a broadcast-oriented system in the sense that every transmission is sent to all connected hosts; hence, each node must selectively process transmissions.

At a higher level, the Internet protocol (IP) provides a mechanism for intra- and inter-network communication. Specifically, it provides an addressing scheme whereby every network node has a distinct address, composed of a network and a local component. For example, the popular network-services organization UUNET has the Internet address `192.48.96.2` (among others). Thus, computers can connect to each other on local networks as well as across gateways to other local networks, hence, the term Internet for inter-network communication. The proper name Internet represents one particular type of internet.

The Internet protocol does not address (no pun intended) reliable data transfer. TCP/IP (Transmission Control Protocol/Internet Protocol) builds reliable transport services on top of the Internet protocol. Whenever several X terminals and workstations share a bus-oriented communication channel such as that provided by Ethernet, there is a potential for collisions of information packets, because each network node has equal access to the network. Transport protocols such as TCP implement a system of checks and balances that guarantee reliable delivery of messages from one network node to another including retransmission of collided messages, strategies for congestion avoidance by dynamically adjusting transmission rates, and so on.

With this limited background in networking, we can describe the X protocol as a simple messaging system that is independent of the physical, network, and transport layers that carry the messages between X clients and the X server. These interclient communication services typically range from memory-resident communication channels for stand-alone workstations to TCP/IP networking via Ethernet between workstations and X terminals.

13.8 Serial Communication

As mentioned, most X terminals support serial communication in addition to Ethernet-based communication. Serial communication is required for traditional modem-based computing over phone lines. There are many individuals who would like to use an X terminal from a remote location that is not connected to the host computer via an Ethernet network. Although using an X terminal via a modem represents a typical serial connection, there are many other environments that are prime candidates for serial X connections. For example, many organizations have serial communication lines in place that were originally installed to support remote computing via ASCII terminals.

Serial connections can use one of several general communication protocols, including SLIP (Serial Line Internet Protocol) and CSLIP (Compressed SLIP). SLIP is, in essence, a mechanism for TCP/IP communication over asynchronous lines. CSLIP compresses a significant amount of the overhead added by TCP and IP, but it is still a general-purpose protocol. In some cases, a serial link via SLIP is adequate for occasional X terminal use. For any type of extended, intensive use, however, an Ethernet connection is highly desirable.

Because serial connections are ubiquitous, but inherently slow, there has been a considerable amount of research into X-specific, serial communication protocols. It is important to understand that the bandwidth, that is, the level of network activity, is much higher for an X terminal than for a character terminal, because of the graphics-oriented nature of X.

Network Computing Devices (NCD) and others have developed XRemote as a designed-for-X remote connection protocol. XRemote is a highly optimized transport protocol that replaces TCP/IP. The latter protocol is, by design, a general-purpose communication facility that wraps each X client-server message inside a significantly larger bundle of information. The overhead associated with general-purpose transport services is not significant for Ethernet networks, but, with serial communication, all communication overhead is significant.

XRemote provides a compression and decompression facility at each end of the X client-server communication. In effect, XRemote interposes a helper process between X clients and the network and between the network and the X server. These helper processes coordinate the compression and decompression of X client and server messages. The reduction in bandwidth is significant; a compressed message is smaller than the original X protocol message.

These helper processes impose a significant burden on the remote computer that hosts the X clients, as well as on the X terminal. On the X terminal, XRemote is implemented in nonvolatile memory. On the remote computer, XRemote is implemented as a standard application. At this time, XRemote is undergoing refinements that address several issues that are beyond the scope of this book.

Concurrently, the X industry is pursuing a more general approach to reducing the overhead of X protocol messages. This technology is commonly referred to as low bandwidth X (LBX). It promises to improve the network performance of X environments in heavily loaded local networks, as well as over serial communication lines.

13.9 The Logical Network Connection

The amount of work required to complete the logical connection to the local network varies depending on the network-readiness of the remote computer to which you've connected an

X terminal. If it is a stand-alone workstation, you may have to set up several files and address other *configuration* tasks such as installing fonts supplied with the X terminal.

At the other extreme, if the remote computer is already supporting other X terminals, the connection may be as simple as adding an entry for the X terminal to its database of recognized hosts (for example, */etc/hosts*), plus setting a couple of options in the X terminal's set-up menu. For example, the */etc/hosts* for one of our file servers includes the following entries:

```
...
192.9.200.11 ncd1
192.9.200.12 ncd2
...
192.9.200.21 hds1
...
192.9.200.61 hp1
...
192.9.200.71 sgi1
...
```

This host database includes entries for HDS and NCD X terminals, as well as for several remote workstations. The first field contains the network node's Internet address. This particular network is a private one, so the addresses are arbitrary (as long as they meet Internet addressing-style requirements). In any case, the network configuration required for your remote computer is likely to vary, so see your system administrator.

Computing devices attached to network nodes must have a way of communicating their addresses to other nodes. Suppose your system administrator has assigned you the address 192.9.200.21 and the lackluster name "hds1" for your new X terminal. Furthermore, this entry has been added to the remote computer's host database, as shown in our previous */etc/hosts* file. Having an entry in */etc/hosts*, however, is not sufficient for a successful connection between your X terminal and the remote computer.

In particular, the X terminal must "recognize" its network address. There are two common solutions: (1) local X terminal storage of the address and (2) an address resolution strategy provided by the host computer. With the first approach, you simply enter the X terminal's network address in a text field during set-up operations; set-up information is stored in updatable, nonvolatile memory (NVRAM).

With the second approach, the host computer automatically determines the address of an X terminal that's attempting a connection via a mechanism called an address resolution protocol (ARP). Many UNIX workstations have one of two common facilities that provide address resolution, BOOTP (Bootstrap Protocol) and RARP (Reverse ARP). BOOTP actually supports other boot operations in addition to address resolution, including downloading the X server.

Your system administrator is responsible for setting up and maintaining these services. We mention them here so that you're aware that these types of operations are required on the host side. Also, the user's manual for your X terminal will probably describe the steps necessary to activate BOOTP or RARP on the remote computer.

If your X terminal stores its X server in ROM and can retain its network address in NVRAM, you may be able to connect successfully after setting its network address (corresponding to its entry in the remote computer's network database). If these settings are insufficient, your network configuration may require modifications to the subnet mask, the specification of a network name server, and other details. This information will be available from your system administrator.

13.10 X Terminal Configuration

In addition to user preferences for the X server, for example, keyboard autorepeat rate, and so on, there are several network configuration options that must be specified for most X terminals. Typically, the default settings are chosen to minimize the amount of work necessary to establish a successful initial connection to the remote computer. Figure 13.1 shows the set-up window for an HDS X terminal, currently running *twm*. The method for invoking the set-up window differs across X terminals. Some X terminals provide a special set-up key; others require you to press a combination of standard keys, for example, **<Ctrl>-<Alt>-<Esc>**; and others, such as HDS X terminals, provide an icon for the set-up window.

13.10.1 Accessing Files on the Remote Computer

An obvious consideration is whether the X server is downloaded from the remote computer or stored locally in the X terminal's ROM. If the X server is stored in ROM, a so-called ROM-based X terminal, using the ROM-based server will probably be the default option. If not, you must specify the remote file server from which the X terminal downloads its X server during start-up operations. Typically, you enter the remote computer's Internet address and the X server's path specification in the appropriate text fields.

Another consideration is fonts. Most X terminals store a small selection of fonts locally, again, to minimize the work required to get the X terminal running. A larger selection of fonts is typically supplied on magnetic tape; these fonts are stored on a remote computer and accessed over the network by the X terminal's X server (on demand). If you want your X terminal to use this larger selection of fonts, you must specify the Internet address of the remote computer that acts as a font server, as well as the path specification for the font directories. Note that the X server and its fonts can reside on different remote computers.

Consider the process of downloading the X server (if necessary). Typically, BOOTP manages the process of downloading the X server, if it is available. If not, the download operation is performed directly by TFTP (Trivial File Transfer Protocol). TFTP is trivial in the sense that it performs a very basic file transfer without the security checks provided by FTP (File Transfer Protocol). The TFTP program is called *tftp(1)*; see its man-page for more information. Note that some X terminals also support X server downloading with the more robust utility *ftp(1)*.

In Section 8.11 we described the X font server. If your X terminal's X server is based on X11R5 or later, you can simply request font service as you would for a workstation; see Section 8.11. Many X terminals are not X11R5-based, however, so fonts must be accessed by specifying a remote computer's Internet address and the path specifications for the font directories. In this case, you should *not* use *xset* with the `fp` command-line option to specify the font directories. X terminals provide a set-up option for specifying font-related information, and this information is retained in NVRAM. The primary reason you should use the set-up menu instead of *xset* to specify your font directories is that the X terminal may automatically append the location of its local fonts to the X server's font path.

If you're not using the font server, *fs* (available beginning with X11R5), fonts are typically downloaded by TFTP, unless the font directories are mounted over the network via NFS (Network File System).

Your system administrator will install the X server (if necessary) and fonts, and notify you of their exact locations, as well as the protocol for accessing these files. Configuring your X terminal involves specifying these locations in the proper text fields, as well as selecting the access protocol, from the set-up window.

Figure 13.1 An X Terminal Setup Screen

13.10.2 Coordinating X Sessions on the Remote Computer

In Section 2.2 we described *xdm*, which coordinates log-in sessions on a workstation. Specifically, *xdm* directly transports the user from the log-in screen to the X environment, with no intervening console or command window.

X terminals employ *xdm* to start an X session on a remote computer with the X terminal as the default display device. XDMCP (X Display Manager Control Protocol), available beginning with X11R4, provides the handshaking necessary to initiate the remote session. Life without XDMCP is now considered unbearable, so we do not discuss pre-X11R4 X terminal strategies. (In times past, you had to log in to the remote computer via a terminal-emulation window and then start X clients manually, directing them to the X terminal.)

From the user's perspective, *xdm* employs a log-in client, *xlogin*, which presents a log-in window and prompts the user for a log-in name and password. You can configure several aspects of the log-in window via X resources, as described in Section 13.11.4. Figure 13.2 shows an *xdm*-managed log-in window.

For anything but the simplest network, there are likely to be several remote computers running *xdm*. There are three ways of resolving the appropriate remote computer: (1) direct, (2) indirect, and (3) broadcast. For a direct *xdm* connection, you supply the Internet address of the remote computer to the appropriate X terminal set-up option. For an indirect connection, you specify a remote computer that passes the *xdm* connection request on to another computer. The remote computer must be configured to redirect XDMCP requests. Also, indirect *xdm* connections are not fully supported prior to X11R5.

Broadcast connections are quite different. You do not have to specify an Internet address for a remote computer. Instead, the X terminal (using XDMCP) broadcasts a request for an *xdm* connection. Typically, the first host to respond to the request then supplies the connection. Some X terminals, however, may provide a chooser box from which you can select the appropriate host from those responding to the broadcast.

13.11 Remote Computer Configuration

Configuring the host computer for X terminal connections is normally handled by a system administrator—these operations require superuser capability. For completeness, however, we overview the process in this section. We should emphasize that host computers vary considerably in terms of their networking services, whether or not they provide the most recent X release, their adherence to the Consortium X standard with respect to system administration-related issues, and so on.

13.11.1 Host Database Facilities

Some workstation environments provide high-level network management services, for example, Sun's NIS™ (Network Information Service). If these services are active, you must use them for entering information such as the network node name for the X terminal. When the local network is a simple one, many system administrators prefer to abandon these higher level services in favor of the older, low-level facilities, such as */etc/hosts* and */etc/ethers* in traditional UNIX workstation environments.

As mentioned in Section 13.9, */etc/hosts* maps Internet addresses to hostnames, sometimes called system names or node names:

```
...
192.9.200.11 ncd1
192.9.200.12 ncd2
...
192.9.200.21 hds1
...
192.9.200.61 hp1
...
192.9.200.71 sgi1
...
```

For a large local area network, the basic task of choosing hostnames can become a significant chore; in the example, we've simply enumerated X terminal manufacturers' names/initials. (You can add aliases that are more meaningful to the right of each primary

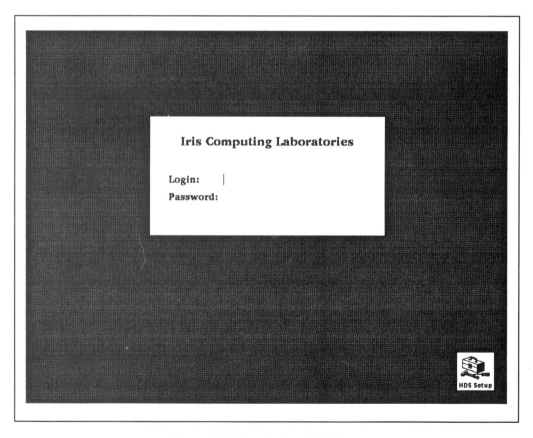

Figure 13.2 An *xdm* Log-in Window

hostname.)

This host database should contain an entry for each known system on the network, that is, for each system with which the host computer intends to communicate. An entry in */etc/hosts* is all that's necessary for normal Internet communication, for example, a remote copy operation between two workstations [using *rcp(1)*]. You can test whether or not the host computer recognizes a particular entry with the utility *ping(1)*:

```
{your system prompt} ping hds1
hds1 is alive
```

[*ping(1)* is not available in all UNIX environments.]

13.11.2 Address Resolution with RARP

If your X terminal depends on RARP for address resolution, you must add an entry for its Ethernet address to */etc/ethers*:

```
8:0:20:8:9b:cb          spectro
. . .
00:00:A7:00:4C:D1       ncd1
00:00:A7:10:7F:8D       ncd2
. . .
00:80:96:00:07:36       hds1
. . .
```

(Ethernet addresses are sometimes stamped on the bottom of X terminals; some X terminals provide this information in their set-up window and on the console during boot operations.)

/etc/ethers maps Ethernet addresses to hostnames, and the latter should be consistent with those in */etc/hosts*. The RARP utility, *rarpd(8)*, matches the Ethernet address broadcast by the X terminal during start-up operations to these entries. If *rarpd(8)* finds a match, it then looks up the Internet address in */etc/hosts*. Once the X terminal has been provided with its Internet address, it becomes a fully functional network citizen.

Of course, for your X terminal to communicate with *rarpd(8)*, *rarpd(8)* must be one of the system processes (daemons) that's started by the host computer during boot operations. In the example, *rarpd(8)* is started in the system initialization file *rc.local*:

```
{your system prompt} grep rarpd /etc/*
/etc/rc.local:  (echo -n ' rarpd'; \
/etc/rc.local:  rarpd ec0 'hostname'; \
/etc/rc.local:  rarpd ie0 'hostname'; \
/etc/rc.local:  rarpd le0 'hostname')                    >/dev/console
```

You can examine the table of current processes to determine if *rarpd* is currently executing:

```
{your system prompt} ps aux
USER        PID %CPU %MEM    SZ  RSS TT STAT START   TIME COMMAND
```

```
. . .
root          121  0.0  0.0    36     0 ?  IW   Apr 23  0:00 rarpd le0 spectro
root          123  0.0  0.0    36     0 ?  IW   Apr 23  0:00 rarpd le0 spectro
. . .
```

Note that in most environments, you must kill and restart *rarpd(8)* for it to recognize
modifications to */etc/ethers*. If you are unfamilar with *kill(1)*, one alternative is to reboot
the host computer. To kill *rarpd(8)* use the -HUP command-line option:

```
{your system prompt} ps aux | grep rarpd
root          121  0.0  0.0    36     0 ?  IW   Apr 23  0:00 rarpd le0 spectro
jsmith       3600  0.0  1.6    32   184 p3 S    12:18   0:00 grep rarpd
{your system prompt} kill -HUP 121
121: Not owner
{your system prompt} su root
Password:
{your system prompt} kill -HUP 121
```

There's nothing like an occasional use of *kill(1)* to let your workstation know who's really
in charge.

13.11.3 Downloading Files with TFTP

In this section we describe the simplest facility for downloading files from the remote
computer to an X terminal, namely, TFTP. For information on BOOTP, see a system
administration guide and/or your X terminal user's manual.

A number of UNIX workstations do not provide BOOTP; hence, *tftp(1)* is a popular utility for
downloading X servers and fonts. Using TFTP presents a minor dilemma. In unsecure
mode, *tftp(1)* creates a large security hole because of the manner in which it accesses files,
a topic that is beyond the scope of this book. If your local network is closed to the outside
world, the lack of security typically is not a problem. In unsecure (unrestricted) mode,
tftp(1) does not require that files reside in any particular directory. Hence, you simply have
to install the X server and font directories at a convenient location and then reference these
locations as part of your X terminal configuration.

In secure mode, *tftp(1)* will only transfer files located within its home directory structure,
which is usually */tftpboot*. Thus, to use *tftp(1)* in secure mode, you must install X terminal-
related files within this directory structure. Installing files within */tftpboot* can be problematic because it is usually located in the root filesystem, which is often too small to
accommodate X server images (executables) and/or font directories.

You can test for the presence of *tftp(1)* and whether or not it is running in secure mode from
the command line:

```
{your system prompt} tftp saturn
tftp> get /home/jsmith/XTerm
Received 869 bytes in 0.3 seconds
tftp>
```

On this particular mininetwork, saturn is running unrestricted *tftp*; hence, we can install font directories at an arbitrary location such as */usr/lib/X11/x-terminals/hds/fonts* for HDS X terminals. It's more likely, however, that you would install an X terminal manufacturer's entire font and X server distribution within one vendor-related directory, for example,

```
{your system prompt} cd /usr/hds/hds-fx
{your system prompt} ls
bin/            extensions/      image_u/        man/
config/         fonts/           include/        rgb/
contrib/        image/           lib/            utils/
```

If you intend to use TFTP for downloading X terminal-related files, it should be activated during the host computer's boot operations. On a Sun workstation, for example, the TFTP daemon is requested in */etc/inetd.conf*:

```
{your system prompt} grep tftp /etc/inetd.conf
#tftp dgram  udp  wait root  /usr/etc/in.tftpd  in.tftpd -s /tftpboot
tftp  dgram  udp  wait root  /usr/etc/in.tftpd  in.tftpd
```

In the example, we've commented out the entry that runs TFTP in secure mode (the -s option) from the directory */tftpboot*, replacing it with an entry that runs TFTP in unrestricted mode from any directory.

If security is an issue, you shouldn't take this issue lightly. See your system administrator, or your computer therapist, before doing what we've done here.

13.11.4 *xdm* on the Remote Computer

In many cases, *xdm* already will be configured and running on the remote computer, and no modifications will be required to support an X terminal. Obviously, however, if *xdm* is not running on the host, you cannot configure your X terminal for *xdm*-based connections.

Typically, *xdm* is run from a system start-up file during boot operations. For example, on a Sun workstation running SunOS 4.x, plus the Consortium X distribution, *xdm* should be run from *rc* or *rc.local*:

```
if [ -f /usr/bin/X11/xdm ]; then
        /usr/bin/X11/xdm;
        (echo -n ' xdm') >/dev/console
fi
```

If your remote computer is not running *xdm*, see your system administrator. The manner in which you start *xdm* differs significantly across UNIX environments.

Section 13.14 describes various *xdm*-related customizations.

13.12 X Terminal Configuration: NVRAM versus a Remote File

Most X terminals have updatable, nonvolatile memory for storing set-up parameters, including the X terminal's network node name, Internet address, location of font directories, and so on. Thus, you can use the set-up window to configure and then save the configuration options in NVRAM for each X terminal on the network. In our opinion, configuring an X terminal from NVRAM is the best approach with one or two X terminals because you can instantly reconfigure selected parameters from the set-up window.

In some environments, for example, when a system administrator must set up and maintain many X terminals, it is easier to save common X terminal configuration parameters in a file on the remote computer. The format for a remote configuration file differs from one X terminal manufacturer to the next. An X terminal user's manual will describe the steps necessary to create this file, as well as the keywords and syntax for each configuration parameter. Note that in some cases you can configure one X terminal manually, and then request that the X terminal generate a remote configuration file corresponding to its current NVRAM settings.

How do you request that your X terminal use the remote configuration file instead of its current NVRAM settings? In some cases you must select this option from the set-up window and specify the remote configuration file's location. With this arrangement NVRAM is being used in a limited way, specifically, to determine the location of a file with configuration parameters that may differ from those currently stored in NVRAM.

Other X terminals automatically examine a configuration file at a particular location in the directory hierarchy for that X terminal's files on the remote computer. This configuration directory may contain a default remote configuration file that's used when no other configuration has been specified. Lastly, some X terminals determine the location of the remote configuration file via BOOTP. Consult your X terminal user's manual.

13.13 Using Telnet

In most cases, an X terminal and a remote host support the TELNET protocol. TELNET is an Internet-related, remote terminal protocol. It allows users at one node to establish a remote TCP connection to a computer at another node. It is a rather primitive analog to *rlogin*, which is demonstrated in Section 2.8.

A Telnet window is useful for establishing a log-in session to a remote computer that does not run X, and hence, does not provide XDMCP-based log-ins. A Telnet window is also useful for testing whether or not your X terminal can communicate with a remote computer. If your XDMCP-based connection is not working properly, you might want to log in via Telnet to ensure that the X terminal and the remote computer can communicate with each other. If you can establish a Telnet-based connection, but not an XDMCP-based connection, there is probably something wrong with your *xdm* configuration.

An X terminal user's manual should include information on how to establish a Telnet session. In UNIX environments, the *telnet(1)* man-page provides information on the remote computer's Telnet support. As one example of establishing a Telnet session, consider the set-up window for an HDS X terminal given in Figure 13.1. The HDS set-up window includes a button for starting a Telnet session. Clicking this button invokes a Telnet window from which we can connect to another computer on the network, concurrent with our existing *xdm*-based connection to a remote computer (see Figure 13.3).

In other words, an X terminal can support one connection to a remote computer via *xdm*, typically, to the computer from which we would like to run X clients. From a Telnet window we can establish log-in sessions to other computers. This Telnet window will run your default command shell. From this command window, you can perform traditional character-based computing, or set the DISPLAY environment variable to your X terminal and then run X clients on this alternate remote computer that display alongside X clients from your primary remote computer. Note that the alternate remote computer must recognize your X terminal, that is, have an entry for your X terminal in its host database.

Another, albeit unlikely, alternative would be to use Telnet instead of *xdm* each time you start your X terminal for a manual, that is, non-*xdm*, connection to a remote computer. As we did in Figure 13.3, you must set the DISPLAY environmnt variable in order to run X clients remotely that display on your X terminal. This type of connection can be used to access a pre-X11R4 X environment without *xdm*, although it would be unusual to discover such a dinosaur.

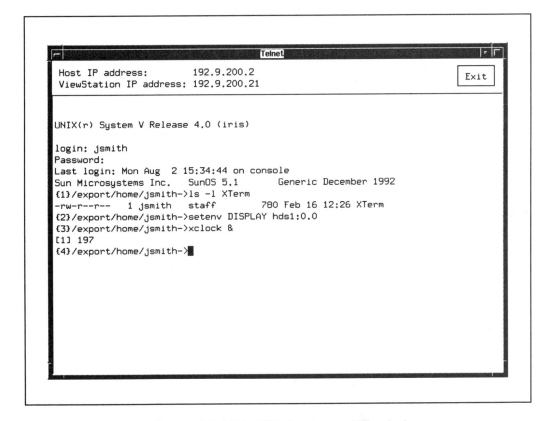

Figure 13.3 A Telnet Window from an X Terminal

13.14 *xdm*-related Customizations

xdm-related data files are stored in a central location, typically, in the directory */usr/lib/X11/xdm*. This section describes each of these files, plus several other *xdm*-related issues.

13.14.1 *xdm-config*

This file, from the Consortium X distribution, contains:

```
DisplayManager.servers:      /usr/lib/X11/xdm/Xservers
DisplayManager.errorLogFile: /usr/lib/X11/xdm/xdm-errors
DisplayManager*resources:    /usr/lib/X11/xdm/Xresources
DisplayManager*startup:      /usr/lib/X11/xdm/Xstartup
DisplayManager*reset:        /usr/lib/X11/xdm/Xreset
DisplayManager*session:      /usr/lib/X11/xdm/Xsession
DisplayManager*authorize:    false
```

The *DisplayManager* class provides resources for setting the names of various *xdm*-related data files. You could, for example, change the error log file so that errors are reported in your home directory (if you're the only user of a stand-alone workstation). In most cases, however, there is no reason to change these files.

The *authorize* resource controls user-based access control, as opposed to the host-based access control provided by *xhost* (see Section 13.15.2). With the current setting, user-based access control is turned off. Some X distributions are configured to enable user-based access control for the local display by including a qualified resource setting before the unqualified *authorize*:

```
...
DisplayManager._0.authorize: true
DisplayManager*authorize:    false
...
```

The resource component _0 refers to the local display; ":0" would be illegal syntax within the left-hand side of a resource specification. The subsequent resource setting ensures that other displays depend on host-based access control.

If you modify *xdm-config*, you should kill the *xdm* parent process, in the manner described for *rarpd(8)* in Section 13.11.2. Typically, there will be multiple *xdm* processes because a child process is started (forked) for every display that is being managed. The file specified by the resource *DisplayManager.pidFile* always contains the ID of this parent process (see Section 13.14.7).

13.14.2 *Xservers*

This file contains a list of displays to manage for any network node not using XDMCP to initiate *xdm* sessions, which is typically the remote computer. (X terminals negotiate for *xdm* sessions with XDMCP.) Of course, if the remote computer is not running *xdm*, this file will probably be empty. If the remote computer is, for example, a UNIX workstation that runs *xdm* all the time (beginning immediately after boot operations), *Xservers* should contain at least one entry:

```
:0 Local local /usr/bin/X11/X :0
```

It is this entry that requests *xdm* sessions on the local workstation. The format of each entry is

```
<display-name> <display-class> <display-type> <X-server> <X-server-arguments>
```

<display-class> is optional, so we could have used:

```
:0 local /usr/bin/X11/X :0
```

Vendors provide their own unique display classes, and *xdm* implementations that recognize their display-class keywords. See the *X* man-page for more information on your X server's command-line options.

If you intend to configure X terminals for *xdm*-based access to a remote computer, but without using XDMCP-based communication with *xdm*, you may need entries for those X terminals here. Typically, X terminal entries include only the *<display-name>* and *<display-type>* fields:

```
ncdu10:0 foreign
```

In some X environments it is possible that you will need a third, comment field for X terminal entries:

```
ncdu10:0 foreign anything
```

The X terminal is responsible for invoking its X server, so the X server is not named here. We should reiterate that, in most cases, you do not need entries for X terminals in *Xservers* because they will be configured to negotiate with *xdm* for a log-in window using XDMCP.

If you modify *Xservers*, you should kill the *xdm* parent process, in the manner described for *rarpd(8)* in Section 13.11.2. Typically, there will be multiple *xdm* processes because a child process is started (forked) for every display that is being managed. The file specified by the resource *DisplayManager.pidFile* always contains the ID of this parent process (see Section 13.14.7).

13.14.3 *Xresources*

This file contains resource settings for *xlogin*, the *xdm* log-in window:

```
xlogin*greetFont: -*-charter-bold-r-normal--25-180-100-100-p-157-*-1
xlogin*failFont: -*-charter-bold-i-normal*140*
xlogin*fail: login failed, please try again...
```

```
xlogin*greeting: Iris Computing Laboratories
xlogin*Font: -bitstream-charter-bold-r-normal--19-140-100-100-p-119-iso8859-1
xlogin*borderWidth: 3
#ifdef COLOR
xlogin*greetColor: #f63
xlogin*failColor: red
xlogin*Foreground: black
xlogin*Background: #fdc
#else
xlogin*Foreground: black
xlogin*Background: white
#endif
```

Most of these resources are self-explanatory; note that the log-in greeting matches our log-in window in Figure 13.2.

Some X environments provide for a robust log-in strategy, namely, a failsafe mode, that can be used to override processing of the user's *.xsession* file. This capability is important and we suggest that you, or your system administrator, add support for failsafe mode, if *Xresources* does not include it already. For the previous *Xresources*, or something similar, add the following translation prior to the end of the file:

```
xlogin*login.translations: #override\
  Ctrl<Key>R:  abort-display()\n\
  <Key>F1:  set-session-argument(failsafe) finish-field()\n\
  Ctrl<Key>Return:  set-session-argument(failsafe) finish-field()\n\
  <Key>Return:  set-session-argument() finish-field()
```

The action finish-field() terminates input to a field, as if you had pressed **<Return>**. The action set-session-argument() sends failsafe as an argument to the session manager, thereby enabling failsafe mode. The current translation invokes failsafe mode when the user presses either **<F1>** or **<Ctrl>-<Return>**.

If the failsafe condition is true, *Xsession* simply starts an *xterm* client without further evaluation of whether or not the user's home directory contains an *.xsession* script. Having this capability is important so that you have a method of logging in if there are errors in *.xsession*. For this capability to operate properly, you must also ensure that *Xsession* processes failsafe requests (see Section 13.14.8).

13.14.4 *Xstartup*

Typically, this file is empty. It contains any start-up commands that the remote computer should execute as root/superuser immediately after the user's log-in is verified.

13.14.5 *Xreset*

Typically, this file is empty. It contains any clean-up commands that the remote computer should execute as root/superuser immediately after the user's log-in is verified.

13.14.6 *xdm-errors*

This file contains error messages. If, for example, *Xresources* specifies fonts that aren't available to an X terminal (because they haven't been downloaded, for whatever reason), this file will contain messages to this effect:

```
Warning: Cannot convert string "-bitstream-charter-bold-r-normal--19-140-100-
100-p-119-iso8859-1" to type FontStruct
Warning: Cannot convert string "-*-charter-bold-r-normal--25-180-100-100-p-
157-*-1" to type FontStruct
Warning: Cannot convert string "-*-charter-bold-i-normal*140* " to type
FontStruct
...
xterm:  unable to open font "6x10", trying "fixed"....
```

If your X terminal is not communicating properly with *xdm*, you, or your system administrator, definitely should take a look at this file.

13.14.7 *xdm-pid*

/usr/lib/X11/xdm/xdm-pid is the default filename for storing the process ID of the parent *xdm* process. You can change this filename with the following resource setting in *xdm-config*:

```
DisplayManager.pidFile: <pid-file>
```

13.14.8 *Xsession*

This file contains a default *xdm* start-up script:

```
#!/bin/sh
#
# Xsession
#
# This is the program that is run as the client
# for the display manager.  This example is
# quite friendly as it attempts to run a per-user
# .xsession file instead of forcing a particular
# session layout
#
if [ -f $HOME/.xsession ]; then
    if [ -x $HOME/.xsession ]; then
        exec $HOME/.xsession
    else
        exec /bin/sh $HOME/.xsession
    fi
else
    twm &
    exec xterm -fn 10x20 -geometry 80x24+20+20 -ls
fi
```

Typically, you provide a start-up script for *xdm* in your home directory that starts your preferred X clients; this file is named *$HOME/.xsession*. See Sections 2.8 and 13.16 for more information.

Here, the commands in *$HOME/.xsession* are executed, if this script exists. If not, the default environment is the window manager *twm* with one *xterm* client. *xterm* is run as a foreground process, so terminating *xterm* would terminate the log-in session.

Some X environments provide for a slightly more robust log-in strategy, namely, a failsafe mode, that can be used to override processing of the user's *.xsession* file. This capability is important and we suggest that you, or your system administrator, add support for failsafe mode, if *Xsession* does not include it already. For the previous *Xsession*, or something similar, add the following prior to the if-then-else that evaluates the presence of a *.xsession* in the user's home directory:

```
#!/bin/sh
...
# session layout
#

case $# in
1)
   case $1 in
   failsafe)
     exec xterm -fn 10x20 -geometry 80x24+20+20 -ls
     ;;
   esac
esac

...
if [ -f $HOME/.xsession ]; then
...
fi
```

If the failsafe condition is true, *Xsession* simply starts an *xterm* client without further evaluation of whether or not the user's home directory contains an *.xsession* script. Having this capability is important so that you have a method of logging in if there are errors in *.xsession*. For this capability to operate properly, you must also ensure that your *xlogin* window provides a key translation that signals a failsafe log-in session (see Section 13.14.3).

13.14.9 Terminating the X Server under *xdm*

If the remote computer runs *xdm* automatically, *xdm* is persistent in its efforts to keep the X server running. By default, if you kill the X server, *xdm* restarts it. There are occasions, however, when you would like to shut down X completely on the remote computer, possibly while configuring X terminals.

One way of terminating the X server is to remove the entry in *Xservers* for the local host:

```
:0 Local local /usr/bin/X11/X :0
```

If you then restart the *xdm* parent process, it will not start X when you kill the X server process. That is, it's perfectly acceptable to have *xdm* running on the remote computer, to support X terminals, even though the remote computer is not currently running X.

Alternatively, you can add the following resource setting to *xdm-config*:

```
DisplayManager.DISPLAY.terminateServer:   true
```

We've covered those aspects of *xdm* that are typically of interest to end-users. There are many other *xdm*-related resources that are used on occasion by system administrators; see the *xdm* man-page for additional information.

13.15 X Display Security

Section 2.8 provides examples for remotely displaying an X client. If other users have access permission for your display, named saturn, they can redirect any X client to saturn with the -display command-line option:

```
{system prompt on jupiter} xroach -display saturn:0.0 &
```

Displaying bugs that scurry across the screen is a rather harmless prank, but it becomes a nuisance if it happens frequently.

There are, however, more serious pranks. An astute X programmer, with access to your workstation or X terminal display, could completely lock up your display, using techniques that we will not discuss here (for obvious reasons). In this situation, you would be unable to save your work indefinitely.

For this reason, X servers normally employ host-based access control wherein the local host—your workstation—is the only one that has access to the display. Host-based access applies to either *xinit*- or *xdm*-based X sessions. Alternatively, for system running *xdm* you can enable a user-based access control mechanism that limits display access to particular users. These topics are considered in this section.

13.15.1 Host-based Access Control

Host-based access, as its name implies, allows any user and any X client from a permitted host to access the display in question. If host-based access control is disabled, all hosts are permitted access:

```
{your system prompt on saturn} xhost +
access control disabled, clients can connect from any host
```

By default, host-based access control is enabled with most X distributions for workstations. If, for some reason, you have disabled your system's access control, you can manually reestablish access control with the following command:

```
{your system prompt on saturn} xhost -
access control enabled, only authorized clients can connect
```

At this point, you could grant explicit access to certain remote computers:

```
{your system prompt on saturn} xhost +jupiter
jupiter being added to access control list
```

Executing *xhost* with no arguments displays its current state and a list of hosts that have access to your display:

```
{your system prompt on saturn} xhost
access control enabled, only authorized clients can connect
jupiter
spectro
```

Depending on the X terminal, its configuration, and the network organization, (1) host-based access may or may not be enabled by default and (2) if host-based access is enabled, the default list of hosts may or may not include the remote computer, even though X clients running on the remote computer can connect:

```
{your system prompt on an hds1} xhost
access control enabled, only authorized clients can connect
hds1
```

With some X terminals, for example, if the network consists of only one remote computer, the host computer's access permission is implicit. With multiple remote computers, the list should include the host computer:

```
{your system prompt on an hds1} xhost
access control enabled, only authorized clients can connect
saturn
hds1
```

To permit X clients on another remote computer to use the X terminal's display, you must add them explicitly:

```
{your system prompt on hds1} xhost +jupiter
jupiter being added to access control list
{your system prompt on hds1} xhost
access control enabled, only authorized clients can connect
jupiter
saturn
hds1
```

The reason that some X terminals do not enable host-based access control is that it is not tremendously useful. In particular, if jupiter and saturn are granted access, any user on these systems can use/abuse your X terminal's display. As a rule, however, it's better to limit access to certain hosts than to permit access by any host on the network, especially if you're directly connected to a large, public network.

Some X terminals provide configuration options for enabling host-based access control, and for specifying which remote computers have access. If your X terminal does not, you can set up host-based access in your *.xsession* script by adding commands comparable to those in the previous examples (see Section 13.16).

For a workstation, as opposed to an X terminal, you can also use *xhost* commands in *.xsession* (or *.xinitrc*). As an alternative, users who have system administrator privileges can create the file */etc/X0.hosts* containing the list of remote computers having access to your display:

```
{your system prompt on saturn} more /etc/X0.hosts
jupiter
uranus
pluto
```

(If you have multiple displays, create the file */etc/X0.hosts* for display 0, */etc/X1.hosts* for display 1, and so on).

Note that if you grant other remote computers access to the host computer's display, this access is *not* propagated to the displays of X terminals connected to the host computer. For example, when you access a workstation from an X terminal, the feeling may be similar to working directly from the workstation, but each X display is distinct—access granted to saturn's display does not extend to hds1's display, even though saturn hosts hds1.

13.15.2 User-based Access Control

At present, X provide a primitive form of user-based access control, formally known as MIT-MAGIC-COOKIE-1; it is useful primarily with *xdm*. Recall from Section 13.14.1 that *xdm-config* may set the *authorize* resource:

```
. . .
DisplayManager._0.authorize:  true
DisplayManager*authorize:     false
. . .
```

These settings enable user-based access control on the local display only. To activate user-based access control for all displays, simply change the second general *authorize* specification:

```
. . .
DisplayManager._0.authorize:  true
DisplayManager*authorize:     true
. . .
```

User-based access is more restrictive than host-based access. When user-based access is enabled, an X server provides display services only to those X clients that have a special key called a *magic cookie*. A magic cookie is, in essence, an *xdm*-generated, host-specific token.

This authorization scheme is enforced jointly by the host computer running *xdm* and the X server managing the target display. When *xdm* starts a user session, it places a magic cookie in a special file, *.Xauthority* by default, in the user's home directory with the following access permissions:

```
-rw-------   1 jsmith          248 Apr 29 15:08 .Xauthority
```

.Xauthority is not a text file, but you can display its contents with the list option:

```
{your system prompt on saturn} xauth list
hds1:0  MIT-MAGIC-COOKIE-1  fe5fac750a7b98f1d657442d62f3b029
saturn:0  MIT-MAGIC-COOKIE-1  41e627d47d72c34079be1f6c35ca3b58
saturn/unix:0  MIT-MAGIC-COOKIE-1  41e627d47d72c34079be1f6c35ca3b58
jupiter:0  MIT-MAGIC-COOKIE-1  bf8cd5eadb7851b6b7248d425390898e
```

xdm also communicates the magic cookie to the appropriate X server, which could be managing a local or a remote display, for example, an X terminal. For the previous *.Xauthority* file, the X server for hds1 would have the magic cookie given in the first entry.

According to the normal file-permission policies in a UNIX environment, when a user executes an X client it has access to this file. Hence, during start-up operations an X client reads the magic cookie for the appropriate display and presents it to the X server, which then verifies it.

X clients executing elsewhere on the network normally do not have access to the magic cookies given in *.Xauthority*, therefore, the appropriate X server prohibits them from using its display. The exception, of course, is when the user's home directory is mounted over the network on multiple computers, that is, when it's shared among network hosts.

Suppose you would like to execute X clients on a remote computer that is not managing your X session via *xdm*. That is, suppose you are either working locally at the workstation saturn, or accessing saturn remotely via the X terminal hds1, but you now want to execute X clients on pluto and display them on saturn, or hds1. (saturn and hds1 could be side-by-side on your desktop). If you perform a remote log-in with *rlogin(1)* to pluto, and then attempt to display its X clients on, say, hds1, each application will fail because pluto cannot provide the magic cookie for hds1's display (X server):

```
{your system prompt on hds1} rlogin pluto
Last login: Thu Apr 29 09:56:56 from saturn
Sun Microsystems Inc.   SunOS 5.1      Generic December 1992
{your system prompt on pluto} xclock -display hds1:0 &
[1] 717
{your system prompt on pluto} Xlib:  connection to "hds1:0.0" refused by
server
```

```
Xlib:  Client is not authorized to connect to Server
Error: Can't Open display

[1]    Exit 1                  xclock -display hds1:0
{your system prompt on pluto} exit
{your system prompt on pluto} logout
Connection closed.
{your system prompt on hds1}
```

To support this type of remote computing, *xauth* provides extract and merge operations, so that you can extract the locally held magic cookie for hds1 and merge it into pluto's authorization file. The easiest way to transfer a copy of the magic cookie is to pass it from one *.Xauthority* file to the other in one command-line operation using *rsh(1)*:

```
{your system prompt on hds1} xauth extract - hds1:0 | rsh pluto xauth merge -
{your system prompt on hds1} rlogin pluto
Last login: Thu Apr 29 16:45:41 from saturn
Sun Microsystems Inc.   SunOS 5.1       Generic December 1992
{your system prompt on pluto} xclock -display hds1:0 &
[1] 733
{your system prompt on pluto}
```

The - command-line options to `extract` and `merge` request that they use standard output and standard input, respectively, so that we can pipe the output from *xauth* on hds1 to *xauth* on pluto. Once pluto's *.Xauthority* file has the magic cookie for hds1's display, we can log in remotely and display pluto's X clients on hds1.

13.15.3 Host- versus User-based Access Control

To enable this type of remote computing with user-based access control requires one lengthy command:

```
{your system prompt on hds1} xauth extract - hds1:0 | rsh pluto xauth merge -
```

With host-based access control the command is simpler:

```
{your system prompt on hds1} xhost +pluto
```

Unless you're working in a closed world, for example, your own private local network, the longer command is worth the extra effort. We suggest that you set the *authorize* resource to `true` for each of your remote computers, and write a shell script for the lengthy *xauth* command that accepts the remote computer's name as an argument, for example,

```
{your system prompt on hds1} send_cookie_to pluto
```

The utility *send_cookie_to* could use the `DISPLAY` environment variable to determine which cookie to send:

```
#!/bin/sh
# File:  send_cookie_to
#
# Function:  Transfer a cookie to a remote computer
#

xauth extract - $DISPLAY | rsh $1 xauth merge -
```

It is important to note that host-based access control overrides user-based access control. That is, if you set up each of your network nodes for user-based access control, but subsequently use *xhost* to permit access to hds1 by any user on pluto, the existing user-based access control will have no effect.

13.16 *.xsession* for X Terminals

With an *.xsession* script in your local directory, you could devise an endless number of configuration possibilities. In this section we provide a single script that uses simple case-structure evaluation to set up the X environment differently for various log-in sessions.

An obvious strategy is to use distinctive names for X terminals and workstations, so that you can distinguish among monochrome and color X terminals, as well as the host work-station during an *xdm*-bases session initiation. It is up to you to devise a classification strategy. An obvious possibility would be to include manufacturer-based distinctions wherein all HDS X terminals include "hds" in their node names, all NCD X terminals include "ncd" in their node names, and so on for X terminals from other manufacturers. Other distinctions would be encoded in these nodenames, for example, a color versus monochrome distinction.

We use the following *$HOME/.xsession* for one of our host computers:

```
#!/bin/sh
#
# Assume that we're using a remote display (X terminal) initially:
#
localDisplay=0

#
# Set up user-based access control:
#
userAccess=1

#
# Monochrome NCDs are category 1:
#
if expr $DISPLAY : "ncd1*"
then
  xsetroot -bitmap /home/jsmith/icon/graytile.bit
  xmodmap -e "keycode 102 = Delete"
  xrdb -merge .Xdefaults-ncd
#
```

```
# Color NCDs are category 2:
#
elif expr $DISPLAY : "ncd2*"
then
  xsetroot -solid "SlateGray"
  xmodmap -e "keycode 102 = Delete"
  xrdb -merge .Xdefaults-ncd
#
# HDSs are color:
#
elif expr $DISPLAY : "hds*"
then
  xsetroot -solid "Salmon"
  xrdb -merge .Xdefaults-hds
# Delete is BackSpace:
  xmodmap -e "keycode 187 = Delete"
# Print Screen is Find:
  xmodmap -e "keycode 124 = Find"
# Pause is BackSpace:
  xmodmap -e "keycode 126 = BackSpace"
# Reverse Control and Caps Lock keys:
  xmodmap -e "remove lock = Caps_Lock"
  xmodmap -e "remove control = Control_L"
  xmodmap -e "keycode 176 = Control_L"
  xmodmap -e "keycode 175 = Caps_Lock"
  xmodmap -e "add control = Control_L"
  xmodmap -e "add lock = Caps_Lock"
#
# XDSs are color:
#
elif expr $DISPLAY : "xds*"
then
  xrdb -merge .Xdefaults-xds
  xmodmap -e "keycode 110 = Delete"
#
# Otherwise, the host workstation (SPARC in this case):
#
else
  localDisplay=1
  #
  #assume Sun Type-4
  #undo the F11 and F12 keysyms for <Stop> and <Again>, respectively.
  #set them to anything outside the range <F1> ... <F12>
  #
  xmodmap -e "keycode 8 = F13"
  xmodmap -e "keycode 10 = F13"
fi
#
# The host workstation (a monochrome SPARC in this case):
#
if test $localDisplay -eq 1
then
```

```
    xrdb -merge Xdefaults.mwm
    xsetroot -bitmap /home/jsmith/icon/graytile.bit
    smail  &
    xterm -sb -geometry 70x30-2-2 -fn 7x13bold -n shell -iconic  &
    xterm -sb -geometry 76x30+5+5 -fn 7x13bold -n shell2  -iconic  &
    xterm -sb -geometry 66x8+2+2 -fn 6x10 -C -ls -n console -iconic  &
    exec mwm
else
    xhost -
    xhost +mercury
    xhost +venus
    xterm -sb -geometry 80x34-1-1 \#+440+2   -fn 8x13bold -n shell -iconic   &
    xterm -sb -geometry 66x8+2+2 -fn 6x10 -C -n console -iconic  &
    exec twm
fi
...
```

Both the X terminal and workstation environments start a window manager in the fore-ground as the final process, so that the X session will end when the window manager is terminated (via a root menu option as illustrated in Chapter 12). To add variety to our perpetual life behind an X display, we use *mwm* in one environment and *twm* the other.

To illustrate activating host-based access control, as described in Section 13.15.1, our script can be modified to execute *xhost* if the value of $userAccess is set to 0.

```
    ...
    if test $userAccess -eq 1
    then
        /home/jsmith/bin/send_cookie_to pluto
        /home/jsmith/bin/send_cookie_to jupiter
    else
        xhost -
        xhost +pluto
        xhost +jupiter
    fi
    ...
```

Specifically, the else clause in the second (and final), top-level *if-then-else* applies to X terminals (the value of $localDisplay is 0). Within this else, a nested if-then-else grants access to the X terminal's display using either *send_cookie_to* (see Section 13.15.3) or *xhost*, based on the value of $userAccess. Without distinguishing among X terminals types, *xhost* first enables host-based access control and then grants access to the X terminal's display to two arbitrary hosts.

We reiterate that this use of *xhost* is provided for illustration only. Normally, as indicated by the value of $userAccess, we prefer user-based access control.

13.17 Local Clients

With respect to X terminals, a local client is an X client that executes on the X terminal's CPU and displays on the X terminal. Normally, X clients execute on the host/remote computer and display on the X terminal; in fact, local display of remote X clients is the primary function of X terminals. For example, a single implementation of an X text editor on the host computer can display on any X terminal. In this sense, local clients provide an alternative to the norm.

X terminal manufacturers provide local clients because some networks are heavily loaded, and because some X terminals depend on a (relatively slow) serial link to the host computer. Local clients reduce network bandwidth because the continual communication between an X client and the X server is local to the X terminal. The disadvantage of using local clients is that they execute within the X terminal's memory, which is fixed (real), not virtual.

That is, X clients executing remotely do so within the host computer's virtual memory system, so there is no danger of running out of memory. Of course, if the host computer has insufficient memory, overall performance could be slow. Because X terminals do not have virtual memory capabilities, there is a limit to the number of local clients that can execute concurrently. Also, note that the X system resources for every X client displaying on an X terminal, local or remote, are allocated from that X terminal's memory, for example, pixmaps, windows, cursors, and others.

Having local clients is advantageous because they provide flexibility in how you configure your system. If you would like to reduce network bandwidth considerably, you have the option of purchasing sufficient memory for your X terminal to support many local clients. If network bandwidth is relatively unimportant, you can run all of your X clients remotely.

Common local clients include window managers, Telnet clients, and standard X clients such as a calculator, one or more clocks, an *xdm*-based chooser box for selecting the host computer, and others. If you want to run one local client, a window manager is a good choice because it is one of the more heavily exercised X clients; hence, it has the most potential for reducing network bandwidth. See your X terminal user's manual for more information on local clients. We do not show an X terminal running a local window manager for obvious reasons—the appearance of a local client implementation of *mwm* is identical to that of *mwm* executing remotely.

13.18 Running a Chooser Program (X11R5)

A number of X terminals provide a so-called chooser box, typically, as a local client, from which an X terminal user can select a host computer from a list of remote computers. Using this facility is more convenient that continually modifying the Internet address in the X terminal's set-up window (when the X terminal is configured for a direct connection). Typically, the chooser box is not present by default; you must enable the local chooser client via a set-up window.

Beginning with X11R5, *xdm* provides a chooser box, *chooser*. This application is usually located in the *xdm* directory, which is */usr/lib/X11/xdm* for many X distributions. *chooser* is especially convenient because it can manage *xdm* sessions for any combinations of remote computers and X terminals—not just X terminals connecting to one of several host computers. Figure 13.4 shows *chooser* executing on the host computer and displaying its chooser box on an HDS X terminal. Some X terminals do not provide a chooser client, so having a general-purpose chooser program is important for supporting every potential display. (HDS does provide a local chooser client, but it's preferable here to demonstrate the common chooser program.)

To activate the host computer's *chooser*, you must include an entry in *Xaccess*, a database that describes the network nodes that can connect to a host computer via *xdm*. (This file has nothing to do with host- or user-based access control—it merely describes the displays that can request a *xdm* log-in window.) When you select a host computer from a chooser box, the request for a log-in session is directed to that remote computer, which then provides an *xlogin* window.

Xaccess can contain three types of entries: direct, indirect, and broadcast. By default, X allows direct or broadcast connection requests from any host computer, which is equivalent to creating *Xaccess* with one entry:

```
*                                    # anyone can request a session
```

Figure 13.4 The X11R5 Host Chooser Box

That is, "*", similar to command-shell filename expansion, matches anything. Any X server can request an *xdm* session from the host computer with this configuration.

To limit *xdm* sessions on saturn to a single network node, say, jupiter, *Xaccess* would include the single (direct) entry:

```
jupiter                         # a very restrictive access file
```

To allow connections on saturn to the workstation jupiter and X terminals from NCD and HDS (whose names encode their manufacturer in the first three characters of their network node names), *Xaccess* would include the following (direct) entries:

```
jupiter                         # a somewhat selective access file
hds*
ncd*
```

If, say, Bob (from the workstation "bobs-machine"), has a history of running X clients that tax a host computer to its absolute computing limit, you can use the special "not" operator, "!", to lock him out:

```
*
!bobs-machine                   # anyone but Bob!
```

Indirect entries allow one host to redirect requests for *xdm* sessions to other computers. For example, to configure saturn's *xdm* to redirect an indirect request by an HDS X terminal for an *xdm* session to "mars", you could use the following entry:

```
hds* mars                       # send HDS users to mars
```

Note that mars must be receptive to *xdm* sessions; its *Xaccess* could allow (direct) connections from an HDS X terminal:

```
hds*
```

Typically, indirect entries are used to allow X terminals to connect to one of several host computers. One remote computer must serve as the redirecting agent, say, saturn. Thus, saturn's *Xaccess* could include the following entries:

```
hds* CHOOSER mars jupiter pluto  # allow HDS users to select a host
```

With this entry, saturn displays a chooser box on the display of any HDS X terminal; the selection box contains three specified entries. Of course, saturn has no authority to make decisions for any of these remote computers. If the user makes a selection, *chooser* simply redirects the request to the appropriate remote computer, which may or may not provide an *xlogin* window, based on (direct) entries in its *Xaccess* file.

An alternative to naming a set of potential host computers is for saturn to broadcast a request for remote computers willing to accept *xdm* connections (a type of "any takers?" redirection):

```
hds* CHOOSER BROADCAST
```

It should be clear that, for a complicated local network, there are many, many potential combinations of direct-, indirect-, and broadcast-based requests.

xdm is quite easy to use, despite its very sophisticated support for virtually any type of display mangement. See the *xdm* man-page for a complete list of its X resources.

A

X Events, Windows, Etc.

In Chapter 1 we addressed the essential components of the X Window System from the user's point of view: the X server, X clients, and the network transparency that allows you run an X client on a remote workstation while displaying (working with) the application at a local workstation. We also emphasized the role of the window manager as an X super-application and X's flexibility with respect to look-and-feel issues. This appendix provides additional lower level information about how X works; this information is not a prerequisite to the preceding chapters.

A.1 Screen-oriented Issues

X is designed for bitmapped displays. That is, X "knows how" to support screen images that are drawn by selectively activating and deactivating individual screen elements, called *pixels* (for picture elements). A screen is composed of a grid (rows and columns) of pixels. If you cannot see this grid on your workstation's screen, because the pixels are too small, the scoreboard at a local sports stadium provides an example of the process of representing images as a system of "dots."

In general, the greater the number of rows and columns of pixels (for a given screen size) the greater the clarity of the on-screen images; this pixel density is called the display screen (or monitor) *resolution*. Most workstations are shipped with a medium-resolution monitor; a common resolution is 1152×900 pixels (1152 pixels horizontally and 900 pixels vertically), which is more than one million dots per screen. High-resolution monitors typically have a resolution of 1280×1024 pixels.

A display's screen also has a depth. A monochrome screen has a depth of one *plane*; a plane is, essentially, an array of data with one array element per pixel. The basic task of displaying the letter "X" on a monochrome screen involves activating the specific pixels that form the

"X" pattern from a rectangular area that encompasses the letter "X" and deactivating all other pixels (or vice versa). A monochrome screen based on cathode-ray tube (CRT) technology typically uses a white phosphor to form a black-and-white pattern of pixels; a monochrome screen based on gas-plasma technology provides orange-and-black patterning; and, an LCD- (Liquid-crystal display) based screen may also provide a black-and-white image. There are, of course, other ways of producing monochrome images. Regardless of the technology, with a monochrome screen you can display the letter "X" using either a light-on-dark or dark-on-light technique.

To manage the pixels on a monochrome screen, a workstation must have a dedicated memory area, sometimes called a frame buffer, with a memory cell corresponding to each screen pixel; this cell records whether or not that pixel is "on" or "off." Thus, a plane is not a physical entity; it is a conceptualization of the bank of memory cells that record the state of a (color) component of each pixel.

A color screen has a depth greater than one plane. That is, to illuminate the pixel at screen position (42,37), it is necessary to do more than simply activate (turn on) that pixel. As with a CRT-based monochrome screen, a pixel is activated by exciting the phosphorescent material in that screen area with a measured amount of radiation. To produce a colored pixel on a color screen, that pixel is radiated by multiple electron guns, each gun selectively activating red, green, or blue phosphorescent material, as necessary to produce the proper color.

To record the color associated with each pixel on a color screen, a workstation must have a multiplane frame buffer. An eight-bit frame buffer has eight bit-planes, that is, eight memory cells per pixel, supporting 2^8 (256) possible color combinations. The color for each pixel is represented in the frame buffer—with respect to a *colormap*. A colormap is a table of information that describes how to translate an application's color specification, say, for a window background, into values that are meaningful to the low-level display hardware and software. In other words, the eight memory cells (eight bits) for each pixel in the frame buffer provide an index into the colormap. Each of the 256 possible combinations of bits, for example, 00000000, 00000001, ..., 10101010, ..., 11111111, references a numerical offset in the colormap; this colormap cell then provides the information necessary for the hardware to display that distinct color. Figure A.1 illustrates this approach to color representation; the diagram highlights the top-left pixel, which is a particular shade of red. For the purposes of the illustration in Figure A.1, the colormap indexes stored in display memory are reduced to two binary digits, e.g., 00000000 is shown as 00 and 00000001 as 01.

With X, different (virtual) colormaps can be associated with different windows, providing different color interpretations. When the window manager gives the keyboard focus to a particular window, the virtual colormap for that window is automatically registered "with the workstation" as the colormap "of the moment." (For a window to receive the keyboard focus simply means that keystrokes are delivered to that window; see Section 3.8.)

Although some workstations support multiple concurrent (hardware) colormaps, most workstations support only one colormap. Because a colormap provides the color interpretation between an X application's window and the hardware, having different windows use different colormaps implies that the colors will be "off," or incorrect, in those windows that use a different colormap than the window that currently has the keyboard focus.

When X (the X server) starts up, it covers the entire screen with a plain, borderless window, often called the *root window*, that serves (visually) as a backdrop for all other windows. (You can set the pattern for the root window with the utility *xsetroot*.) Actually, the root window is more than a visual backdrop for other windows. X is a hierarchical window system, as described in Section A.2. When X starts up, it associates numerous default "characteristics" with the root window, for example, a default colormap. When an application creates its windows, they inherit a colormap from their parent (in the window hierarchy). Thus, by default, X applications use the default colormap. For the user, the implication is that all applications/windows use the same colormap and retain their true colors regardless of which window has the keyboard focus, unless an application installs an alternate colormap for its window(s).

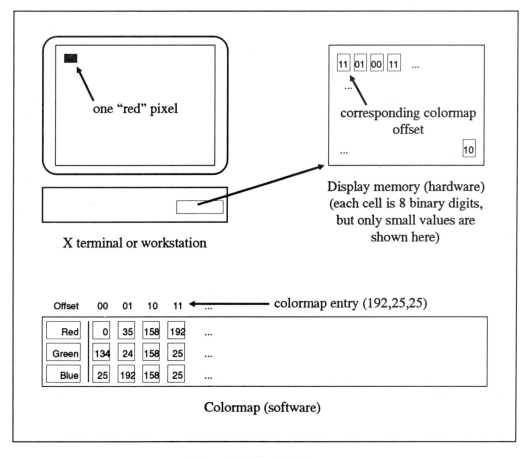

Figure A.1 The X Colormap

A.2 Drawables

With X, there are two types of drawables: (1) pixmaps and (2) windows. Essentially, a *drawable* is an X resource that accepts various graphics requests such as drawing a point, line, or rectangle, copying an area of one drawable to another drawable, and so on.

We mentioned that X uses a hierarchical, or (upside-down) tree-oriented, window system. Every window is part of the window hierarchy that originates from the root window; see Figure 1.14. An application can create windows that are children of the root window, often called *top-level* windows, as well as windows that are children of its top-level windows, and so on.

Parenthetically, when we say that an application's window is a child of the root window, we deliberately ignore the fact that most modern window managers actually *reparent* application windows; that is, window managers interpose their own window(s) so that they can provide window decorations to application windows. Also, note that there will be multiple window hierarchies if a display has multiple screens, say, one monochrome and one color screen—one per screen.

A *pixmap*, on the other hand, is not a window and is not part of the window hierarchy. A pixmap is an off-screen memory area that accepts graphics requests, much like a window. Pixmaps are not subject to exposures, as described previously for windows. In some cases, applications will produce output directly to a window; in others situations, applications use pixmaps to build an image and then copy the "finished product" to the window. This approach is especially useful when the computations required to produce the graphics are complex, but the application design requires that the image appear immediately (without the user having to watch as it is being drawn).

Another use for pixmaps is for ongoing storage of a window's contents. That is, the application maintains the current, proper image for a window as a pixmap. Then, each time there is an exposure in the window, for example, when the user is moving windows around on the screen (raising partially obscured windows), the application responds to the notification of an exposure by refreshing the window (or a portion of the window) from the pixmap.

Strictly speaking, it is improper to think of a pixmap as a window that you cannot see, because (1) a pixmap is not a window and (2) windows are not always visible. X allows you to drag a large window over top of a smaller window, totally obscuring the latter, but it is still "there," and it is still a window (part of the window hierarchy). Also, X allows an application to *unmap* its windows. To unmap a window is to remove it from the screen; the window, however, still exists. For example, pop-up windows such as dialog boxes are frequently mapped and unmapped for user interaction. Also, an application window is in an unmapped state when it is iconified.

Icons, by the way, are windows, like an application's main window. The window manager is responsible for creating an icon to represent an application; it also provides a default image for the icon. Typically, a user can substitute an alternate icon (image) for an application or class of applications using a window manager configuration parameter. Many applications supply their own icon images and "suggest" that the window manager use them. The window manager, however, is the ultimate authority with respect to icons and it can simply ignore an application's suggestions.

Lastly, we should mention that the organization of windows in the window hierarchy is quasi-independent of the organization of windows on your screen. That is, you can drag a word processor's main window and drop it on top of a spreadsheet's main window; the fact that the word processor's window is now obscuring the spreadsheet's window does not change their parent-child positions in the window hierarchy. It's common to refer to windows as being stacked on top of each other (when you have a lot of them). Most window managers allow you to manipulate the stacking order of windows through menu options ("Raise", "Lower", "Rotate", and so on) and with keyboard and mouse shortcuts, for example, clicking on a window's border to raise it to the top of the stack.

The concept of manipulating windows on your screen much like papers on your desk is distinct from X's concept of a window hierarchy. X's hierarchical window organization provides a powerful window management strategy, wherein child windows inherit characteristics from their parents, are clipped by their parent windows, and so on. For a programmer, this hierarchy simplifies tasks such as creating menus and other user-interface components that are composed of many little windows. For the user, the hierarchical nature of X is somewhat transparent; noticeable exceptions include the way in which child windows inherit (application) resources from their parent windows, for example, background color, and the manner in which certain events such as mouse button operations and keystrokes in an application's child windows can be propagated (in effect, delivered) to the parent window.

A.3 X Window System Resources

With X, the term *resource* is used in two ways. First, X has a facility for configuring applications wherein configuration parameters are managed as database entries, using the term database quite loosely. These parameters are called *application resources* in this book, when necessary, to distinguish them from system resources. (X toolkit programmers use the term *application resources* in another way, but here we will avoid distinctions that are awkward, confusing, and largely irrelevant to the typical user; see Section 7.3).

An application can define its own resources that override resources by the same names that may exist at a higher level; for example, an application may define its own unique interpretation of a resource such as *cursorColor*. In many cases, users can define resources generically or at the application level. For example, an X user might set the resource *background* to plum with no application-specific qualifications, so that all applications use a plum background color (on a color workstation, of course). An X application can simply adopt this default background when it starts up or provide its own default value. Beginning with Chapter 5, we address how to set application resources as well as rules of precedence in resource matching and other resource-related issues.

The second use of the term resource is for essential X entities such as windows, pixmaps, graphics contexts (a data structure that described various graphics parameters such as foreground color, drawing strategies, and so on), (software) cursors, fonts, and colormaps. X requires system resources in the same sense as an operating system. OS resources include the process table, virtual storage information (paging table), device tables, and so on. Resources are software entities; that is, they are created, managed, and destroyed by resource management routines; all of this activity is based in computer memory. X system resources are not "free"; every time X allocates another resource, the amount of available memory decreases.

Users sometimes fail to recognize that X applications use both operating system and X resources. The X server allocates memory on behalf of applications as necessary to represent windows, pixmaps, and so on. An X server running on a UNIX workstation gets its memory from the operating system; more precisely, it requests access to physical memory via the operating system, which manages all physical memory. An X terminal does not have an operating system; it is a dedicated X display station. Thus, an X server for an X terminal directly manages the physical memory in the X terminal—directly allocating X resources from this physical memory.

All applications, including X applications, use memory for manipulating data, for example, tables of numbers and a customer's database record. This type of storage is allocated by the operating system at the application's request *from the machine on which the application is running*. Thus, if you're using X on a stand-alone workstation, as you start up more and more X clients, the memory used for both application data tables and X resources is the workstation's memory. If, however, you're using X from an X terminal, your X applications are running on a workstation (or file server) and displaying remotely on the X terminal; hence, your applications are using system resources on the workstation and on the X terminal.

As an aside, our comments here highlight the fact that X resources such as pixmaps and windows are allocated by the X server using local memory, not necessarily on the machine where the application is executing. In particular, the X client and the X server do not pass a window (the data structures that collectively constitutes a window) back and forth over the network during window-related operations. The window is represented in the X terminal's physical memory, and both the X server and X clients reference that window using a window ID.

For a user in an X terminal environment, if you continue to start X clients without terminating existing X clients, there is a point at which the X server will have allocated most of the X terminal's physical memory, and additional applications cannot be started. This condition does not arise in a stand-alone workstation environment because the X server's requests for memory will be honored through the operating system's virtual storage strategy. (A virtual storage strategy is a memory allocation scheme whereby the operating system can manage applications requiring memory that exceeds the physical limits of the workstation. The operating system, essentially, "juggles" applications; it automatically moves [swaps] inactive applications to disk in order to make room in memory for applications that switch from an idle to an active state.)

For the user, the significance of this distinction is that with a workstation you will not run out of memory if you need to start a lot of applications, even though the workstation's performance may become sluggish. If you use an X terminal, however, you must recognize that you could encounter a situation in which you need to start a large number of applications, but cannot do so because of insufficient memory. If the nature of your work is such that it's critically important that you never get into this situation, be sure to monitor your physical memory usage and add whatever amount is necessary to provide a margin of safety.

A.4 Event-driven Window Systems

The event-driven nature of X is not particularly significant for X users; we mention it here, however, for completeness. We've mentioned that X clients communicate with the X server via a communication channel using a messaging scheme called the X protocol. The question is: How (logically) and when do they communicate?

X clients do not poll the X server, like children continually asking their teacher: "Is it my turn yet?" Obviously, it would be quite wasteful of computing resources (CPU time) to poll the X server simply to determine if there are any events of interest to that X client. It is not uncommon for users to have 10 or more X applications running, on average, throughout the day. Similarly, the X server does not poll its X clients asking: "Is there anything I can do for you?"

Instead, X clients issue directives to the X server during start-up operations that indicate exactly which categories of events are of interest (on a window-by-window basis). The X server keeps a record of these event registrations for all active X clients, passing along event notifications as requested by each X client.

There are four types of communication messages between the X server and an X client: (1) request, (2) reply, (3) event, and (4) error. Requests are issued by X clients; examples include "draw a rectangle that is 300 pixels in width and 100 pixels in height in the window with ID 1234567 beginning at coordinate (400,200)" and "clear the window with ID 7654321." An X client does *not* wait for a confirmation that a request has been completed successfully because (1) doing so would double the network load with respect to most requests by X clients, and (2) X assumes that it is running on a network that has a reliable network transport mechanism (that is, reliability is handled at a lower level).

The second type of communication is a reply by the X server to an X client's request. That is, certain requests do require a response from the X server, for example, "determine and return the current coordinates for the mouse cursor" and "what are the current attributes (dimensions, location, and so on) of the window with ID 1234567?"

An event notification is the third type of message, again, from the X server to the X client. Events include button presses, keystrokes, mouse cursor movements within a window, mouse cursor movement across window boundaries, and others. By the way, moving the mouse generates many, many events. For this reason, applications should not register an interest in (mouse) motion events unless they really intend to use them. Unfortunately, some ill-behaved X clients register for motion events even when they do not use them. If you have an X terminal with a network activity light on the keyboard, you can often spot applications that waste network resources in this manner. For example, is there constant network activity when you move the mouse pointer around in your X word processor's main window, even though you are not pressing a mouse button? If so, register a complaint with the developer's technical support department.

Lastly, an error message may be issued by the X server to an X client's error handler. In many cases, the default action is for the application to terminate. X applications should intelligently process error notifications, because, in many cases, it may be too severe an action simply to terminate in response to an error notification.

A.5 Operations That are Not Strictly Screen Oriented

It should be clear that, given the complexity of a modern window system, there are many X server-related tasks that are not strictly related to screen operations. We've mentioned the resource database facility and it is one of the best examples of an X feature that is *not directly* related to screen operations. Because X manages databases of information related to application configuration parameters, called application resources, it provides a common, consistent mechanism whereby applications can set user-controlled parameters. With X, application configuration parameters can be set on a system-wide basis from application-specific files located in standard system locations, on a user-by-user basis from a file in each user's log-in account, or using a combination of both approaches.

X's window-oriented interclient communication is another example of a task that is not strictly screen oriented. A window manager can use X's interclient communication facility to inform an application that it now has the keyboard focus (keystrokes will be delivered to the specified window). Likewise, a programming debugger could use X's interclient communication to inform a text editor to redisplay a computer program with the cursor at an arbitrary line (the location where an error has been detected). X's interclient communication facilities are also used for copy and paste operations between X applications. At first glance, a paste operation may appear to be a screen-related operation, because it may lead to a change in what is displayed in a window. Actually, however, X simply provides a low-level mechanism for delivering the data that will be pasted; the application is responsible for receiving the data, merging it with its existing data, and updating the window, if necessary.

A.6 The X Consortium and Standard X Releases

The origin of X is largely associated with the Massachusetts Institute of Technology (MIT). Many individuals and companies, however, have directly and indirectly contributed to the development of the X Window System. Fairly early in X's developmental history, the X Consortium was established to provide a vendor-neutral organization to oversee continued development of X. The Consortium makes decisions regarding any changes of course in X's design, including modifications and enhancements provided with each new release. (The X Consortium is now independent of MIT.)

The development of the windowing environment that became X essentially began in the mid-1980s. It proceeded through 10 major (developmental) releases before it and the UNIX community were ready for large-scale acceptance of a GUI environment for UNIX workstations. As we've mentioned, although X was first developed, tested, and accepted in UNIX workstations environments, it is a hardware- and OS-neutral graphical window system. Commercial acceptance of X coincided with X11R4, the fourth release of the 11th version of X. X11 Release 5 (X11R5) added a considerable number of features, including a color management system and a font server, plus many underlying improvements to X11R4. At the time of this writing, X11R6 is on the horizon.

In many X environments, you can determine which X release your workstation is running by issuing the command *xdpyinfo* (X display information) in a command window. Typically, there will be many lines of output so you may want to combine this command with *head* to extract the beginning lines of output; otherwise, you'll have to scroll back through

the output to find version-related information. The following command extracts the first 9
lines of output from *xdpyinfo*:

```
{your system prompt} xdpyinfo | head -9
name of display:      :0.0
version number:     11.0
vendor string:     MIT X Consortium
vendor release number:     5000
maximum request size:   262140 bytes
motion buffer size:   256
bitmap unit, bit order, padding:     32, MSBFirst, 32
image byte order:     MSBFirst
number of supported pixmap formats:     1
{your system prompt}
```

This information indicates that the X server is part of the standard X Consortium distribution
of X. The version is 11 and release number is 5000, that is, Release 5, hence, the popular
abbreviation "X11R5".

The encoding of the release number is not consistent across all X vendors. For example,
consider the output from the same command, but on a Sun workstation running its standard
X environment, OpenWindows [Sun Microsystems, 1992]:

```
name of display:      :0.0
version number:     11.0
vendor string:     X11/NeWS - Sun Microsystems Inc.
vendor release number:     3010
maximum request size:   65535 longwords (262140 bytes)
motion buffer size:   100
bitmap unit, bit order, padding:     32, MSBFirst, 32
image byte order:     MSBFirst
number of supported pixmap formats:     2
```

Here, the release number reflects the OpenWindows version, 3.0.1; for OpenWindows 3.1,
the release number is 3100. OpenWindows is Sun's implementation of the combined X and
NeWS servers, plus various standard X clients and the OpenWindows Deskset, a loosely
integrated suite of applications. This version of Sun's X11/NeWS server is actually based on
X11R4, not X11R5.

B

Properties

There are essentially two areas in which the property concept becomes somewhat noticeable to users: (1) the use of *xrdb*'s to establish the RESOURCE_MANAGER property for the root window, which is evaluated as a resource repository and (2) the use of properties for communications between the window manager and X clients.

A property is simply a collection of information, in a recognized format, that is associated with a window. An X application could, for example, store information that it requires at some later point as a property of the main application window; these data could be stored using any appropriate format, for example, integer, string, pixmap, and others. X programming books, for example, Nye and O'Reilly [1992], describe property management in detail.

For our purposes, it is sufficient to examine the properties associated with several windows. *xprop* reports property-related information:

```
{your system prompt} xprop -root
CUT_BUFFER0(STRING) = "the property concept"
WM_ICON_SIZE(WM_ICON_SIZE):
                minimum icon size: 16 by 16
                maximum icon size: 50 by 50
                incremental size change: 1 by 1
_MOTIF_WM_INFO(_MOTIF_WM_INFO) = 0x2, 0xc0001f
_OI_CONN_CACHE(PIXMAP): pixmap id # 0x0
```

The -root command-line option requests the properties associated with the root window. Without this option, *xprop* presents a cross-hair cursor and allows you to click on the target window.

By convention, property names are in uppercase text. In this case, the root window has a few properties. The most interesting one is CUT_BUFFER0, a data repository used by some X clients, especially older X clients, for simple clipboard-like operations. Here, the property CUT_BUFFER0 (in string format) contains the text "the property concept."

In this system's default configuration, it does not run *xrdb* during start-up operations to store X resources on the root window—there is no RESOURCE_MANAGER property for the root window. To see the RESOURCE_MANAGER property, we can store two X resources in a text file, say, *test.resources*, and then use *xrdb* to establish this property.

Here are the resources from *test.resources*:

```
{your system prompt} more test.resources
xclock*geometry:   120x120
xcalc.Mode:   rpn
```

Next, *xrdb* sets the RESOURCE_MANAGER property:

```
{your system prompt} xrdb -merge test.resources
```

Now, we can execute *xprop* and click on the root window for a property report:

```
{your system prompt} xprop
RESOURCE_MANAGER(STRING) = "xcalc.Mode:\trpn\nxclock*geometry:\t120x120\n"
CUT_BUFFER0(STRING) = "{your system prompt} "
WM_ICON_SIZE(WM_ICON_SIZE):
                minimum icon size: 16 by 16
                maximum icon size: 50 by 50
                incremental size change: 1 by 1
_MOTIF_WM_INFO(_MOTIF_WM_INFO) = 0x2, 0xc0001f
_OI_CONN_CACHE(PIXMAP): pixmap id # 0x0
```

Note that, regardless of how you specify resources, *xrdb* builds the RESOURCE_MANAGER property (as a string) with a tab character preceding the resource value ($\t$) and a newline character ($\n$) separating each resource specification.

If your system uses *xrdb* during start-up operations to load the contents of a file such as *.Xdefaults* or *.Xresources*, it is likely that this property will be much larger. The point, however, is that, regardless of its contents, the X resource manager consults this resource repository (if present) just as it does traditional resource files. See Section 6.3 for additional information on the resource evaluation process.

Next, consider the use of properties for communications between the window manager and X clients. In the previous output from *xprop*, it is clear that even the root window has one traditional window manager property, namely, WM_ICON_SIZE. The conventions for the names, contents, and formats of window manager-related properties are established by the ICCCM, as mentioned throughout this book (see Section 3.1).

We can see other window manager-related properties by using *xprop* on an X client's main application window:

```
{your system prompt} xprop
WM_STATE(WM_STATE):
                window state: Normal
                icon window: 0xc000e2
_MOTIF_WM_MESSAGES(ATOM) = _MOTIF_WM_OFFSET
WM_PROTOCOLS(ATOM): protocols   _MOTIF_WM_MESSAGES, WM_DELETE_WINDOW
_MOTIF_WM_HINTS(_MOTIF_WM_HINTS) = 0x1, 0x3e, 0xffffffff, 0xffffffff
WM_CLASS(STRING) = "xrolodex", "XRolodex"
WM_HINTS(WM_HINTS):
                Client accepts input or input focus: True
                Initial state is Normal State.
                bitmap id # to use for icon: 0x240005b
WM_NORMAL_HINTS(WM_SIZE_HINTS):
                program specified location: 0, 0
                program specified size: 432 by 290
                window gravity: NorthWest
WM_CLIENT_MACHINE(STRING) = "spectro"
WM_COMMAND(STRING) = { "xrolodex" }
WM_ICON_NAME(STRING) = "xrolodex"
WM_NAME(STRING) = "xrolodex"
```

Here, we selected the application *xrolodex*, but any application would have similar properties. Although it is beyond the scope of this book to examine properties in detail, it should be clear that the property concept provides a simple communication mechanism between X clients, in particular, between the window manager and other X applications.

C

Resource Repositories

X clients include resource management that consult the following resource repositories in the order described here.

I. Application-related Resources

1. If the environment variable XFILESEARCHPATH exists, process the specified file.

If not, check a system-wide application-defaults directory such as */usr/lib/X11/app-defaults* or *$OPENWINHOME/lib/app-defaults* for the X client's class file. (X toolkit applications evaluate the colon-separated list of locations (see Section 7.3):

```
/usr/lib/X11/%L/%T/%N%S:/usr/lib/X11/%l/%T/%N%S:/usr/lib/X11/%T/%N%S
```

2. If the environment variable XUSERFILESEARCHPATH exists, process the specified file.

If not, then if the environment variable XAPPLRESDIR exists, check the specified directory for the X client's class file. (X toolkit applications evaluate the colon-separated list of locations (see Section 7.3):

```
$XAPPLRESDIR/%L/%N:$XAPPLRESDIR/%l/%N:$XAPPLRESDIR/%N:$HOME/%N
```

If not, check the user's home directory (*$HOME*) for the X client's class file. (X toolkit applications evaluate the colon-separated list of locations (see Section 7.3):

```
$HOME/%L/%N:$HOME/%l/%N:$HOME/%N
```

II. Server-related Resources

If the RESOURCE_MANAGER property exists for the root window, process relevant resources. (See Appendix B.)

If not, check the user's home directory for the dot file *.Xdefaults*.

III. Host-related Resources

If the environment variable XENVIRONMENT exists, process the specified file.

If not, check the user's home directory for the dot file *.Xdefaults-<hostname>*.

IV. -xrm Command-line Resources

Next, process command-line resource specifications, if any.

V. Command-line Options

Next, process toolkit and client-specific command-line options.

Note that resources from each numbered category are loaded/merged according to the rules described in Section 5.6.

D

Event and Translation Information

Copyright Notice

Translation Table Syntax

The syntax for the subsequent translation table uses EBNF notation with the following conventions:

In this table, all terminals are expressed in bold Courier, e.g., **#override**.

Nonterminals are expressed in medium Courier, e.g., `production`.

Informal descriptions are enclosed in angle brackets, e.g., `<ISO Latin 1 character>`. Also,

    [**a**] is either nothing or **a;**
    { **a** } is zero or more occurrences of **a;**
    (**a** | **b**) is either **a** or **b;** **and**
    \n is the newline character.

The syntax of a translation table is:

translationTable = [directive] { production }

directive = (#replace | #override | #augment) \n

production = lhs : rhs \n

lhs = (event | keyseq) { , (event | keyseq) }

keyseq = " keychar {keychar} "

keychar = [^ | $ | \ ] <ISO Latin 1 character>

event = [modifier_list] <event_type> [(count[+])] {detail}

modifier_list = ([!] [:] {modifier}) | None

modifier = [~] modifier_name

count = (1 | 2 | 3 | 4 | ...)

modifier_name = @ <keysym> | <see modifier list below>

event_type = <see event types table below>

detail = <event specific details>

rhs = { name ([params]) }

name = namechar { namechar }

namechar = { a-z | A-Z | 0-9 | _ | - }

params = string {, string}

string = quoted_string | unquoted_string

quoted_string = " {<Latin 1 character> | escape_char} [\\\\ ] "

escape_char = \\"

unquoted_string = {<Latin 1 char except space, tab, ,, \n,)>}

Note that the params field contains a list of string values that will be passed to the specified action procedure. Also, an embedded quotation mark is legal in a quoted_string, if the quotation mark is preceded by a single backslash (\). Lastly, the three-character sequence "\\"" is interpreted as "single backslash followed by end-of-string."

List of Modifier Keywords

Modifier	Abbreviation
Ctrl	c
Shift	s
Lock	l
Meta	m
Hyper	h
Super	su
Alt	a

List of Modifier Keywords

Modifier	Abbreviation
Mod1	
Mod2	
Mod3	
Mod4	
Mod5	
Button1	
Button2	
Button3	
Button4	
Button5	
None	
Any	

Event Modifier Abbreviations

Abbreviation	Meaning
Ctrl	KeyPress event with Control modifier
Meta	KeyPress with Meta modifier
Shift	KeyPress with Shift modifier
Btn1Down	ButtonPress for Button1
Btn1Up	ButtonRelease for Button1
Btn2Down	ButtonPress for Button2
Btn2Up	ButtonRelease for Button2
Btn3Down	ButtonPress for Button3
Btn3Up	ButtonRelease for Button3
Btn4Down	ButtonPress for Button4
Btn4Up	ButtonRelease for Button4
Btn5Down	ButtonPress for Button5
Btn5Up	ButtonRelease for Button5
BtnMotion	MotionNotify with any button modifier
Btn1Motion	MotionNotify with Button1 modifier
Btn2Motion	MotionNotify with Button2 modifier
Btn3Motion	MotionNotify with Button3 modifier
Btn4Motion	MotionNotify with Button4 modifier
Btn5Motion	MotionNotify with Button5 modifier

Modifier Abbreviations in Key Sequences

Modifier	Abbreviation
Control	^
Meta	$

In key sequences, a backslash (\) can be used to quote a double quote ("), a circumflex (^), a dollar sign ($), another backslash (\), or any other character.

Events with Modifiers

Modifiers can be used for the following event types (and their abbreviations):

KeyPress
KeyRelease
ButtonPress
ButtonRelease
MotionNotify
EnterNotify
LeaveNotify

Event Translation Qualification Rules

If no modifiers are specified, and None is not specified, any modifier can be present for that event.

If the modifier list begins with an exclamation point (!), the specified modifiers must be in the correct state and no other modifiers can be present for the event. If no explamation point is specified, the specified modifiers must be present in the correct state for the event, but nonspecified modifiers are irrelevant.

If a specified modifier is preceded by a tilde (~), that modifier must not be present for the event. If None is specified, which is equivalent to an exclamation point with no specified modifiers, no modifiers can be present for the event.

If the modifier list begins with a colon (:), standard modifiers in the event (Shift and Lock) are applied in mapping the event keycode to a keysym. This mapped keysym must exactly match the specified keysym and other, nonstandard modifiers for the event must match the modifier list. Following this rule, :<Key>a is distinct from :<Key>A and :shift<Key>A is distinct from :<Key>A.

If the modifier list begins with both an exclamation point and a colon, the specified modifiers must be in the correct state and no other modifiers, except the standard modifiers, can be present for the event.

If a colon is not specified, standard modifiers are not applied; therefore, :<Key>a is *not* distinct from :<Key>A.

Summary of Event Qualification Rules

No modifiers:	None <event>
Any modifiers:	<event>
Any modifiers except this one:	~mod1 <event>
Only these modifiers:	! mod1 mod2 <event>
These modifiers and any others:	mod1 mod2 <event>

Event Types

Type	Meaning
Key	KeyPress
KeyDown	KeyPress
KeyUp	KeyRelease
BtnDown	ButtonPress
BtnUp	ButtonRelease
Motion	MotionNotify
PtrMoved	MotionNotify
MouseMoved	MotionNotify
Enter	EnterNotify
EnterWindow	EnterNotify
Leave	LeaveNotify
LeaveWindow	LeaveNotify
FocusIn	FocusIn
FocusOut	FocusOut
Keymap	KeymapNotify
Expose	Expose
GrExp	GraphicsExpose
NoExp	NoExpose
Visible	VisibilityNotify
Create	CreateNotify
Destroy	DestroyNotify
Unmap	UnmapNotify
Map	MapNotify
MapReq	MapRequest
Reparent	ReparentNotify
Configure	ConfigureNotify
ConfigureReq	ConfigureRequest
Grav	GravityNotify
ResReq	ResizeRequest
Circ	CirculateNotify
CircReq	CirculateRequest
Prop	PropertyNotify
SelClr	SelectionClear
SelReq	SelectionRequest
Select	SelectionNotify
Clrmap	ColormapNotify
Message	ClientMessage
Mapping	MappingNotify

E

Keysyms

There are too many keysyms to provide a complete listing in this book. In this appendix we list miscellaneous and Latin 1 keysyms, to provide a quick reference to common keysyms. For a complete listing see */usr/include/X11/keysymdef.h*.

BackSpace	Down	Help
Tab	Prior	Break
Linefeed	Next	Mode_switch
Clear	End	script_switch
Return	Begin	Num_Lock
Pause	----------	----------
Scroll_Lock	Select	KP_Space
Escape	Print	KP_Tab
Delete	Execute	KP_Enter
Multi_key	Insert	KP_F1
----------	Undo	KP_F2
Home	Redo	KP_F3
Left	Menu	KP_F4
Up	Find	KP_Equal
Right	Cancel	KP_Multiply

KP_Add	F14	R10
KP_Separator	L4	F31
KP_Subtract	F15	R11
KP_Decimal	L5	F32
KP_Divide	F16	R12
----------	L6	F33
KP_0	F17	R13
KP_1	L7	F34
KP_2	F18	R14
KP_3	L8	F35
KP_4	F19	R15
KP_5	L9	----------
KP_6	F20	Shift_L
KP_7	L10	Shift_R
KP_8	F21	Control_L
KP_9	R1	Control_R
----------	F22	Caps_Lock
F1	R2	Shift_Lock
F2	F23	----------
F3	R3	Meta_L
F4	F24	Meta_R
F5	R4	Alt_L
F6	F25	Alt_R
F7	R5	Super_L
F8	F26	Super_R
F9	R6	Hyper_L
F10	F27	Hyper_R
F11	R7	----------
L1	F28	space
F12	R8	exclam
L2	F29	quotedbl
F13	R9	numbersign
L3	F30	dollar

percent	E	e
ampersand	F	f
apostrophe	G	g
quoteright	H	h
parenleft	I	i
parenright	J	j
asterisk	K	k
plus	L	l
comma	M	m
minus	N	n
period	O	o
slash	P	p
0	Q	q
1	R	r
2	S	s
3	T	t
4	U	u
5	V	v
6	W	w
7	X	x
8	Y	y
9	Z	z
colon	bracketleft	braceleft
semicolon	backslash	bar
less	bracketright	braceright
equal	asciicircum	asciitilde
greater	underscore	----------
question	grave	nobreakspace
at	quoteleft	exclamdown
A	a	cent
B	b	sterling
C	c	currency
D	d	yen

brokenbar	Ccedilla	ae
section	Egrave	ccedilla
diaeresis	Eacute	egrave
copyright	Ecircumflex	eacute
ordfeminine	Ediaeresis	ecircumflex
guillemotleft	Igrave	ediaeresis
notsign	Iacute	igrave
hyphen	Icircumflex	iacute
registered	Idiaeresis	icircumflex
macron	ETH	idiaeresis
degree	Eth	eth
plusminus	Ntilde	ntilde
twosuperior	Ograve	ograve
threesuperior	Oacute	oacute
acute	Ocircumflex	ocircumflex
mu	Otilde	otilde
paragraph	Odiaeresis	odiaeresis
periodcentered	multiply	division
cedilla	Ooblique	oslash
onesuperior	Ugrave	ugrave
masculine	Uacute	uacute
guillemotright	Ucircumflex	ucircumflex
onequarter	Udiaeresis	udiaeresis
onehalf	Yacute	yacute
threequarters	THORN	thorn
questiondown	Thorn	ydiaeresis
Agrave	ssharp	
Aacute	agrave	
Acircumflex	aacute	
Atilde	acircumflex	
Adiaeresis	atilde	
Aring	adiaeresis	
AE	aring	

F

OSF/Motif Virtual Bindings

This appendix lists the high-level, or virtual, bindings that OSF/Motif environments employ (instead of mapping operations directly to keysyms). Unless otherwise modified, these bindings are in effect for *mwm* as well as applications built from the X toolkit and Motif widget set. Note that tables similar to those presented here are also available on-line in many OSF/Motif environments as part of the *VirtualBindings(3X)* man-page.

F.1 Modifying Virtual Bindings

OSF/Motif provides numerous default, or fallback, bindings for its virtual buttons, keys, and keysyms. Note that vendors sometimes modify these default virtual bindings; thus, a particular commercial software product may not interpret button- and key-press events exactly as described here—see the documentation for your Motif-based software for complete descriptions of button and key mappings.

Users normally specify virtual event mappings in two locations: (1) the file *.motifbind* in your home directory and (2) via the resource *defaultVirtualBindings*. Many X environments automatically provide a *.motifbind* file; each line in the file should contain one virtual-to-X-server binding:

```
...
osfBackSpace    :    <Key>BackSpace
osfDelete       :    <Key>Delete
osfInsert       :    <Key>Insert
...
```

Note that keysyms beginning with "osf..." are not present in non-Motif environments. Also, because X server keysyms vary greatly across workstation vendors, the entries in a

.motifbind file vary significantly from one Motif environment to another. See Section F.3 for examples of four common *.motifbind* files. Lastly, note that virtual bindings in *.motifbind* are global; that is, they are not application specific.

Recall from Section 7.5.1 that we provided a rather low-level approach to configuring Motif applications to interpret **<Delete>** as a backspace key:

```
*XmText.translations:  #override\n\
  <Key>osfDelete:  delete-previous-character()
```

In this example we've omitted an application name from the resource specification; thus, this translation will apply to all Motif applications, unless overridden elsewhere with an application-specific resource setting.

In Section 7.5.1 we alluded to a higher level solution to modifying **<Delete>** so that it performs a backspace operation. One approach is to add the following binding for the virtual keysym osfBackSpace to *.motifbind*:

```
...
osfBackSpace          :    <Key>Delete
...
```

With this binding, pressing (the physical key) **<Delete>** requests the virtual OSF backspace operation.

The second common location for virtual bindings is the resource *defaultVirtualBindings*; thus, this mechanism supports application-level configuration of virtual bindings. Hence, adding the following resource setting to the appropriate resource file (see Chapters 6 and 7) would accomplish the same thing as the previous entry in *.motifbind*:

```
...
*defaultVirtualBindings: \
  osfBackSpace : <Key>Delete\n\
  ...<other virtual bindings>...
...<other resource settings>...
```

It is imporant not to confuse the Xt-supported *translation* resource with the Motif-supported *defaultVirtualBindings* resource; in particular, the syntax for the two resources is different. The latter resource requires virtual binding specifications that mirror the format used in *.motifbind*; the translation manager is not involved in processing the value field for *defaultVirtualBindings*.

F.2 OSF/Motif Tables of Virtual Bindings

Virtual Modifier Bindings

The following table lists the virtual modifiers, as referenced in the *mwm* man-page:

Virtual Modifier	X Server Modifiers
MAlt	Mod1
MCtrl	Ctrl
MShift	Shift

Recall that the Mod1 modifier is one of five generic modifiers defined by the X server. OSF/Motif suggests that Mod1 be assigned to the **<Alt>** or **<Meta>** key(s). See Section 7.5.4 for a complete description of modifier states.

Virtual Button Bindings

The following table lists the virtual buttons, as referenced in the *mwm* man-page, and their default mappings to (physical) button-press events:

Virtual Button	X Server Button Events
BCustom	<Btn3>
BDrag	<Btn2>
BExtend	Shift<Btn1>
BMenu	<Btn3>
BSelect	<Btn1>
BToggle	Ctrl<Btn1>

See your Motif-based software's documentation for a description of operations that use these virtual button bindings.

Virtual Key Bindings

The following table lists the virtual keys, as referenced in the *mwm* man-page, and their default mappings to (logical) OSF keysyms and (physical) key-press events:

Virtual Key	OSF and X Server Key Events
KActivate	<Key>Return
	Ctrl<Key>Return
	<Key>osfActivate
KAddMode	<Key>osfAddMode
KBackSpace	<Key>osfBackSpace
KBackTab	Shift<Key>Tab
KBeginData	Ctrl<Key>osfBeginLine
KBeginLine	<Key>osfBeginLine
KCancel	<Key>osfCancel
KClear	<Key>osfClear
KCopy	<Key>osfCopy
	Ctrl<Key>osfInsert

Virtual Button	**OSF and X Server Button Events (cont.)**
KCut	`<Key>osfCut`
	`Shift<Key>osfDelete`
KDelete	`<Key>osfDelete`
KDeselectAll	`Ctrl<Key>backslash`
KDown	`<Key>osfDown`
KEndData	`Ctrl<Key>osfEndLine`
KEndLine	`<Key>osfEndLine`
KEnter	`<Key>Return`
KEscape	`<Key>Escape`
KExtend	`Shift<Key>space`
	`Shift<Key>osfSelect`
KHelp	`<Key>osfHelp`
KInsert	`<Key>osfInsert`
KLeft	`<Key>osfLeft`
KMenu	`<Key>osfMenu`
KMenuBar	`<Key>osfMenuBar`
KNextField	`<Key>Tab`
	`Ctrl<Key>Tab`
KNextMenu	`Ctrl<Key>osfDown`
	`Ctrl<Key>osfRight`
KPageDown	`<Key>osfPageDown`
KPageLeft	`Ctrl<Key>osfPageUp`
KPageRight	`Ctrl<Key>osfPageDown`
KPageUp	`<Key>osfPageUp`
KPaste	`<Key>osfPaste`
	`Shift<Key>osfInsert`
KPrevField	`Shift<Key>Tab`
	`Ctrl Shift<Key>Tab`
KPrevMenu	`Ctrl<Key>osfUp`
	`Ctrl<Key>osfLeft`
KPrimaryCopy	`Ctrl<Key>osfPrimaryPaste`
	`Mod1<Key>osfCopy`
	`Mod1 Ctrl<Key>osfInsert`
KPrimaryCut	`Mod1<Key>osfPrimaryPaste`
	`Mod1<Key>osfCut`
	`Mod1 Shift<Key>osfDelete`
KPrimaryPaste	`<Key>osfPrimaryPaste`
KQuickCopy	`Ctrl<Key>osfQuickPaste`
KQuickCut	`Mod1<Key>osfQuickPaste`
KQuickExtend	`Shift<Key>osfQuickPaste`
KQuickPaste	`<Key>osfQuickPaste`

Virtual Button	OSF and X Server Button Events (cont.)
KReselect	`Ctrl Shift<Key>space`
	`Ctrl Shift<Key>osfSelect`
KRestore	`Ctrl Shift<Key>osfInsert`
KRight	`<Key>osfRight`
KSelect	`<Key>space`
	`Ctrl<Key>space`
	`<Key>osfSelect`
KSelectAll	`Ctrl<Key>slash`
KSpace	`<Key>space`
KTab	`<Key>Tab`
KUndo	`<Key>osfUndo`
	`Mod1<Key>osfBackSpace`
KUp	`<Key>osfUp`
KAny	`<Key>`

OSF Keysym Bindings

See Section F.1 for explanations and formats for the file *.motifbind* and the Motif resource *defaultVirtualBindings*. This section documents the default bindings of OSF keysyms to X server keysyms.

OSF Keysym	Default Binding
osfActivate	`<none>`
osfAddMode	`Shift F8`
osfBackSpace	`Backspace`
osfBeginLine	`Home`
osfClear	`Clear`
osfCopy	`<none>`
osfCut	`<none>`
osfDelete	`Delete`
osfDown	`Down`
osfEndLine	`End`
osfCancel	`Escape`
osfHelp	`F1`
osfInsert	`Insert`
osfLeft	`Left`
osfMenu	`F4`
osfMenuBar	`F10`
osfPageDown	`Next`
osfPageUp	`Prior`
osfPaste	`<none>`
osfPrimaryPaste	`<none>`

OSF Keysym	Default Binding (cont.)
osfQuickPaste	\<none>
osfRight	Right
osfSelect	Select
osfUndo	Undo
osfUp	Up

F.3 Sample *.motifbind* Files

The following *.motifbind*, or something similar, is often installed in Hewlett-Packard's
PA-RISC X environment:

```
osfCancel       :    <Key>Escape
osfLeft         :    <Key>Left
osfUp           :    <Key>Up
osfRight        :    <Key>Right
osfDown         :    <Key>Down
osfEndLine      :    <Key>F7
osfBeginLine    :    <Key>Home
osfPageUp       :    <Key>Prior
osfPageDown     :    <Key>Next
osfBackSpace    :    <Key>BackSpace
osfDelete       :    <Key>DeleteChar
osfInsert       :    <Key>InsertChar
osfAddMode      :    Shift<Key>F8
osfHelp         :    <Key>F1
osfMenu         :    <Key>F4
osfMenuBar      :    <Key>F10
osfSelect       :    <Key>Select
osfClear        :    <Key>Clear
osfUndo         :    <Key>Undo
osfPrimaryPaste :    <Key>InsertLine
osfQuickPaste   :    <Key>DeleteLine
```

The following *.motifbind*, or something similar, is often installed in IBM's RS/6000 X
environment:

```
osfCancel       :    <Key>Escape
osfLeft         :    <Key>Left
osfUp           :    <Key>Up
osfRight        :    <Key>Right
osfDown         :    <Key>Down
osfEndLine      :    <Key>End
```

```
osfBeginLine       :       <Key>Home
osfPageUp          :       <Key>Prior
osfPageDown        :       <Key>Next
osfBackSpace       :       <Key>BackSpace
osfDelete          :       <Key>Delete
osfInsert          :       <Key>Insert
osfAddMode         :       Shift<Key>F8
osfHelp            :       <Key>F1
osfMenu            :       <Key>F4
osfMenuBar         :       <Key>F10
```

The following *.motifbind*, or something similar, is often installed in Silicon Graphics' X environment:

```
osfCancel          :       <Key>Escape
osfLeft            :       <Key>Left
osfUp              :       <Key>Up
osfRight           :       <Key>Right
osfDown            :       <Key>Down
osfEndLine         :       <Key>End
osfBeginLine       :       <Key>Home
osfPageUp          :       <Key>Prior
osfPageDown        :       <Key>Next
osfBackSpace       :       <Key>BackSpace
osfDelete          :       <Key>Delete
osfInsert          :       <Key>Insert
osfAddMode         :       Shift<Key>F8
osfHelp            :       <Key>F1
osfActivate        :       <Key>KP_Enter
osfMenu            :       <Key>F4
osfMenuBar         :       <Key>F10
```

The following *.motifbind*, or something similar, is often installed in Sun Consortium X environments that have been equipped with Motif:

```
osfCancel          :       <Key>Escape
osfLeft            :       <Key>Left
osfUp              :       <Key>Up
osfRight           :       <Key>Right
osfDown            :       <Key>Down
osfEndLine         :       <Key>R13
osfBeginLine       :       <Key>F27
```

```
osfPageUp           :     <Key>F29
osfPageDown         :     <Key>F35
osfBackSpace        :     <Key>BackSpace
osfDelete           :     <Key>Delete
osfInsert           :     <Key>Insert
osfAddMode          :     Shift<Key>F8
osfHelp             :     <Key>Help
osfMenu             :     <Key>F4
osfMenuBar          :     <Key>F10
osfCopy             :     <Key>F16
osfCut              :     <Key>F20
osfPaste            :     <Key>F18
osfUndo             :     <Key>F14
```

The following *.motifbind*, or something similar, is often installed in OpenWindows X environments that have been equipped with Motif:

```
osfCancel           :     <Key>Escape
osfLeft             :     <Key>F30
osfUp               :     <Key>F28
osfRight            :     <Key>F32
osfDown             :     <Key>F34
osfEndLine          :     <Key>R13
osfBeginLine        :     <Key>F27
osfPageUp           :     <Key>F29
osfPageDown         :     <Key>F35
osfBackSpace        :     <Key>BackSpace
osfDelete           :     <Key>Delete
osfInsert           :     <Key>Insert
osfAddMode          :     Shift<Key>F8
osfHelp             :     <Key>Help
osfMenu             :     <Key>F4
osfMenuBar          :     <Key>F10
osfCopy             :     <Key>F16
osfCut              :     <Key>F20
osfPaste            :     <Key>F18
osfUndo             :     <Key>F14
```

G

X Toolkit Command-line Options

This appendix provides a quick reference for the command-line options recognized by Xt-based applications, including Motif applications; see the X man-page for a complete reference.

Command-line Option	Example

`-display <display>`

[the X server host, display number, and screen number]

    `-display saturn:0.0`

`-geometry <geometry>`

[the initial size and location of the application window]

    `-geometry 100x200+5+5`

`-bg <color>, -background <color>`

[the background color for the application window]

    `-bg ivory`

`-bd <color>, -bordercolor <color>`

[the border color for the application window]

    `-bd HotPink`

`-bw <number>, -borderwidth <number>`

[the border width for the application window (may be overridden by window manager)]

    `-bw 2`

Command-line Option	**Example**

`-fg <color>, -foreground <color>`   `-fg black`

[the foreground color for the application window]

`-fn <font>, -font <font>`   `-fn 8x13bold`

[the font for the application window]

`-iconic`   `-iconic`

[requests that the application start up in iconic form, if possible]

`-name <application-name>`   `-name myterm`

[the instance name to use for this application during resource evaluation]

`-rv, -reverse`   `-rv`

[exchange the foreground and background colors, if possible]

`+rv`   `+rv`

[do *not* exchange the foreground and background colors, even if possible]

`-selectionTimeout <milliseconds>`   `-selectionTimeout 25`

[the length of time in milliseconds that the current application (session) will wait for another application (session) to respond to a selection request, for example, delivering the primary selection for pasting into the current application]

`-synchronous`   `-synchronous`

[turns off buffering of X client requests to the X server (useful during debugging only, not with commercial/completed software)]

`-title <string>`   `-title "xterm -- saturn"`

[the suggested title for the application window's title area (the window manager may ignore this suggestion)]

`-xnllanguage <language[_territory][.codeset]>` `-xnlanguage English_Canada`

[the language, territory, and codeset for resolving resources]

`-xrm <resourcestring>`   `-xrm '*cursorColor: magenta'`

[a resource setting from the command-line that overrrides resource settings from other files (does *not* override command-line options; see Appendix C)]

H

Miscellaneous X Freeware

Chapter 4 describes several X clients including traditional X applications shipped with all X distributions as well as vendor-specific applications. This appendix provides a sampling of freeware X clients that are available from a variety of anonymous FTP (file transfer program/protocol) sites, such as *ftp.uu.net*. For readability, each X client is described on a separate page. In lieu of a lengthy description of each application, we present screen shots that provide a visual description of their basic functionality.

Note that in many cases multiple authors contribute to the development of a freeware application. For brevity, however, in our summary of each X client we list only the author(s) mentioned in its man-page, if any, including references to authors of other applications from which an X client is derived. For applications that are described further in other books, we provide a reference as well.

The collection of applications presented here was assembled somewhat randomly; the only criteria for inclusion were that the X clients compiled and ran without obvious problems on a Sun SPARCstation running SunOS 4.1.2 with the Consortium X11R5 software distribution, and that they have obvious practical utility. Also, because we are intimately familiar with our own software, we've included several clients developed at our site. There are, of course, many other useful freeware X clients including clients such as *xfishtank*, *xphoon*, and *xroach* that are not shown here because they are not easily represented by a simple screen-shot.

See your system administrator for X clients that are popular at your site, as well as a list of anonymous FTP sites and the appropriate public directories containing retrievable software. (Look for a directory named "contrib" within an X directory.) Appendix I illustrates the general process of "FTPing" a file from a remote site.

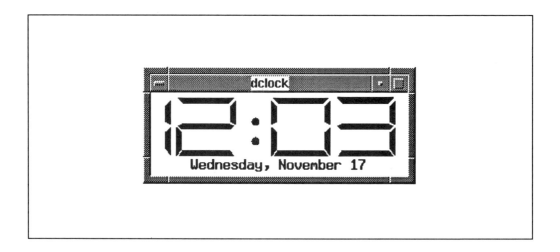

Application: *dclock*

Author(s):   Dan Heller, Steve Reinhardt

Description: A highly-configurable digital clock

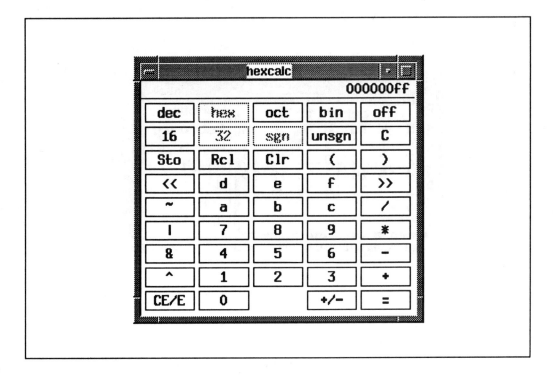

Application:	*hexcalc*
Author(s):	Tom Jarmolowski
Description:	A programmer's hexadecimal calculator

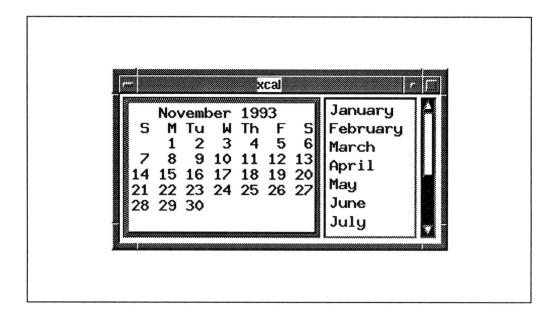

Application:	*xcal*
Author(s):	Dan Heller; see Heller [1991] pp. 366-367
Description:	An X interface to the UNIX program *cal(1)*

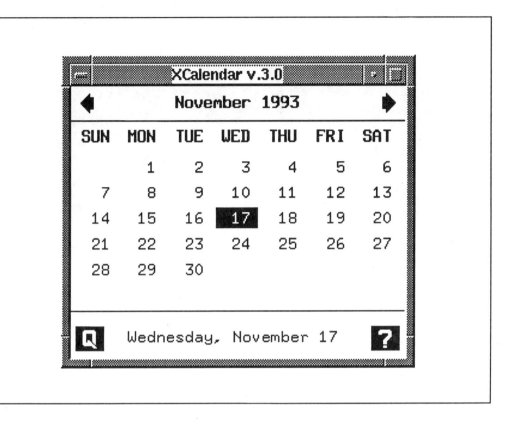

Application:	*xcalendar*
Author(s):	Roman J. Budzianowski, Richard Bingle, Beth Chaney
Description:	A calendar with notebook-style storage of daily information

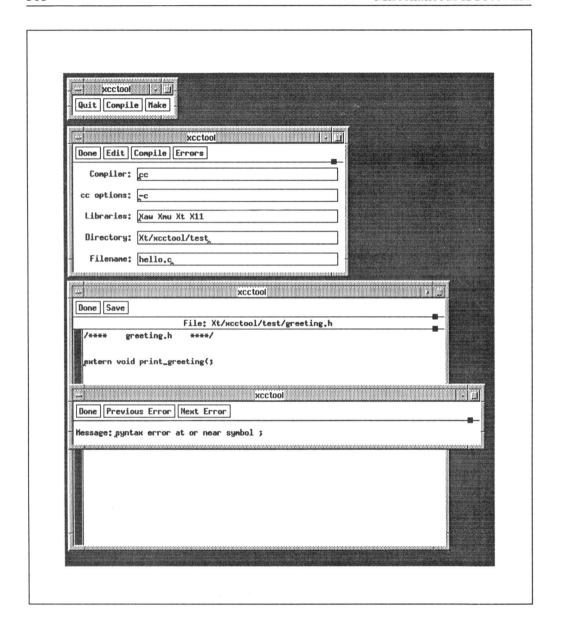

Application: *xcctool*

Author(s):   Jerry Smith

Description: A compiler and make/project tool for programmers

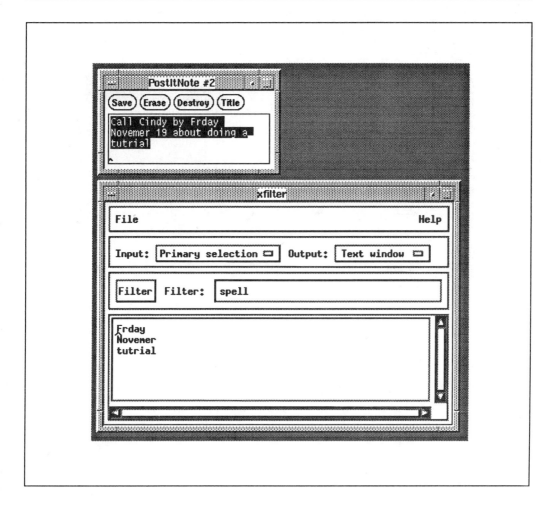

Application:	*xfilter*
Author(s):	Jerry Smith; see Smith [1992]
Description:	An X interface to UNIX filters

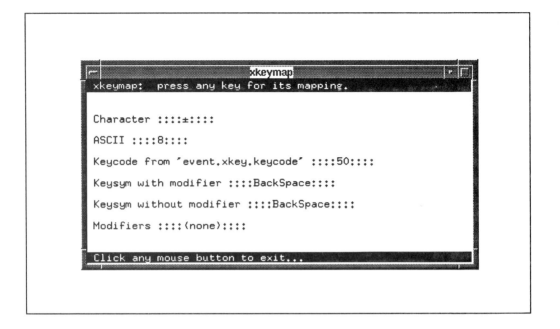

Application:	*xkeymap*
Author(s):	Jerry Smith
Description:	A utility for reporting key-related information

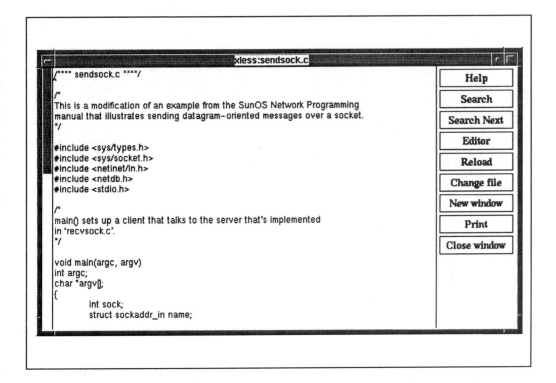

Application: *xless*

Author(s):   Carlo Lisa, Chris Peterson, Dave Glowacki

Description: A file browsing application

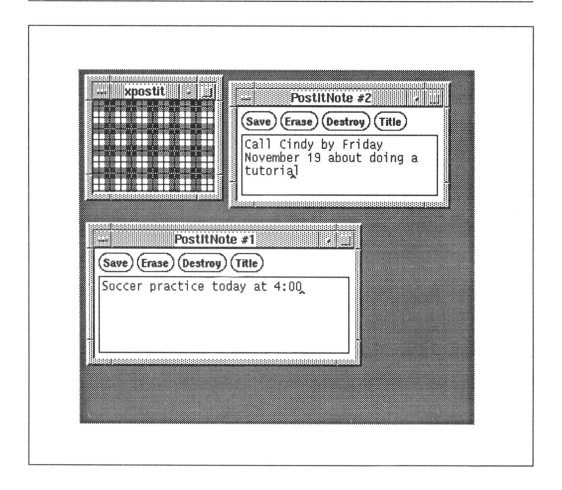

Application: *xpostit*
Author(s):   David A. Curry
Description: A note utility based on Post-it® notes

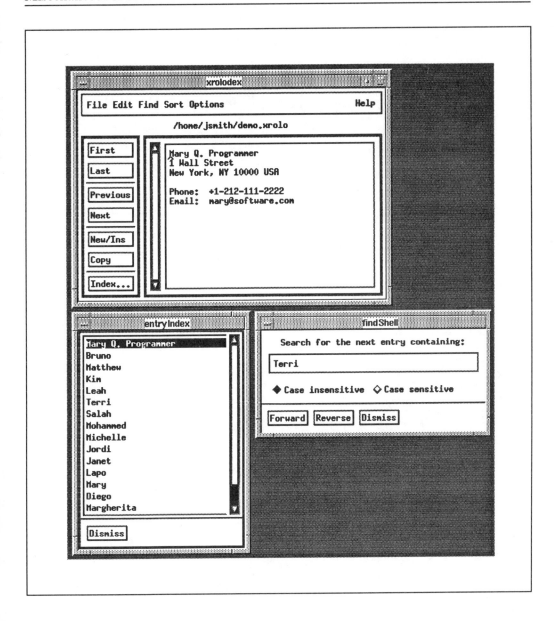

Application: *xrolodex*

Author(s):   Jerry Smith; see Smith [1992]

Description: A card-file utility following the Rolodex® model

I

The FTP and Software Building Process

This appendix includes command-window output that illustrates an FTP (file transfer program/protocol) session in which a file is "FTP'd" from a remote site. You can FTP a file (for example, freeware X software) from any FTP site for which you have access, represented here by *<ftp-site>*. In this example, selected output has been deleted to reduce the volume and the possibility for confusion. In addition, this command-window session illustrates the general process of uncompressing, unarchiving, and building an X application after you've retrieved it from a remote site. If you are not a programmer, you may have to seek help in building an X application, especially those that require modifications to adapt them to your X environment.

First, execute *ftp(1)* with the FTP address as a parameter:

```
{48}/export/home/jsmith/demo->ftp <ftp-site>
Connected to <ftp-site>.
220 <ftp-site> FTP server (Version XX) ready.
Name: anonymous
331 Guest login ok, send e-mail address as password.
Password: jsmith@spectro.com
230 Guest login ok, access restrictions apply.
```

For *<ftp-site>*, you can use either a domain name, for example, *ftp.uu.net*, a common FTP site, or an Internet address, for example, 192.48.96.9. Of course, you must know the address of an FTP site that has the software that you would like to copy.

Next, you should switch to binary mode before retrieving the software (the default is ASCII):

315

```
ftp> binary
200 Type set to I.
```

Next, switch to the directory containing the public files:

```
ftp> cd /vendor/spectro
250 CWD command successful.
ftp> ls x*
200 PORT command successful.
150 ASCII data connection <other stuff>...
xcctool.tar.Z
xkeymap.tar.Z
xrolodex.1.1.patch1
xrolodex.1.1.tar.Z
xrolodex.1.2.tar.Z
xrolodex.tar.Z
226 ASCII Transfer complete.
remote: x*
107 bytes received in 0.058 seconds (1.8 Kbytes/s)
```

Here, we change to a known directory at *ftp.uu.net*, specifically, */vendor/spectro*. Then we list all files beginning with "x". At *ftp.uu.net*, the directory of contributed X software is */packages/X/contrib*. Note that any time *ftp(1)* transfers data, including the result of the remote *ls(1)*, it provides data transfer statistics.

Next, we get/retrieve a compressed (".Z") archive (".tar") file, in this case, for the X client *xkeymap*, and then terminate the FTP session:

```
ftp> get xkeymap.tar.Z
200 PORT command successful.
150 Binary data connection for xkeymap.tar.Z <other stuff>...
226 Binary Transfer complete.
local: xkeymap.tar.Z remote: xkeymap.tar.Z
14664 bytes received in 0.15 seconds (96 Kbytes/s)
ftp> quit
221 Goodbye.
{49}/export/home/jsmith/demo->ls
xkeymap.tar.Z
```

At this point, we can uncompress and unarchive the distribution file on our local workstation:

```
{50}/export/home/jsmith/demo->uncompress xkeymap.tar.Z
{51}/export/home/jsmith/demo->tar xf xkeymap.tar
{52}/export/home/jsmith/demo->ls
xkeymap/
{53}/export/home/jsmith/demo->cd xkeymap
{54}/export/home/jsmith/demo/xkeymap->ls
Imakefile      display.h      key.h          screen.h        simplewin.h
```

```
display.c    key.c         screen.c      simplewin.c   xkeymap.c
```

Next, we run the X utility *xmkmf*, which simply creates a *makefile*, that is, a project file for building the software, from the generic makefile template, *Imakefile*:

```
{55}/export/home/jsmith/demo/xkeymap->xmkmf
imake /usr/openwin/lib/config
```

Lastly, we use *make(1)* to build the software and use *ls(1)* to show that the process succeeded:

```
{56}/export/home/jsmith/demo/xkeymap->make
cc -O -I/usr/openwin/include -I/usr/openwin -DSYSV -c display.c
cc -O -I/usr/openwin/include -I/usr/openwin -DSYSV -c key.c
cc -O -I/usr/openwin/include -I/usr/openwin -DSYSV -c screen.c
cc -O -I/usr/openwin/include -I/usr/openwin -DSYSV -c simplewin.c
cc -O -I/usr/openwin/include -I/usr/openwin -DSYSV -c xkeymap.c
rm -f xkeymap
cc -o xkeymap display.o key.o screen.o simplewin.o xkeymap.o -O -lXext -lX11

{57}/export/home/jsmith/demo/xkeymap->ls -l xkeymap
-rwxr-xr-x  1 jsmith   staff      24884 Nov 17 13:24 xkeymap*
{58}/export/home/jsmith/demo/xkeymap->
```

In your X environment, you may have to perform specific tasks to install the software and its man-page, if any, into known executable-file, or "bin," directories. See your system administrator.

References

Adobe Systems. *PostScript® Language Reference Manual.* Reading, MA: Addison-Wesley, 1990.

Asente, P. J. and Swick, R. R. *X Window System™ Toolkit.* Burlington, MA: Digital Press, 1990.

Benson, A. and Aitken, G. *OI™ Programmer's Guide.* Englewood Cliffs, NJ: Prentice Hall, 1992.

Dvorak, J. C. The bonehead vs. the power user. *PC Magazine, 11*, No. 16, 93, 1992.

Heller, D. *Motif™ Programming Manual.* Sebastopol, CA: O'Reilly & Associates, Inc., 1991a.

Heller, D. *XView™ Programming Manual.* Sebastopol, CA: O'Reilly & Associates, Inc., 1991b.

Hewlett-Packard. *HP™ Visual User Environment 3.0 User's Guide.* Part Number: B1171-90061. Corvallis, OR: Hewlett-Packard Company, 1992.

Iris Computing Laboratories. *ie™.* Santa Fe, NM: Iris Computing Laboratories, The Spectro Group, Inc., 1993.

Kochan, S.G. and Wood, P.H. *UNIX® Networking.* Carmel, IN: Hayden Books, Howard W. Sams & Company, 1989.

Linton, M. and Price, C. Building Distributed User Interfaces with Fresco. Proceedings of the 7th X Technical Conference, Boston, Massachusetts, January 1993. Published in *The X Resource, 5,* 1993.

MIT X Consortium. *Athena Widget Set--C Language Interface.* Cambridge, MA: MIT X Consortium, 1991.

Mui, L. and Pearce, E. *X Window System Administrator's Guide.* Sebastopol, CA: O'Reilly & Associates, Inc., 1992.

Network Computing Devices (NCD). *PC-Xview® for DOS User's Guide.* Part Number: 1270.2. Beaverton, OR: NCD PC-Xdivision, Network Computing Devices, Inc., 1992.

Nye, A. and O'Reilly, T. *X Toolkit Intrinsics Programming Manual.* Sebastopol, CA: O'Reilly & Associates, Inc., 1992.

Open Software Foundation (OSF). *OSF/Motif™ Programmer's Reference.* Englewood Cliffs, NJ: Prentice Hall, 1992a.

Open Software Foundation (OSF). *OSF/Motif™ Style Guide.* Englewood Cliffs, NJ: Prentice Hall, 1992b.

O'Reilly & Associates. *X Toolkit Intrinsics Reference Manual.* Sebastopol, CA: O'Reilly & Associates, Inc., 1992.

Ousterhout, J.K. and Rowe, L.A. Hypertools: a revolution in GUI applications. *The X Journal*, 2, No. 4, 1993.

Quarterdeck Office Systems®. *DESQview/X™ User Guide.* Part Number: 500US-DX0100. Santa Monica, CA: Quarterdeck Office Systems, Inc., 1992.

Quercia, V. and O'Reilly, T. *X Window System User's Guide.* Sebastopol, CA: O'Reilly & Associates, Inc., 1992.

Rosenthal, D. *Inter-client Communication Conventions Manual.* In Scheifler, R. W. and Gettys, J. *X Window System™.* Burlington, MA: Digital Press, 1992.

Scheifler, R. W. and Gettys, J. *X Window System™.* Burlington, MA: Digital Press, 1992.

Silicon Graphics®. *IRIS Essentials.* Part Number: 007-1342-030. Mountain View, CA: Silicon Graphics, Inc., 1992.

Silicon Graphics®. *Indy™ Workstation Owner's Guide.* Part Number: 007-9804-010. Mountain View, CA: Silicon Graphics, Inc., 1993.

Smith, J. D. *Designing X Clients with Xt/Motif™.* San Mateo, CA: Morgan Kaufmann Publishers, 1992.

Solbourne Computer®. *Using the Window System.* Part Number: 105463. Longmont, CO: Solbourne Computer, Inc., 1991.

Sun Microsystems®. *OpenWindows™ Version 3.1 User's Guide.* Part Number: 801-2555-10. Mountain View, CA: Sun Microsystems, Inc., 1992.

UNIX® System Laboratories. *OPEN LOOK® Graphical User Interface.* Englewood Cliffs, NJ: Prentice Hall, 1992.

X/Open. *Common Desktop Environment: Functional Specification.* Document Number: S306. Berkshire, United Kingdom: X/Open Company Limited, 1993.

Index